Dear Lisa and Dal 8/9/23

my book of happy memories."

Lots of Love and God Bless you,
Pixie
X

By **JOAN ELLIS GETCHELL COLE**

12.25.1907 - 12.19.1943

This book was compiled by Joan Ellis Getchell Cole's daughter
Joan Shaw Cole Pendergast

with her great-grandchildren
MacKenzie (Max) Ellis Pendergast & Jack Brennan Cox

outskirts
press

My Book of Happy Memories
All Rights Reserved.
Copyright © 2022 Joan Ellis Getchell Cole
v6.0 r1.0

The opinions expressed in this manuscript are solely the opinions of the author and do not represent the opinions or thoughts of the publisher. The author has represented and warranted full ownership and/or legal right to publish all the materials in this book.

This book may not be reproduced, transmitted, or stored in whole or in part by any means, including graphic, electronic, or mechanical without the express written consent of the publisher except in the case of brief quotations embodied in critical articles and reviews.

Outskirts Press, Inc.
http://www.outskirtspress.com

ISBN: 978-1-9772-3073-7

Cover Design @ 2022 MacKenzie Pendergast and Giuseppe Butera.
Painting by Richard Kinnicutt of Sakonnet Harbor before the 1938 Hurricane.
All rights reserved - used with permission.

Outskirts Press and the "OP" logo are trademarks belonging to Outskirts Press, Inc.

PRINTED IN THE UNITED STATES OF AMERICA

*Dedicated to
the memory of my mother,
Joan Ellis Getchell Cole*

"Don't you have an album,
An annotated album
With snapshots of the kiddies and photographs of you,
That I can pour a while on
With fixed and glassy smile on?
Don't you have an album?
Oh, God, of course you do!"

- Phyllis McGinley

On the front of Mom's blue and tan striped scrapbook.

"He who honors his mother amasses a great fortune."
Ecclesiastes / Sirach 3:4

This is on the front of my first collection of Mom's writings I gave to my children for Christmas in 1988.

"The glory of God is a man fully alive.
The life of a man is the vision of God."
- St. Irenaeus

Mom was filled with the joy of being alive.

Table of Contents

Introduction   May, 2021   i

PART I - *Younger Years*

Poems – *Dad, A House on Prospect Street*   5
                                            Date Unknown
Letter to "Mother Darlingest"   Date Unknown   7
Letter to her "Dearest dearest Mother"   9
                                            Date Unknown
Brown Journal   1922   10
Red Journal   1926-1927   16
Poem - *Golf*   Date Unknown   19
Excerpt from *Johnnycakes and Cream*   21
                                            Date Unknown

PART II - *A Young Woman*

"Dearest Vee"   Date Unknown   27
Shaw to Mr. H. Eugene Getchell   April 28, 1931   29
Joan letter to her family from Smith   1931   32
Joan letter to Mr. Cole   1931   34
Mary Cole to Edith Getchell   June 15, 1931   36
Graduation/Engagement Ann.   May/June, 1931   38
Blue Travel Journal – trip to Italy   March, 1932   39
Poem - *Papa's Sore Back*   1932   41

PART III - *Early Married Years*

Wedding Invitation   1934   45
Wedding Ann. in Woonsocket Call   March 24, 1934   47
Account of wedding events by Joan   March, 1934   49

"I think by now we own half the town!" April 8, 1934		53
Morning Prayer Scrapbook entry	1934	57
"My role as engineer's wife...!"	1934	58
Silvia Laveen: "Howdya do!"	1934	62
"I feel just like Atlas..."	April 24, 1934	66
"No word so far."	1934	70
Post Card - "Everything swell."	April 27, 1934	72
"We're moving nearer you!"	April 30, 1934	73
"Dear Each + Every One"	May 4, 1934	75
A Poem To Edie from Joan	1934	79
"Life goes on very smoothly."	May 4, 1934	80
Shaw to his Mother - "Mother dear"	May 13, 1934	82
Scrapbook - "En route from Beaver Falls" May, 1934		85
"We had such a charming weekend..."	1934	87
Postcard - "What a life!"	May 28, 1934	90
"This has been such a gay weekend!"	1934	91
"Love in a Garret on Garret Road" September 19, 1934		93
"Picture me at this setting..."	1934	97
"Enfin! We are proud tenants..."	1934	99
"Being only about 11:00pm..."	Fall, 1934	103
"It was such fun to come home..."	1934	106
"Such a homecoming as I had!"	1934	108
Letter from Eugene Getchell	October 17, 1934	110
"Welcome to your city house!"	Fall, 1934	113
Scrapbook - "Our main line sojourn..."	1935	116
"Another blizzard rages outside..." January 8th, 1935		118
"I see by the itinerary..."	February 23, 1935	123
Fredonia - "We aren't here..."	April 6th, 1935	128
"Many thanks for sending the trunks..."	1935	130
"Dearest Mother..."	1935	132
"Shaw has departed for night work..."	April, 1935	134
"This is dedicated to the lowly hog."	April, 1935	137
Shouts from the Shelter Box	1935	

Pitometer Wife's Greeting		140
Give this poem a title to suit yourself		141
The Zero Hour		143
"The Hoopers have been with us..."	May 1, 1935	145
"Dearests - Welcome home!"	May 7, 1935	147
"205 needs shining up a bit."	1935	149
Home is Where we Hang Our Hats	June, 1935	153
"I am perforce writing with pencil..."	1935	164
"Such a flood of letters arrived..."	July, 1935	167
"I turn to the US weather chart..."	August, 1935	170
"Another weekend and wash day..."	1935	176
"Minneapolis 'came through'..."	1935	180
"I am en route to Woonsocket..."	Fall, 1935	183
"Mother never allows ink in bed..."	Fall, 1935	185
"Mother is safely home..."	Fall, 1935	187
Mother Edith to Joan	November 7, 1935	189
Edith E. Getchell Obituary	November 12, 1935	190
"I am writing this note in the ladies..."	November, 1935	193
Shaw to Joan from Frackville	December, 1935	194
"Our sixth bed in six nights!"	April 25th, 1936	195
H. Eugene Getchell Obituary	April, 1936	198
"Woonsocket Citizen Takes his Own..."	April 25th, 1936	200
"Dearest Craigs..."	1936	203
Woonsocket Call Articles	1935, 1936	204
"We break up our Woonsocket home"	Summer, 1936	206

PART IV - *Motherhood*

"Dearest Mart..."	December, 1936	218
"My 36 diapers are hanging on the line!"	December, 1936	220
"Pixie is 2 months old today..."	December, 1936	223
"The Pixie gives great promise..."	December 7, 1936	225

"Well we're back to earth again..."	December, 1936	229
"One weekend is hardly over..."	Fall, 1937	232
Shaw and Joan to Shaw's Mother	October 11, 1937	234
Thanksgiving 1937	Fall, 1937	238
"Dearest Aunty, I had a long letter..."	August 30, 1938	242
Lists Written at Truesdale Hospital	August, 1938	244
"Dearest Aunty, I had a letter..."	September, 1938	249
Woonsocket Call - Sakonnet Hurricane	September 23, 1938	251
Woonsocket Call - Hurricane	September 30, 1938	256
"Dearest Ceci..."	September, 1938	258
Pixie's Baby Book - Hurricane	1938	262
Bruce's Baby Book - Hurricane	1938	265
Little Stories		
Faits Accompli	1938	267
Bon Voyage	September, 1940	269
Youth Today	November, 1941	274
The Leisured Class	February, 1942	276
Fireside Chat	September, 1942	278
Denouement	February, 1943	279
The Bergere	April, 1943	281
Swan Song	April, 1943	285
"I had my turkey and now my baby!"	November 27, 1943	286
"Dear Multípara para 3 grava 3..."	December 1, 1943	288
"Dear Mart..."	December 3, 1943	291
War Time Bedpan Technique	November, 1943	293
"Dearest Aunty, thanks for your letter."	December 8, 1943	295
"Vee Dearest..."	December 7, 1943	297
Poor Butterfly	1943	299
Picture and Death Notice	December 19, 1943	302
Markings of Mercy Excerpt	(December 19, 1943)	303
Shaw to Vivian after Joan's death	January 3, 1944	307
In Loving Memory of Joan Cole	February 1944	310

Appendix

Appendix A - Biography of John Waldo Ellis	313
Appendix B - *Birds of a Feather*	317
Appendix C - *Johnnycakes and Cream*	323
Appendix D - A genealogy for Grandpa Cole	325
Appendix E - Biography of John Adams Cole	330
Appendix F - Article from Water Works Engineering	332

Introduction

May, 2021

Before introducing my mother and her writing to the rest of the readers that find this book in their laps, I want to speak first to my family.

To my sisters, Heather, Cesca, Prissy, and Susu, my deceased brother Bruce, my cousins, all of our children, and all of our grandchildren, I just want us all to get to know Joan - Mom, Grandma, Aunt Joan, Aunt Dodo, Aunt Wanie. She died so young and we all grieved her death. Our knowing her got cut short when we were kids, and two generations never knew her - our children and grandchildren. As the second eldest living Getchell-Cole relative, I take great pleasure in passing on to you most of her writings and some family pictures.

This book is the story of her life in her own words.

My Mother, Joan Ellis Getchell Cole was born on Christmas Day, December 25, 1908 to Edith Almira Ellis Getchell and H. Eugene Getchell, in Woonsocket, Rhode Island. The second of four daughters, she grew up in a very loving family at 205 Prospect Street, which her mother entered as a bride from her own home across the street.

Mom Joan grew up in Woonsocket, went to public schools, was a Girl Scout, and wrote poems and many extensive diaries. She went on to Northampton School for Girls, a boarding school in Springfield, Mass., for High School and then to Smith College in Northampton, Mass., from where her mother, sisters and future mother-in-law graduated. On March 24, 1934 she married E. Shaw Cole, a graduate of Dartmouth College and the Thayer School of Engineering. He became a Water Works Engineer for his Father's company, the Pitometer Company in New York City. They evaluated Water

Systems and surveyed them for leaks in many towns throughout the country.

As newlyweds Shaw and Joan lived in several towns and cities as my Dad hunted for water leaks in pipes. They stayed anywhere and everywhere from two weeks to a few months setting up new homes each time. Mom wrote a ton of letters to her family who would send them around to each other. Many of these letters are included here. She wrote a piece which she entitled, "Home Is Where We Hang Our Hats" describing their nomadic life. She also wrote poems for a little Pitometer Newsletter called "Shouts From The Shelter Box" about her husband's work, and later in her life, she wrote short essays for "The League's Latest".

Mom's Mother, Edith, suffered from Tuberculosis for some years and died from it on November 10, 1935. Joan's Father Eugene died six months later by his own hand, on April 25, 1936, suffering from grief and a broken heart.

Joan and Shaw had me on October 9, 1936 in Tuxedo Park, N.Y., while they were still traveling for Shaw's work.

Eventually Shaw and Joan bought a house next door to Mom's sister Celie French and her family - Uncle Bud, Wayne who was my age, and David who was the youngest - on Wildwood Avenue in Montclair, New Jersey. It was less than an hour from New York City, from which my Dad commuted to work at the Pitometer Company, at 50 Church Street.

My brother Getchell Brewster Cole was born on August 29, 1938 just before the Hurricane of 1938. Mom wrote about the hurricane in Bruce's baby book and in mine. She also wrote several short essays as Editor of the Junior League's Latest newsletter and kept scrapbooks full of pictures and stories. We moved to 21 Erwin Park Road in Montclair in 1942.

My sister Heather Dunclee Cole was born on November 27, 1943. Since Mom had to stay in bed in the hospital for ten days, she wrote more little stories. She was bedridden more when she got home because of a sore back. They called it lumbago. I think it was the blood clot that took her life on December 19, 1943, just three weeks after Heather was born.

For years I have been collecting my Mom's writings. People have sent them to me in letters as well as printed stories. A few times over the years I typed them up or copied them and gave them to my children for Christmas.

Mom's maiden name was Getchell, and we Getchells are still in touch. Last June, many members of our big family (there are over one hundred of us in total) celebrated the fiftieth reunion of our "Getchell Day". Every five years or so Chris and Mary Rawson have hosted us for a day of games, fun, and food at their house in Little Compton, (Sakonnet) Rhode Island. Last year our Day included a family remembrance service of sorts for my brother Bruce who died April 18, 2018 in Naples, Florida.

A few winters ago I got the idea to read through Mom Joan's writings and maybe put them together for living relatives, of which I am presently the second eldest. On March 29th, 1992, my husband Jack, Vivian (my mom #2), and I, found a metal trunk in the attic at 21 Erwin Park Road. Inside were lots of little packets of my mother's letters and her diaries bundled in 1935 Woonsocket Call newspapers and tied up with string. Her letters reveal a very loving family of Grandma Edith, Grandpa Eugene, Mart, Joan, Celie, and Genie Getchell… and then happy couples as the girls got married.

Joan wrote several times about publishing a story. She even provided the title! In a letter she wrote to her family she asks her sister Celie to store her letter in her trunk drawer, so she could put it one day in "my book of happy memories." Mom had to wait a long time for her story to be published but here it is!

This book is really a family affair. My grandchildren MacKenzie (Max) Ellis Pendergast, third child of John and Judene, and a theater director/educator is my editor, and Jack Brennan Cox, second eldest and twin of Joan and Ray Cox, a High School athlete, musician, and scholar, is my assistant editor and typist. Both Max and Jack worked tirelessly on our project for over three years. Grandma Joan's award-winning penmanship had to be transcribed into Word for the publisher. (She was a prolific writer and all her many words had to be found and organized first.)

Of course, we had a lot of fun. Max would come up from New York City for hunks of time until Covid 19 grounded us and weekly video calls took over. I would pick up Jack after high school at least once a week, get fast food somewhere, and he would type for a couple of hours, as I read text out loud. They are both amazing people.

It is with great humility and some trepidation that I turn these letters, diary entries, stories, poems and musings over to you, dear reader.

I hope we have chosen what Mom would have wanted published.

And we hope you will enjoy…

" my book of happy memories."

Part I
Younger Years

The first part of this book is a collection of writing from Joan's youth - letters and poems and journal entries written while in her early school years, at Northampton School for Girls, and while attending Smith College.

In 1916, my grandfather, H. Eugene Getchell, bought two houses on the harbor at Sakonnet Point in Little Compton in Rhode Island - "Harbor Edge", or "The Big House" as we called it, and the cottage behind it, which we called simply "The Cottage". His father had already bought property in the area a few years before.

In her journal, a small brown leather-bound diary, written between 1918 and 1926, my mother describes her youth in Sakonnet - summers at the beach, the golf course, and late night fireside chats, falling in and out of love.

Ever since, houses have shifted (we have said goodbye to Harbor Edge and The Cottage and occupy "The Captain's House" across the yard instead) and family has moved far and wide, but Sakonnet has remained our gathering place. My mother went there throughout her childhood, my own childhood was there, I watched my children run through the surf and kick up the sand, and they in turn have taken their children, my grandchildren, to the crab pools and picked wildflowers with them by the water. And now my great-grandchildren have seen the same jagged rocks and smelt the same salty air.

Reading my mother's early writing, so much of which she wrote while in the places I still know and love, has given me both joy and the secret feeling of awe one gets at reading the youthful thoughts of one's parent as a child, before they became a mother and their world became yours. In her younger writing you can hear her writing style begin to form - unique, full of jokes and observations and funny quips.

Family photo with Eugene, Edith, and daughters Martha and Joan

Four Getchell sisters; Joan, Martha, Genie, and Celie

YOUNGER YEARS

**Poems written during her school days while
at Northampton School for Girls**

Dad

I often wonder what I would do
Without a peach of a Dad, like you.
You're always nearby when I've been bad
Either to scold me or help me, Dad.

I often wonder what would happen to Jo
If she didn't have someone to hand her the dough
Yes – all that she has, or ever had
Is all on account of her wonderful Dad.

But it isn't your gifts – or it isn't your dough
That makes me love, love, love you so
It's what you are, and what you do
In other words, Dad, it's just plain you!

Untitled

There is a house on Prospect Street which holds a family dear
A family full of happiness and always full of cheer.
Mother, Father, and four girls comprise that happy crowd,
And every child and grownup of each other is most proud.

Although Genie is the youngest, she leads everyone,
And if she don't have her way – she surely makes things hum!
But just the same we love her – as she loves her bouncing ball –
And although she's often naughty, her quaintness charms us all.

MY BOOK OF HAPPY MEMORIES

Next comes Celie darling – with her sweet and cunning ways.
Who's always full of happiness – and like sunshine casts bright rays.
The smartest and the dearest one to me is darling Mart
She'll always lend a helping hand and never shirks her part.

You see I haven't mentioned Jo – though at present she's happy and gay
But there's nothing special about her, so I wouldn't know what to say.
But best of all are the parents – that complete that loving home,
For without that Father and Mother, those children would feel quite
   alone.

> When you take a salty bath
>   We will not cramp your style,
> For there's loads and loads of water there
>   And it's yours for many a mile.
> But when you take a soap suds bath
>   We warn you of its scarcity –
> For Zeus did not equip our well
>   With Neptune's great capacity

Joan wrote this poem years later and made copies for every family bathroom in Sakonnet. This one hangs in my house to this day, and even my grandchildren have memorized it.

A letter written from Joan to her mother

Date unknown

Mother darlingest —

 <u>Please</u> don't ever go away again. I can't possibly tell you how lonely the house seemed without you that Monday + Tuesday before you came back from Hanover. I never before realized what a comfort it was to be able to run into your room a million times a day + share with you my thoughts and doings. Does it alleviate your unhappiness just a little to know what a comfort it is to us all to know that "Mother is always home." How keenly I realized during those two days that Mother is home itself. Your two little ears are always waiting to hear us spill over our enthusiasms, and that makes coming home such a pleasure for me. When I'm away I am constantly saying to myself — "Edie would appreciate that little bit," or "that's just what Mother would choose." So when I am home, I get a double pleasure by being able to say it to you in person. No sir, Edie, the place for you is home, where you have become indispensable to us all. When we were little we considered you necessary to answer our physical wants, but now you are so much more valuable for you are our mental audience.

 I couldn't get to sleep Sunday night because you were so unhappy and I was heavy-hearted all day Sunday for fear you were feeling terrible. But I kept thinking of the sunny smile you gave me when I kissed you goodbye and that reassured my unhappy thoughts. Just so long as you can smile, everything is O.K. with me, Edie, but if the time ever comes when it's too hard for even you to do so, will you promise to send for me? For I feel that making people smile is my chief purpose in life and you are my favorite raw material.

With a heart full of love and so <u>much</u> admiration for you,
Joan

P.S. Wipe your tears, too.[2*]

---

[2] *This letter is spotted with tears from Joan, the writer, or her mother Edith, the recipient. The TB took its toll on Edie both mentally and physically.

A letter written from Joan to her mother

Friday

Dearest dearest Mother,

I thought I'd write you a little personal note for my letters leave out many messages to you since they are practically public property.

I think of you so often, Edie dear, and now that Genie is absent how I wish I could be around to help make you comfy. When is she coming back and how are you managing without her?

Oh but I'm sorry the C.S.[3] didn't work. Maybe it <u>is</u> all baloney, and then again, it may work yet. I have so much faith and hope that you will come out of this unhappy fog soon. So <u>many</u> people have been through perfectly horrible unhappiness and have emerged with something gained.

At least you have the satisfaction of knowing that all of your family is well and contented. In answer to a letter to Dad concerning this Worcester dame he said he loved you so much that your just being around kept him happy + his only unhappiness lay in your mental distress. So kiddo, let's hope you'll get over the idea that you've got to be on your feet to be useful.

Here is my latest iron in the fire. I'm writing an article which I <u>hope</u> will be published in Harper's! You mustn't tell a <u>soul</u> cause it's a <u>private secret</u> + they probably won't accept it. Maybe the Smith Quarterly will, though.

There now I feel better for having had a little private chat with you. Give Dad a private kiss for me, too.

Lots + lots of love to you, Edie. I think of you so very often and it's always loving thoughts.

Good-by-
Joannie

---

[3] Joan's mother was being treated for tuberculosis. I am unsure what "C.S." is, though likely a tuberculosis treatment that her mother tried.

When I read these diary entries from her brown leather journal, I can't help but cringe at her youth and giddiness, remembering many diaries of my own from that age… but I love seeing her as a young woman, always in and out of love with some boy or other, playing golf and tennis, swimming all day and dancing all night. Rather than overwhelm a reader with names and places and daily details, we have selected some bits of her diary to include. (Max Pendergast)

Brown Diary

Joan Getchell

Her thoughts, words, and deeds – <u>private.</u>
P.S. Mostly thoughts – on <u>love</u>
The beginning of Joan's eventful life at Sakonnet

Not readable without my permission and then you probably won't be able to read it

June 1922 (Age 14)… I have had a wonderful time this week – the boys have been down most every day. Tro Horton is visiting the Chases and he is the peachiest peach I ever met, wonderful looking and a marvelous dancer…

July 1 1922… Had a <u>marvelous</u> time at dance tonight. Didn't sit down once all evening except in intermission…

July 2 1922…Tonight I was wishing someone would come down when Dick arrived on the scene. We went over to Mack's (store at the Point) got some candy and then sat out on the pier (there was a pier in front of their house) and chewed the rag…

July 5… What a rotten day! And yet I had a peach of a time… Tonight I went to Serena Smith's dance. Gee! What a ripping time!

July 8… Whew! The end of a perfect day! I played about 70 games of tennis today.

July 10… At last my golf is getting better!… I'm to play in a tournament tomorrow. Wish me luck!

July 11… This aft I played in the tournament and won second prize! Two golf balls!

July 12… Dickie's gone! I don't know what I'll do with myself till Sat.

July 13… We all went for a ride and I ate too much candy! Gee! But I feel sickish. Here's hoping I don't feed the fishes.

July 14… Why did I eat that candy? As a result I have been sick almost all day…

July 15… At last! Dickie's back! This morning I was supposed to play tennis with Francis Smith but couldn't cause my racket busted…

July 18… Who'd a thunk it? "Little Joannie won the grave-yard tournament and made a 49!! Look me over!…"

July 20… Just home from Doris' dance. Greenburt and I had good fun. Just the right crowd, and also Dickie was awful nice to me.

July 22… I'm awful tired and sort of peeved. I do wish Dicky liked me a lot. If he liked me as much as I like him, well ———. This morning Bob and I went fishing and I caught a flounder + a tautog.

July 25... Tonight we lent Bob the car and Dot, Mart, Dick, Bob and I all went. Dunt came home with us and I slammed my finger in the door. I'm sensible.

July 27... This morning Mart, Dot and I went up to the Club.... Dicky was sort of nice to me but Dunt was darling. He wrote a letter to Hal Gross and said he liked me best! Thrills.

July 28... Oh Joy, oh rapture! Dunt gave me his M.B. (Moses Brown School) pin!...

July 30... I had the most marvelous sail this morning! Mr. Flint gave a sailing party and everyone went.

Memoranda... opposite page
In reading this revelation of my soul over I find I have not said
but about half of what I really did. You will have to imagine the rest.
<u>Please be Kind</u>.

August 1... Gee! August 1st! Only a month more of fun. You can bet I'm going to make the most of it.

Good by darling diary_____I'm through!!!!

September 9... Ah! Darling Diary! Why did I stop revealing my heart, soul and liver (?) to you? Oh boy! What I didn't write! And also what I didn't do! That's really all foolishness cause I really only kissed one boy this summer – darling Tro Tro. Oh Boy! Will next summer ever come? Not for ages – but when it does come!—-! I hope I go to loads of Pro Dances this winter but nobody knows and darn it! Nobody seems to care!

September 11... "School days, school days! Reading and writing arithmetic (only don't have such childish studies!) taught to the rule of the hickory stick!" da da ta ta— Yep! I'm back again to the old grind!

October 9... Climbed trees. Mrs. Hanlon curled my hair... Nothing doing much.

November 29... I do believe I'll continue to confide in you, strange to say. I'd just as soon tell you everything cause I know you can't tell a darn soul – unless you "stink out loud" if I may be so vulgar.

December 1... Had a peach of a time today cause I didn't have to go to school... Tomorrow I may see Dickie! Gee but I've got some crush on him! It's almost love!

December 4... Oh Boy! I got my report card today and was I surprised. Oh no! I didn't flunk anything strange to say...

December 5... Gee but I'm having fun! I've just finished reading "snappy stories"... after dinner read and thought of Dicky, and then thought of Dicky some more.

December 7... Such an exciting day! Of course I went to school and had a peach of a time but had to stay ages cause I was naughty. Aren't I devilish?...

December 8... Gee! But my seat is wet! I have just come in from sliding...

December 9... Once again my seat is wet! And once again have I been sliding.

December 10... Ye Gads! Just had a peach of a row with Mother. She said I didn't know anything about Latin and I said I did. No one won...

December 11... Two weeks more and then Christmas! Ain't it grand?...

December 25... Merry Christmas! I'm fifteen years old today!

Memoranda (no date)

To think that the best, most exciting, most thrilling year of my life has come to an end! Honor bright! I never have had such a good time in all my young life, as I have this year and all - yes, every bit on account of Richard Hunt Chase! Ah! He has been the big hit of my life! I don't know what I would have done at Sakonnet without him – but I also would have passed away if I hadn't him to think of in Woonsocket! I have seen quite a lot of him this fall and Oh Boy! What a time I did have when I visited him.

If anyone should happen to read this – don't think it is <u>bosh!</u> - cause it isn't, I'm <u>very</u> serious.

And also my darling diary – I have meant to be faithful to them but when one has so many important things to think of – one simply can't be .

Well – as I said before, the year is over! – but this next year is going to be very exciting too – at least it is – if I can help it – so to begin with I have made two new year's resolutions –

Namely –
<u>First</u>

I hereby promise that I will try not to get peeved at mother and be respectful to her at all times because she is my mother.

<u>Second</u>
Short but sweet!
<u>Vamp</u> <u>Dick</u> <u>Chase</u>.
Amen

P.S. I hereby repent of everything I have said about anybody in this "Book Of Thoughts" which is against them.

P.P.S.S. I write in here for the last time closing with these words –
"May I never be base –
To my Mother's sweet face –
And here's hoping the best
May come of the rest" –
(meaning Article Two of my New Year's
constitutions – concerning Dick Chase)
Finis
Joan Getchell
Jan. 1, 1923 – 15 Years Old

Just a word to my <u>Descendants</u>

If, in the years to come you – my noble descendants – should happen to read this please don't be shocked! Also, never fall in love!

If by chance this book should roam,
please don't read but send it home to
Joan Ellis Getchell
205 Prospect Street
Woonsocket, R.I.

Red Journal[4]

December, 1926... My first day of vacation - spent very profitably! Left school at 10am... I came up to bed and had a lovely time thinking about vacation as I was falling asleep...

December 18th... Home again with all the family... Dick is coming out tomorrow. He looks *wonderful* in a derby. Never realized it before today...

December 19th, Woonsocket... Al came over later and we all sat in front of the fire and talked. They went about 10 and Mart and I sat downstairs and gabbed about sex and being in love. She says it's wonderful - "you feel so sort of warm inside." She claims Dick and I don't really love each other yet and I guess she's right...

December 20th... Never had more fun in my life than this evening. We all felt silly and acted it...

December 21st... It's over - but oh - what a party... Heart missed a beat when I saw Ash... Wore my new black evening dress. Love it... Dick ushered me in. He looked darling and so sweet to me. Started dancing and never felt so peppy in my life. Orchestra gorgeous + best men in world... After supper the orchestra got going - and did they go! I requested so many things they got to know me and after the dance Mr. Whitstein, the leader, came up to me and said, "Anytime you ever want a piece I would love to play it for you. I always love to satisfy people who act as if they were having a good time. I hope you're at my dances often!"... While I was dancing with Ash I said, "I'm getting such a rush from you tonight it almost seems natural."... The boys went upstairs to

---
[4] When writing her red journal Joan was just turning 19 in December 1926, spending Christmas in Woonsocket and then the following summer in Sakonnet and Cape Cod.

bed and Dick and I stayed down and talked for a while. Oh how I do love him!...

December 22nd... Had to get up at nine-thirty this morning so they could get eleven o'clock to New York... We came home about twelve and when I got in I sat up in the front hall and wrote to Ash. Couldn't help it...

December 24th... After dinner I read my diary of four years ago to the family and I thought they would die laughing...

December 25th... Christmas and my birthday spent with the family...

December 27th... Marvelous dance and marvelous men!... After dinner we played bridge and then went over to dance at Essex Country Club. Wonderful place for dance and gorgeous orchestra...

December 29th... After luncheon we all went to Palace to the theatre and saw very good vaudeville. Came home afterwards and Jimmy taught me the tango. He is so attractive...

December 30th... Charlie came for me and we went to the theatre. When we got home he came in for a minute and wanted to stay but I didn't dare let him for more than one reason. He is darling though and it's going to be hard to be good this summer. I think I'm being perfectly fair with him because he knows I like Dick. When he asked me if I loved him I said I loved no one in the world.

December 31st... Twelve o'clock came at the wrong time and I was dancing with Hal. The lights went out and I nearly died when he kissed me. Dick arrived just too late...

January 3rd, 1927... Slept until twelve + then Mart and I had a bath in the same tub. I'm sure I got most of the water...

January 4th... Spent all day trying to realize that Dick and I must call it off. Had a grand old blubber and next day Mrs. Chase came out and Mother she and I talked it all over and decided it was best. If I write all about it I will weep so guess I won't.

March 30th... Went down to Sakonnet this morning with Mother and Jerry... I think I've picked a congenial crowd, and a decent one too...

March 31st... Decided to go to Newport to movies so Gorden went back to Providence + we went to Newport only to find movies closed also! We drove all over the town and drove into all the estates which were open...

June 25th... So relieved to be away from school and with some men once again! Summer is starting in well!

June 26th... Poured guns all day. After breakfast we all went for a walk and became soaked after which we all went in swimming. Water simply freezing but no wetter than we were...

June 27th... We all went out and picked strawberries for a while after breakfast...

July 1st... Played golf with Mother this morning and then went over to the beach. Phil and Dick pushed me off - darn their hides!

Typing up these letters for my Grandma over the last three years has been very eye opening to me. Learning about my different family members who I have never met before has really put a perspective of the past in my head that I never thought I could experience. And of course, a very common theme in almost all the letters I've typed: golf. Around Christmas a couple of years ago, I remember one of my cousins asking me what the letters I typed were about. And to that I answered one word only: golf. (Jack Brennan Cox)

Golf

From way down in Sakonnet
I hear the loud loud call
Of my good, old banged
up driver,
And my little old golf ball.

I just know each hole is wondering
When the dickens I'll ever come –
And take a great big chunk
Out of every gosh darn one.

But just wait until I get there
I'll show 'em something new –
I'll have learned to play so
Gosh darn good
That I'll get a forty-two!

Forty-two – yep! Forty-two.
Maybe you think it's a lie
Well – if you don't believe me
Just wait till by and by.

My balls will go so straight
And my balls will go so far
That every single hole I play,
I'll make in less than par! (pa)

An excerpt about golf from *Johnnycakes and Cream* written by Joan's sister Genie[1]

Johnnycakes and Cream
Oral Histories of Little Compton, R.I.

Compiled and Edited by
Lucy A. O'Connor
Printed by America House Design & Communications, Newport, R.I.
(99) *Used with permission*

Eugenie Rawson
Born 1915

...I wasn't a golfer. Martha, my oldest sister and I, I think, kind of fought against golf. Dad loved it and was a great golfer. Joan and Celie played a lot and at the dinner table it was golf, golf, golf. And I don't know whether Martha and I just sort of backed away or what happened. Well, finally, I guess it was Richie that got me going and then I'd just walk around with him 'cause he wanted someone to verify his scores. At the Club... we had lots of fun with those plays. I was the kid sister in most of them. They were sort of petering out by the time I got older but I remember them because of Martha, Joan and Celie. But Celie can really go through every one of them... the one about when you had to go to the beach and the clothes we had to wear at the beach. Oh my, yes. Celie's the one - she can remember the words to every single one of those songs in the musical comedies that they had. I remember one particular one I was in and Dick Chase who was my sister Joan's beau, he and someone else had a prize fight in this play and he was knocked out and I had to go

---
1   An additional excerpt from *Johnnycakes* about the family's Sakonnet origins is located in Appendix C.

on and drop rose leaves over him. And I don't know - there'd been a rehearsal and I thought it was great fun but the night of the play when I went onstage and saw him out cold I burst into tears 'cause I was very fond of Dick.

A Handwriting Contest that Joan Won in May, 1928

Part II
A Young Woman

In her early 20s, Joan travelled with her mother Edie, who suffered from tuberculosis, to Europe, and attended Smith College. She also fell in love with and became engaged to Edward S. Cole, my father, who everyone called Shaw.

Some of my favorite letters here, one to her friend Vee, one written by Shaw to Joan's father Eugene, and the other by Joan to her soon-to-be-in-laws the Coles, speak so beautifully of their love for each other.

Letter from Joan to her friend Vivian Craig

Sunday Morning

Dearest Vee,

    Honestly, this is the most wonderful place to stay. Everyone is so darn nice + I feel so at home. I'm so sorry you weren't here tho. I'd like nothing better than a long, long talk with you. Here goes a long, long letter instead.

    I take it you went to New Haven with Jack. Please write and tell me what you did because I'm going to start now for at least three pages about what I did.

    Vee, if you could see this man I was with. He is without a doubt the smoothest individual I know and yet he isn't smooth like Paul. You'd never guess he was anything but an awful good egg but I've never yet known a woman who didn't fall for him. I was sure I wouldn't because I think he <u>must</u> have loads of them but of course I am – I'm crazy about him. Or at least, the craziest I've been about anyone since Dick. And he looks exactly like Richard Dix. That ought to be enough of a description of him. I hate these women who write to you and do nothing but rave about their men but I have to in this case because I want to get it off my chest. Now, I don't know what to do about him because I've never met anyone like him before. Do you suppose I ought to give him a lot of time or be sort of indifferent? I'm so damn afraid I'll lose him!

    We went to the Copley both nights and it was glorious! Everyone at college said it was usually so wet it was disgraceful but this time it was really respectable last night and fairly so the night before. I had heard great tales about how the men just passed out on the dance floor but I didn't see one. By the way, I saw Gretchen Andres there with her brother and I told her there was a letter addressed to her on your mantle. (I also saw a letter from Al Martell! Is he functioning?)

    The game was wonderful since Dartmouth won by so much. You

were on the winning side too, weren't you? I guess we know what men to go with. (The only one who asked me was Shaw, but nevermind.)

I must tell you something funny. Before I came to Boston I had felt sort of "wupsy" and so I hadn't eaten a thing except a potato + a cup of coffee for two days. Shaw's roommates' family were staying at the Copley and asked us up for a little cocktail party. Well! In the first place I'm not very used to cocktails + in the second place they don't sit so well…[5]

---

[5] The rest of this letter is missing.

A YOUNG WOMAN

Letter from Shaw Cole to Joan's Father, H. Eugene Getchell

April 28, 1931
Hanover, N.H –

Dear Mr. Getchell,

Joan and I have just spent a very happy weekend together here in Hanover, after which I drove her back to Northampton. We were pretty busy a good part of the time with food, dancing, etc. but we did find time to do some serious talking –

I hope I am not good enough at hiding my feelings and intentions to surprise you with this letter, for I must long before this have shown that I loved Joan very much. What the etiquette is today with regard to making your intentions known, I am a bit uncertain about, and although I have for some time had in mind writing you I thought it would be much wiser to be sure of the subject matter.

Today I am much surer of everything than I have been before and feel more able to lay my case before you – Joan and I love each other. We want to get married and start a life together as soon as is wisely possible. If I were to try to tell you what a wonderful girl she is I would be attempting something you are already aware of and I am sure I could not do her justice. It would be much better for me to tell you that I have never been so convinced of anything nor that I have ever been so serious and earnest about anything as I am about marrying her and doing my best to make her the happy person she deserves to be.

As for myself, I hope I have been able to make a sufficiently good impression on you so that you will think I have both the qualifications and the ability to marry Joan and make her happy. I hope I have not too many illusions about myself but I feel equal to the responsibility which I want to assume. There is no halo about my head and my ambitions and aims in life are not such that I could write a book about them. If I can do justice to my home training and supplement that with sound judgment where changing conditions make it seem wise I will have achieved I believe a great deal and lived a pretty fine life.

A letter today from my Father gives me more information about my job than I have had before. I have a wonderful opportunity, I think, to make a good living and it is my ambition to someday have shown sufficient ability to continue the fine business Father has developed.

I hope that you will not feel I have waited too long before giving you my feelings about Joan or that I am being too hasty, and that you will be in favor of that which my heart is so set on. Please give my kindest regards to Mrs. Getchell and (believe me),

Ever sincerely yours –
Shaw Cole

Shaw and Joan's father, H. Eugene Getchell

Letter from Joan to her family from Smith College

1931, Monday

Dearest High Hats –

Boy, I hope it's warmer there than here today. Everything is out to be blossoming beautifully according to my horticulture teacher, so I know Mother can rave all over again about the "new spring tools".

Hanover was wonderful this weekend. Aunty was fine + had enjoyed her visit as well as Louise. Shaw + I stayed there for dinner Sunday + had a lovely time.

I hope you'll be excited to hear that Shaw knows more definitely about his job and much to our surprise + great joy the future looks bright + early. About next June seems to be our date. Shaw is writing Papa for my hand + if you all approve, we will surprise all of our friends by announcing our engagement around this 4th of July.

It will be a ringless affair because I refuse to let Shaw work for a long time to buy me a hunk of rock which will just hinder us from getting married sooner. I don't care two hoots about a diamond chip – I'd much rather wait + get one nice one. Also we think a family wedding would be the best both for financial and sentimental reasons. I want my 3 sisters + Mary Cole + Shaw has 4 boy cousins so it will be strictly family + very nice.

If you had any idea of taking me to Europe – thank you very much, I'd love to go. Whatever you + Dad do next Spring I would like to do with you because I love you and will miss you terrifically when I am married. We don't know where we'll be living so I want to stick around you people while I can!

I'm going on my Horticulture Trip to Groton & Boston this Thursday + Friday. Be sure to put our allowance in won't you because I don't know how much this trip will cost. I hope we don't stay at the snooty hotel you + I stayed at Mother.

We had a faculty dinner tonight + I sat between Miss Cook and Mrs. Scalss + had a grand time.

I hope you are all having wonderful weather + a wonderful time. Think of us working up here!

Best love to you all,
Joan

Letter from Joan to her future father-in-law, Mr. Cole

Wednesday

Dearest Mr. Cole,

Yours was the nicest letter I've ever received from a boy – except for Shaw's!

It makes me so happy to know that you and Mrs. Cole approve of me. I love Shaw so <u>much</u> that I can easily imagine what he means to you, therefore it makes me feel extra happy to have you glad that I am the girl he has chosen.

Shaw and I have had such glorious times together and I just beam with joy when I realize that this is only the beginning of it all. Life with him is such a wonderful thing to look forward to, and I can hardly wait to begin.

I can so easily picture all of the "ups" in married life but I can't seem to imagine any of the "downs." Of course we won't have much money at first, but we don't seem to care about that, and if he has to go from town to town on business, if I can go with him once in a while, that's all I ask.

It all seems so ideal to me, Mr. Cole. All of my Mother's family were engineers, as you are.[6] All of my family are Smith advocates, as Mrs. Cole is and I hope Mary will be. Both our families are from New England and neither of us are rolling in wealth. Consequently, Shaw + I have loads of the same ideas, but enough different ones to make it interesting! And we both love New England so that when Shaw's business ceases demanding that he be in other parts of the world, back to New England we'll come and have a little house right in the midst of it.

Shaw says you mentioned something about the liquor problem. We had just discussed it all this weekend + decided that we would never serve or accept any at all because it involves both unhappiness

---

6   More information on the Ellis and Cole engineers can be found in the appendix.

\+ expense. It seems to worry him a little because he feels that business seems to demand it somewhat.

We have just loved having the car this spring and I have a sentimental attachment for it because we have had such glorious times in it. Thank you so much for letting us have it – but you're such a grand Father that you would realize our wants, but you can't ever realize how much I love and want Shaw -

Lovingly,
Joan

Letter from Mary Cole, Shaw's mother, to Edith Getchell, Joan's mother

June 15, 1931
133 Belleview Ave
Upper Montclair, N.J.

My dear Mrs. Getchell –

Shaw has been with us for the past week – partly killing time and partly recovering from the tonsil operation.

Much of our thought and conversation has turned upon Joan and their relationship. I understand that tonight she is to carry on the Smith tradition and run around the table after class supper with the other engaged girls and Shaw assures me that no one will be in the least surprised.

We are greatly pleased that Joan feels a life interest in Shaw. From our much too slight acquaintance with her we have come to value highly her sterling qualities and recognize her brilliant mind. She may find Shaw's more moderate pace + mental activity disappointing but in so far as I am able to appraise them, they seem to supplement each other pretty well and I am sure we should look forward to a life of happiness for them.

We shall gladly welcome Joan into the bosom of our family and I am looking forward to the days when we may become better acquainted.

You must feel very proud of her achievements at College where she has taken such conspicuous roles.

I have been somewhat disheartening to Shaw with his new ambitions. I find that Mr. Cole's business, like most others, has been affected by the present depression, and that at the moment he may have to mark time.

It may not be long before he has a taste of what life after college really is. Shaw has plenty of faults and much to learn – but he is a dear son.

I had hoped we might see much of you this summer, but I understand a trip is in prospect which may take you away. It sounds most delightful.

Hoping that we may catch a glimpse of you before you go or after you return and in anticipation of our future common interests.

Cordially yours,
Mary R. Cole

Joan and Shaw's engagement announcement was sent on golf cards.

Engagement and Graduation Announcements

Class of 1927, Northampton School for Girls Newsletter
ENGAGED:
Joan Getchell to Shaw Cole of Montclair,
New Jersey, Dartmouth, 1930;
Thayer School of Engineering, 1931

Smith College
The Evening Bulletin, Providence
Monday, May 25, 1931

Five R.I. Girls to get Diplomas at Smith College

...Miss Getchell also prepared at the Northampton School for Girls and while in college majored in religion. She was a member of Telescopium, a club composed of those students doing especially outstanding work in the field of astronomy. Miss Getchell was also secretary of her class freshman year, author of the Rally Day show of her class, and is to be toastmistress at the class supper held as part of commencement week activities.

WE SEE BY THE PAPERS AND CURRENT PUBLICATIONS...
Joan Getchell spent a few weeks at Easter in Naples with her sister who is a Smith Junior-in-France. She will be in Paris until June, and then in England on a golfing tour until the end of July. She hopes "to walk off the gangplank into a wedding dress if business has risen from depression to elation." Address, Raymond Witcomb, Paris.

Entries in a Travel Journal, blue-covered, that she kept in 1932

March 4 '32
New York
2nd class "Roma"
Leaving Shaw!

Minimum second class rates. Nice purser gave us a 3 port hole suite, same price. Sleep + oblivion. Considered snooty by passengers. Stared at as if curiosities by male element at females. Cable from Shaw. Flowers filled all three rooms + many indescribable gadgets sent us were all stuck in drawers.

Asleep in the deep! Some more asleep in the deep.

March 13

An ocean - beautiful day. Saw whale, porpoises + snow capped mountains.

March 14

Sicily, Palermo beautiful. Toured all around - exquisite mosaic chapel.[7] Monreale. Lunch beautiful Hotel Iqiza with all of the tourist agents! Heavenly garden - most romantic. Drove all around all afternoon + sailed that night. Sat in bar, + talked with the jewelry salesman!

---

7   *(On the back of the picture of Vee, Joan, Edith & Celie In Grandma Edith's handwriting)* "Taken today – March 31 – in front of Santa Croce – Florence, where Michelangelo, Galileo etc. etc. are buried. I look cadaverous, too, in the picture but don't feel that way. So glad to get Dad's letter, so full of news. You are leaving from us (?) by this time. It takes so long for letters. It makes me happy to know you go to Martha's often – too cold & lonesome at home. Bought you all presents to-day! Everything beautiful in Florence." *(Added by Joan)* "Just kissed Mother and her nose is very cold - healthy sign."

Vee, Joan, Edith, and Celie

A Young Woman

Papa's Sore Back - a poem written to Joan, Edith, Celie, and Vivian from her Father and her sister Genie

Papa had a sore back,
Had to lie in bed,
Had to use a bedpan,
By a nurse was fed.

Went to the hospital
All wrapped in cloth,
Curses on the doctor,
With him he was wroth.

Wore it just about a week,
Purgatory was Heaven,
Had him take the damned thing off,
Just like throwing seven.

"Three weeks" and home again
Bed pan and all,
Who to do the honors
Joe sure had first call.

Now that phase is over,
Papa is a man;
Toddles like a baby,
Just the best he can.

Every day in every way,
He gets better and better;
Now he feels good enough
To write you this letter.

Hope it finds you sitting up,
And reaches you fast mail;
When you start to read it,
Better be near the rail.

Genie and I are the authors,
How quiet she can be!
But no one more interested
Could be than she.

Now we're all exhausted,
Bees buzzing in our bonnet,
Trust you'll like our spasm,
We call it a Sonnet.

Sonnet to our loved ones,
On the briny deep,
Prayers for you every night,
Before we go to sleep.

Part III
Early Married Years

My mother and father had a very interesting start to their marital bliss. My father, Shaw, like his father before him (and for a short period my sons John and Michael Pendergast, and also their cousin Michael van Duren), worked for The Pitometer Company. As they worked with Pitometers all over the country, the job entailed constant travel, and it left my parents uprooted for the first few years of their marriage. They travelled all over the country. They would spend anywhere from a week to six months in any given town whilst Shaw, my father, finished whatever project or test the water system there required.

Hearing my mother describe all of these small American towns and all their abodes is like travelling back in time and far away. Her descriptions are delightful and vivid.

Towards the end of their nomadic life, Joan's mother passed away from tuberculosis, shortly after a visit from Joan. Her father died a few months later, having killed himself in his hospital room (he was hospitalized for a throat ailment) of grief over his wife's death. I cannot imagine the toll this must have taken on my mother, but in the years following, as all her children were born, she maintained her positive embrace of life and all its twists and turns.

I'll let my mother tell the rest!

Mr. and Mrs. Herbert Eugene Getchell

request the pleasure of your company

at the marriage reception of their daughter

Joan Ellis

and

Mr. Edward Shaw Cole

on Saturday, the twenty-fourth of March

at half after four o'clock

Two hundred and five Prospect Street

Woonsocket, Rhode Island

The favor of a reply is requested

Joan and Shaw's wedding invitation

Joan and Shaw on their wedding day

Early Married Years

Article written on the occasion of their wedding on page 12 of the Woonsocket Call[8]

March 24, 1934

"Joan E. Getchell Bride Today Of
Edward S. Cole Is Seventh To Wear Veil
Which Is Family Heirloom; Simple Ceremony"

Before an improvised altar, banked in Southern smilax, gleaming by the soft light of ivory cathedral candles in silver candelabra, in the living room at the home of Mr. and Mrs. H Eugene Getchell at 205 Prospect Street, their daughter, Miss Joan Ellis Getchell and Edward Shaw Cole, son of Mr. and Mrs. Edward Smith Cole of 133 Bellevue Avenue, Upper Montclair, N.J. were united in marriage at 4 o'clock this afternoon. The ceremony, performed by Rev. E. Dean Ellenwood, pastor of the First Universalist Church, was a simple one, witnessed only by families and intimate friends of the bride and bridegroom. Window boxes of spring bulbs, tulips, daffodils and freesia, and vases of acacia, forsythia and stately calla lilies, lent their beauty to the floral decorations of the living room.

The bride was lovely in her mother's wedding gown of white satin in a princess model, trimmed with duchess and rose point lace, worn by the bride's sister, Mrs. W. Roland Harrall, at her wedding. Her veil, trimmed with lace, a family heirloom belonging to Mrs. John Rockwell, aunt of the bridegroom, was worn by Mrs. Rockwell at her wedding and also by Mrs. Edward Smith Cole, mother of the bridegroom, on a similar occasion. Today's bride is the seventh bride to wear it. She carried an old-fashioned bouquet of gardenias.

Miss Mary Lucile Getchell, sister of the bride and Miss Vivian A.

---

8   * Founded in 1892, The Woonsocket Call is an American daily newspaper published seven days per week in Woonsocket, Rhode Island, covering northern Providence County, Rhode Island, and some adjacent towns in Massachusetts.

Guerin, bridesmaids, wore gowns of pebbled chiffon in pastel green, the ruffled trimmings on the long skirts extending from the waist line and continuing to form a train. With the gowns they wore small hats of brown marline and their arm bouquets were of acacia and daffodils. John Rockwell Cole of Upper Montclair, brother of the bridegroom, served as his best man.

Many guests attended the reception, following the ceremony, at 4:30 o'clock, with the bride and bridegroom assisted in receiving by their parents and the bridal attendants. Music for the reception was by Mrs. Marden Platt, harpist of Providence and the Laura Carr Company of Providence catered. The ushers were Thomas N. Barrows of Cedarhurst, L. I. and Donald Cruickshank of Ottawa, Can.

The bride was educated at the Northampton School for Girls, Pembroke College, Royal Victoria College and Smith College. The bridegroom was educated at Williston Academy, Deerfield Academy, Dartmouth College and the Thayer School of Engineering. He is associated with the Pitometer Company of New York City as hydraulic engineer.

Joan's written account of all the events right before and after her wedding to Shaw in March 1934

March 22-26, 1934

March 22 – Thursday – arrival of Shaw with Craig – after short trip of 250 miles I insisted on Shaw's taking me for a ride in our new car. Supper party at B. Ingraham's. Dad + __ having date – many cocktails played games. Arrival of Aunt M. + Louise. Mart + Doc arrived.

March 23 – Guick's arrival in morning having wired his old girl not to come. Thousands of presents. Decorators putting up smilax. Belgian drinks by Dad – lunch Celie Shaw John Guick + me… 11 o'clock called on minister. Insisted on ceremony being short + to the point. Bedlam until rehearsal, Arrival of Tom, Franny Holliday, Mr. and Mrs. Cole, Harriet. 4:00 rehearsal. Celie playing wedding march. Many wise cracks. Minister cornering Mrs. Cole after rehearsal – long conversation. Dressed for Genie's dinner at 7:30. Soup + nuts, cocktails to cordials. Getchell dinner arrived + movies taken. Barkley Club table for 24. Wedding march played. Arrived late. Many Boston friends on hand outside of party. Bride + Groom last to arrive home.

March 24 – Florists – more presents. Pack + dressed for Macky's luncheon. Vee stuck pin in eye – some doubt as to whether she could be in wedding. Tom feeling horrible. Movies at luncheon, very wet ones of bride + groom. Dressed for wedding. Photographers. Arrival of wedding party + cousins Irene ½ hour early. All grouped in nursery. Dad handing out whiskey to lend moral support. Shaw perfectly dry. Guests arrive. The wedding party silly – clogging – remembering + jazzing wedding march. 4:00. Mr. Ellenwood giving dissertation to Shaw about German situation. Wedding march. Billy Robinson during hush – "Is Joan coming in now?" Procession + ceremony. Some tears. Reception complete to bride + groom. Just one "So glad you came after another." Distinct loss of appetite. Cutting of cake most assuredly made of plaster of Paris + lacking orange blossoms especially sent from Fl for occasion. Bride throwing bouquet with bunch of old maids in sight. Meredith Perkins caught it. Very touched in more ways than one. Bride just took off wedding veil when B. Ingraham burst in + said "Oh! I just came – put it on again for me." Shaw in attic. I ready much before him. Rushing through Dad's room together. Jennie yelling after me – "don't be scared Joan – don't be scared." Rushing out midst much confetti. Unsuccessful movies because of canopy. Leaping into car. Steaming up P. street to music of trailing cans just married sign put on backwards. Discovery of lack of luggage. Changing cars. Doc arriving with luggage. Genie's crowd arriving + dousing us with confetti. Off – snowstorm. 5 inquiries as to whereabouts of Wayside Inn. Reading of telegrams on route. Arrival at here. Confetti dripping out. Joan surprised herself by being embarrassed. Shaw going for cigs. Escorted into lovely room. Dining table set for 2. Candles. Appetite returned – delicious dinner with Chianti. Arrival of Mart + Doc's telegram "Goodnight."9*

March 25 – Breakfast in room. Telegrams. Message from Aunt Alice. Morning paper. Beautiful day. Note in rafters. Scratches on windows. Leaving gift of corkscrew from Henry Ford – unbeknownst to him. Hostess calling after me my cousin Ellis at home + would like to see me – saw her. In to Copley for cocktails + lunch at Merry go round to commemorate first date there. To Elys in Chestnut Hill for going away party. Coffee + liqueur for ladies – highballs for gents. Escorts to boat. Entrance to Suite P. Refusal on part of steward to open bar. Arrival of Woonsocket contingent looks on entrance. Departure – very gala. Boat held over for passengers waving. Alone on deck watching Boston recede. Forced in by cold. Planned to dinner dance. Few waves changed

---

9 * See photo of another telegram from Celie & Bud.

Joan's mind. Flat sudden urge to bathroom. Copley mushrooms. Flat again. Hopes for recovery when arrived at Canal. Shaw calling to find out time – no canal – hopes fade. No recovery. Later partial recover, etc. – oblivion for Joan. Bath for Shaw at 3 A.M. to get money's worth. No food. Joan didn't care.

March 26 – Awakening to find New York harbor. New lease on life for Joan. Starvation – big breakfast – many stares. Landing – Macy's. Out to L.I. and week of retreat.

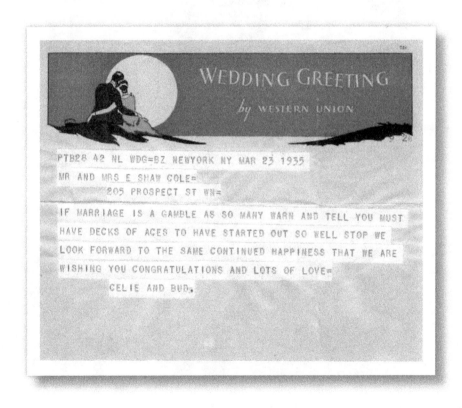

Joan and Shaw

Early Married Years

Letter from Joan to her family

April 8, 1934

Letter No. 1
General Brodhead Hotel
120 Rooms All With Bath. Reasonable Rates
SEVENTH AVE. AT TWELFTH ST.
Beaver Falls, PA

Dearests,

I think by now we own half the town! We are more than pleased with what we find. Our friend Mr. Gaver is our patron saint. He is a very dear friend of Mrs. Conyngtous (a friend of Mrs. Cole's), has lived here all his life, and since his wife died two years ago, has been living here at the hotel. He met us for lunch yesterday noon + brought along a young married couple who are living here at the hotel, + yesterday afternoon he drove us all over Beaver and Beaver Falls. He used to have a bathtub etc. factory here and evidently made lots of money because his old home here in Beaver Falls, which he took us through, is a beauty and he has an equally fine one in Beaver, two miles from here. He knows everyone in town by his first name and has been more than nice to us.

Also two other friends of his have dropped in to see us and a Mr. Bernie, the head of the water works dept. took us in hand yesterday morning and helped us find a place to live. I've also called up Adiu Capron's wife + became acquainted with her. So you see we've had a splendid welcome + don't feel like lost sheep in the least.

We have decided where we're going to live and hope to move in tomorrow. It was recommended by Mr. Bernie + while it isn't exactly artistic as to furnishings it will be very comfortable. There is a dining living room and separate kitchen on the ground floor with a cute little back porch of our own (hope to eat out here soon) which opens out onto some nice lawn with our garage nearby. The bedroom and bathroom is upstairs. Our landlady is very nice and - a Mrs. La Veen - Christian. The location is <u>ideal</u>. It's in Patterson Heights, the nice section and we're about 100 yards from the golf club. It's a nice little nine hole course + we've already joined under some spring rates which we wouldn't be able to get after April - fifteen dollars for both of us. Ten dollars initiation + 5 dollars a month for both of us. We had dinner there this noon. <u>W</u>onderful food. It seems that they have women's tournaments each week and mixed foursomes occasionally so it's apparently a very active club. Several people spoke to us at the club this noon so I guess word has gotten around that a couple of green newlyweds are in town.

Before I forget I wanted to give you our address and phone number. It's 513 Fifth Avenue Patterson Heights Beaver Falls + the phone is 510-R. Phone under Paul La Veen's name. We aren't having a separate one put in. Forgot to tell you the rent is thirty dollars per month including garage.

Patterson Heights is certainly a height! It's sort of a bluff overlooking the Beaver River + all of the country is really <u>beautiful</u>. We are right off the main route from Pittsburgh to Cleveland, Cleveland being 115 miles from here.

The town is <u>very</u> dirty + the water very hard (is it borax that softens it?) but it is much cleaner up high where we are. There are some lovely homes both here and in Beaver Dash. Some Pittsburgh people live out here. The town itself isn't much but the people seem <u>awfully</u> nice.

Now, I don't think we'll want much stuff sent because the pitometer man tells us we will only be here three months. I imagine the ten cent store can supply most of our wants but if I find we can't do without some of the things, we'll send for them when we get established + know what we want.

I wish you'd ask lots of questions if you want to know things because everything is so new + different I can't remember all I want to tell you.

I hope everything is going splendidly at home. I could wax very sentimental about you both but it would end up in tears for all of us + I wouldn't want that for either of us. I don't want Shaw to think I'm lonesome and unhappy because I'm gloriously happy and feel as if we're living a great adventure.

Tomorrow night my role as cook starts. Thank heaven for the toast master! When Mrs. La Veen was showing me the kitchen I tried hard to look intelligent but finally broke down and told her that all I could make was Hollandaise Sauce so none of the gadgets meant anything to me as yet. I did see an ice box that requires real ice and some sort of gas range. I'm glad I didn't bring any elaborate linens because I wouldn't want to insult them by putting them on the mission sideboard!

From tomorrow on I expect to bury myself in my thank you notes so I'm afraid my bulletins will be puny post cards for a while. My only reading matter will be the cook book and I've already absorbed this month's Good Housekeeping!

How the people sound their R's down here. In fact even the beggars are different. One approached us as we came into the hotel and said, "Buddy, I'm not asking you for money - all I ask is that you take me across to the drug store and buy me a cake of "Lifebuoy soap"! I guess he's one of the "four out of five have it"- he looked it!

Our car is _such_ a joy. Living here would be a problem without one - but as it is it looks as if we didn't have any problems at all because we're young + healthy + very much in love.

My dearest love to you all + don't think of us with any pity because everything is the nuts - my next letter will probably tell you about the muffins that were muffed + the omelet that dropped through to the cellar!

Much love again -
Joan

The Bernies live two doors from us. She is lovely and will help me out with domestic details. They are from Biddeford, ME. Also have a lovely house + garden. Hope for some flowers from her!

An Excerpt from Joan's Scrapbook

1934

The following little framed inspiration greeted me each morning when I opened my eyes.

Morning Prayer

Now I get up to do my work
   I pray, Oh God, I may not shirk.
If I should die before the night
   I hope, My Lord, the work's alright.

I found this a slightly discouraging eye-opener, and I soon read it with different, and very disrespectful, intonations. With great difficulty, I restrained my desire to frame the following -

Evening Prayer

I'll say I rose and did my work
   At least the part I dared not shirk
I'm so tired I could die tonight
   Oh yes, My Lord! - I worked alright!

Letter from Joan to her family from Pennsylvania

Monday, 10pm

Dearest mother et al -

My role as engineer's wife has started full blast! We just came from the movies and Shaw went down to the office to see about getting the boys going on the night work. He found that Harry Ingersol, head of the Pit. Job, had missed his train from Pittsburgh so has to wait for the next train to arrive. In the meantime, I came up here rather than wait out in the car. Incidentally there is a revival meeting going on in a wooden tabernacle near the office and they are making <u>some</u> noise.

There are quite a few strange sects in + near town. There are many orthodox covenanters whom I haven't found out much about as yet. All I know is they don't vote because the word God is used in the constitution of the U.S. Then there are the Amish Dutch who devote their time to farming only. We see them in their produce wagons – the men all in black with long hair + the women in gray bonnets. They think buttons are evil for some reason or other!

Sunday we went into Pittsburgh for dinner at the Ingersols. They are <u>peaches</u>. He's one of the better Pit. engineers and they've lived fourteen different places and had four children while doing it - 2 of which have died. The two children they have are <u>darlings</u> + they are a lovely family. She gave me lots of useful dope on moving from place to place. We had a wonderful dinner + stopped in Beaver on the way home to call on the Capoons but found them out. They have a very nice looking brick house.

Wed. night we are going to the Bernies for dinner. He's head of the water company here + they are originally from Biddeford. They have a very pretty house a few doors down - in fact to our minds they have the only pretty one in B. Falls. There are some expensive ones but they are all of homely yellow brick. Brick is much cheaper here because painted houses get so filthy!

Everything is dirty here! This morning the woman next door took her clothes in because a mist started to fall. The rain brings the dirt from the air down on to the drying clothes even. Downtown here there is most always a heavy fog of smoke & mist but up where we are it's lovely.

We really were <u>very</u> lucky to find a place up on the Heights. It is the only available house up there and + we're so glad we could get it. When I first saw it I thought I'd die if I ever had to live among such horrible looking furniture but Shaw + I were just saying tonight how much we'd grown to love it. The kitchen is so complete + Mrs. LaVeen a dear. I really think she'd cook all of my meals if I so much as suggested it! We're <u>more</u> than comfortable + I hope we get a break like this one everywhere we go.

I'm really amazed at my growing skill as a cook. Tonight we had baked ham with cloves, brown sugar + pineapple all cooked together, candied sweet potatoes, cauliflower + a dessert which I meant to be brownies but turned out to be a kind of gingerbread. I make special sauces for everything which pleases Shaw most to death. I've made mayonnaise + French dressing + have some kind of lunch salad each day. If he comes home at noon we just have soup, different kinds of toasted sandwiches made right on the table + salad. Yesterday I had 2 egg whites which I thought I'd use up, so attempted to make a cake. All went well until I suddenly realized I had mixed the recipe with the one farther down the page which was an angel cake – so the result was interesting to the eye but not the palate! The funny part of it is that I just <u>love</u> to cook. Of course, I'm <u>terribly</u> awkward about things – I'm forever dropping the things I'm paring into the swill! But, I think it's sort of like taking a course in chemistry and I always did like to "mix" things. I get perfectly panicky trying to get all of the things onto the table when they are done, and I have yet to get everything done at once, but I guess that will come with experience. Each morning after the breakfast dishes I pour over the cook books for the day's menu and I get so absorbed I have to force myself upstairs to make the beds.

We're trying to eat on a dollar a day including Shaw's .25 for lunch + you'd laugh to see us figuring out how much each meal cost before we finished it! I've estimated how long a loaf of bread lasts, a can of coffee etc. and we find it's loads of fun.

I haven't done any washing as yet but we're planning to send out the sheets + Shaw's good shirts etc. It's <u>so</u> hard to get things clean! Oh I found a soap that makes suds at last. Mrs. Ingersol told me about it, + I've taken to rubber gloves which is a great help.

Pretty soon now we're going to start playing golf when Shaw gets home from work + then have a late dinner.

Have you read "I went to Pitt College"? I have it here but can't feel right about reading until I get my thank you notes done. The authoress was in my class at Smith, you know. The country around here is full of mines + each farm seems to have its own small mine in its backyard. It looks as if there is a great deal of poverty around here, but everything is so dirty it's hard to tell whether the houses are run down or not.

We have a cute little back porch with a huge forsythia bush + pussy willow tree in front of it so when it gets warm we hope to eat out there. The view from the bluff is really beautiful + when things get greener it will be even more lovely.

Sat. afternoon I went with Shaw while he did some Pitt work + now I really feel pretty intelligent about my husband's business. We have such a swell time together + so far there has been <u>none</u> of that much talk of adjusting. We're so thoroughly congenial in every way + I don't believe we'll ever get each other's goats!

You've all been so wonderful about writing! Mother, please stick to postcards because I know how writing tires you. I can just hear you say - "darn this pen!"

Yes - about all the dresses you mentioned. Don't worry about the old rag problem. Mrs. Cole made me a nice bundle.

Honestly I'm <u>so</u> busy. I don't see how Jen ever does all the things she does in one day. I never thought that a day lasting from 7 AM to 10 PM would go quickly but it just flies!

Shaw goes on night work pretty soon + then I'll have him home all day - asleep most of the time to be sure but at least under the same roof. Our meal time will have to be readjusted but so far I haven't made him any picnic lunches.

Now mother be sure to fix your little fence up cute. I expect it to look like a penthouse when I come home.

Here's Shaw-
Goodynight-

Much Love
Wanie

My Book of Happy Memories

Excerpt from Joan's scrapbook

1934
Beaver Falls continued

Landlady – Silvia LaVeen. "My friends call me 'Silver'."

"Howdya do! Come right in and I'll show you around. Excuse my old dirty apron, but I was just about to get ready for a funeral. (*Heard various excuses for the same dirty apron daily throughout my sojourn there.*) The apartment is a mess – fired the last couple who were here because he was a drinker – even found gin bottles under the bed – but as I say I'm not one for wasting my life dusting + chasing dirt. Life's too short. Besides I can't use my right wrist very much – see it won't bend. I killed my Mother four years ago – yes it was a bad accident. I was unconscious for three days + the car was ruined. I couldn't go to the funeral so my husband had a lovely picture taken. It don't look at all like a funeral picture (*I viewed it later + it was so funereal I could fairly smell the flowers!*). Excuse me but the phone just rang... Well, Mrs. Cole, that just shows I'm easy to get on with! That was the girl whose husband drank that we had to throw out so you see we parted friends. Yes sir – we're close friends even so" etc. etc. etc.!

"Silver" – the loquacious! Merry as Tinkerbell, lively as a sparker, folksy as a bean supper and a gift of gab the envy of a Fuller Brush man. Very energetic – thought herself "just a little mischief" and ever so pleased with herself for being such a live wire. One minute she would be on her knees scrubbing the kitchen floor + the next she would rap on my door – "Look at me. You'd never know I was the same girl, would you! I look some different when I'm dressed up to go out, don't I!" – Only visible difference big red earrings, red beads + lots of red mouth.

<u>Most</u> ardent telephone conversationalist – calls all her friends every morning, tells each her proposed activities for the day and invariably

Early Married Years

states her menu. An integral part of each call, "Beaver Falls 610R you're welcome. Hello. Agnes? I can tell by your voice you don't feel good – now do you? – You see, I could tell. Well, I was just washing that old runner on the end table in Paul's room – the one over by the…, and I said to myself I guess I'll call Agnes – yes I guess I will. Did your stew come out good? Um hum. Mrs. Cole just passed me on the stairs and I smiled at her. I think I'll have some nice fresh asparagus today along with that warmed oven cornbeef I told you about yesterday – etc. etc. …… Well, gudby!" – Punctuated every other sentence with – "Are you <u>busy</u>?" Then rushes quickly on for fear her audience might reply in the affirmative! Even when wrong number calls she manages a lengthy conversation. It was a two party line + I'm sure she answered the wrong ring once in a while through sheer inability to resist temptations.

Her most absorbing subject was her day's menu. Her grocer would hear it all over the phone and again when he delivered. The garbage man who brought her rhubarb would listen til his mouth watered visibly! I not only heard it told to all of these, but I was also given a private audience and know she always carried out her plans as stated – because I could <u>smell</u> it, and finally when we met on the back stoop with our garbage I could see what was left!

I did my washing with her every Monday. The first time we compared underwear, the second, menus (of course) and the third (+ each subsequent Monday) operations! She couldn't have any children so I learned at great length why and where she was abnormal. Gave me much worthwhile visualizations on "how to wash." Considered me a helpless child of the idle Rich and said it was a shame I was brought up so ignorantly of domestic lore. Told me <u>she</u> didn't iron her sheets in summer. Upon asking her if she thought it was cooler or something she said "No but it's supposed to take all of the vitamins out." – so doubtless Shaw will have scurvy, come Fall. She was a little ashamed of the few socks and shirts her husband used per week compared to Shaw, and when I pulled a strange looking object from the wringer she commented "I can't seem to get my husband to wear pajamas. He still prefers the old fashioned nightshirts." She always chose the best looking clothes – preferably mine, because new – to hang facing the neighbors. Saw some small finger towels of mine + said "How <u>do</u> you pronounce those hossy-something napkins?" After much thought I gathered she meant hors d'oeuvres. When she surveyed her hanging wash she always said – "Well that sure looks like a hunksys wash!"

She was terribly proud of herself for respecting the privacy of my rooms – always saying – "See, Mrs. Cole, I'm knocking. I'm not coming in. Yes. So, I don't interfere, do I?" Oh no dearie – not with your body – but your voice!

She just gurgled over her own sense of humor – often saying, "I'm a funny girl, aren't I!" Typical joke: "Man came to farmhouse and knocked on the door, 'Is your Pa in?' 'No, he's down in the orchard with the pigs. You'll know him because he has a hat on.'"

She was too kind to shut the door in any salesman's face and was also delighted to find a willing ear. The salesman finally abandoned all hope of saying his peace + also all hope of getting to the next doorbell. Did my heart good to see one try and get away for a change. Silvia never refused a beggar food or money and I heard her get sucked under more than once. However, having bought 3 supposedly oriental rugs from a peddler and some stock in a New Jersey cemetery which she found were transferred to ownership in a certain number of graves – she must be used to getting gypped by now!

Favorite expression upon accomplishing anything, "Well, <u>that</u> baby's born!" Confided in me that she knows she shouldn't say it but it just slips out! – Her hobby was "underwear." "I suppose it sounds silly from a big woman like me."

When we first came she asked me if we liked to dance and play bridge whist. – "Wouldn't we like to go to the Eastern Star Lodge annual covered dish supper at $.75 a plate?" I was on the spot!

Censor came one day + she snickered to me afterwards. "I told my

Early Married Years

age alright but I thought I better lie about my husband's, so I told him 2 years younger."

When dressed to go out she invariably knocked on my door and said, "Oh, Mrs. Cole – do you think this rig is alright to wear downtown?" – Even if it was brand new. Just her way of displaying her wardrobe to me.

Used to read all her mail out loud to me; had great faith in fortune telling ladies ("I don't know, they just seem to be connected with the above somehow.") and the same faith in the stock market. Took down every quotation from the radio at 5:00 PM each day but didn't have the faintest idea "what you'd call what my husband does." Forever calling the beauty parlor to see if she could stop in to have her whiskers removed.

Her sister – Gloria Guppy – whom "Silver" described as being more "profusive" than she, arrived home from the South (to occupy this house) with Helen Louise, her 12-year-old cross-eyed blessing. Gloria, lazy, sloppy, grey-haired soft-soaping widow but slave to the cross-eyed 12 yr. old, who played the uke + <u>many</u> duets with "Mumma." She was the only issue of combined families therefore as spoiled as Roquefort cheese. Gloria quite apt to put on the dog – feeling more on my plain because she goes south winters – considers her sister quite provincial. When we were introduced, she beamed on me + said – "Anything I can do to add to your pleasure while you're here" – a noose around the blessing's neck would have added greatly to our pleasure.

Item 4 in the household was Silvia's husband. Very nice looking – meek and slightly deaf (that was his story anyway) – the radio either his entertainment or sole refuge.

Silvia, with all her interesting qualities, was kindness personified, and as she wished us all luck upon our departure, I waved goodbye and made a little niche for her among my pleasant memories.

Letter from Joan to family - one month married

April 24, 1934
Monday

Dearests "To whom it may concern",

I feel just like Atlas when he handed the world over to somebody or other - very cramped but extremely uplifted, because I've done my first washing. It consisted of practically everything Shaw owns, and two sheets. However, Mrs. LaVeen's washer made things very easy and she was more than helpful in giving me the lowdown on ironing + sprinkling. I must have been a sight to marvel at while ironing Shaw's shirts, for I tackled the wrinkles from every angle of the room + fairly played hopscotch over the ironing board. I find I was a little generous with the starch, + the finished collars + cuffs looked like slightly bent celluloid. He'll probably feel like ye knight of old in his shining armor when he wears them too!

To the lucky family who get this pencil copy let me state that I've started the carbon copy system, + it bewilders me to think of all the people I am writing at once!

I've forgotten when I last wrote but don't think I've told you about going to the Bernies for dinner. They are loads of fun and we had a wonderful meal - a roast, and I was so glad because I am not up to one yet. We both ate like horses which they seemed to enjoy, and afterwards we had a nice game of bridge. She has been married before + I think her two children aren't his. (Not very clear!)

Then Thursday night we had dinner at the Ingram's (Getchells - he was a classmate of Shaw's). They are very fine people + also served a very fine dinner even though they are on the Hay diet.

Sunday afternoon we played 18 holes with Mr. Garver + had him to supper afterwards. He stayed until 10:30 which we thought quite flattering. My golf was abnormally good and I managed a swell drive on the first tee + luckily plenty of caddies were standing around so I ought to be pretty famous by now. Mr. Garver can't wait for me to win all the tournaments! In fact he calls me Glenna.

Tonight Harry (Pitt engineer) was here for dinner + pleased me to death by eating everything in sight. My "Cabbage Au Gratin" turned out to be quite something. Per usual my potatoes were a failure - overdone this time.

We have finally gotten in touch with the Capron's (other newlyweds) + though we haven't met yet I talked with Adin on the phone + I find he stutters quite badly. We are going over sometime this week.

We've made quite an improvement in our dining-living room by having the old oaken table removed. It was so big that it took up most of the room and now that it's departed the room takes on more of a salon air. We eat on the card table and overflow the food on to the standing tray you sent us. It's much nicer this way.

My latest cooking casualty was very disastrous. I had brewed the most wonderful goulash of leftovers - ham, pineapple, maple syrup etc. and I was stirring it over the gas in a Pyrex dish when suddenly a pop! - and the whole business just vanished down into the regions of the gas pipes. I suddenly concluded that it couldn't have been Pyrex after all.

My cooking is getting on splendidly. I made some brownies the other day that were so chewy I thought I made a batch of elastics by mistake. My greatest problems so far are how one "tries out" salt pork and how to make bread crumbs! It simply won't crumb for me.

Shaw is at present out taking a reading of something - at least that's his story. Did I tell you he took me out with him and showed me the shelter box etc. After explaining what the different gadgets were I said, "I understand everything so far, but what's this rod sticking down in the ground?" "That my dear, is a pitometer".

Well, dear public - in order to answer all your questions I'll have to write each family individually from now on so tra-la until my next carbon copy chapter.

Mart - thanks for the recipe. We had it tonight and it reminded us of the double dates we had with you and Doc.

Celie thanks <u>ever</u> so much for the letters. I hope to be able to write you one before we leave here!

Dad - many thanks for all the stuff you sent. One of the coffee cups was broken and since we have sixteen it doesn't matter, but if you have that kind of insurance I just assume collect.

Mother darling - I'm so glad about your two rides. We had snow yesterday so don't believe you're out today. Mother - Carolyn Agar came to the tea on the wrong day!

<u>Could</u> you do me a favor? Send me my: I. Vielle flannel, II. my new JGC dye (Beehive dresses in big box about third drawer full of jewels etc. - it's in a very small Tiff box), III. two pillowcases, IV. Anthony Advase if no one is reading it, V. my light brown skirt which Jenny was fixing, VI. blue and brown Taffeta 2 piece dress, VII. snapshot of family among my pictures in beehive, VIII. brown napkins with orange stripe (Add ones I bought G. Lafayette), IX. my other house dress in wash. X another suede card cover.

I'm about to make up my mind about wedding pictures. Think I'll get some close ups from Somerville buddy.

Probably will think of a thousand things to say tomorrow morning so we'll leave this space.

I have - Dad, give us an estimate on those parcel post charges. The Pit Company pays for it we find.

A letter from Mr. Cole just now gives a glowing report of many new jobs including Minneapolis, which is a great help. All of the engineers are busy and they are taking back an old one. So I guess we happen to board at the right moment!

A month ago today we were married. What a lot I've learned about domesticity in one month. I feel positively like a home making center.

We're having smothered pork chops tonight. It may turn out to be just suffocated pig but it sounds swell.

I feel as if we weren't a bit far away from you all. Your letters are swell, but mother, <u>please</u> just write cards.

Best Love,
Joan

Letter from Joan to her Mother

Thursday

Dearest -

No word so far. A letter from Mr. Cole says Case[10] is in Montreal until this Saturday, so we won't hear until after that. Case asked Mr. Cole whether we would prefer Minneapolis for six months or Amsterdam. I'm glad he said Amsterdam!

Had a wonderful golf foursome last evening with Mr. Garver + a Mr. Bingham. I came through in the pinches + we (B and me) won two up.

I'm all excited about leaving. Shaw says I'll get sick of this business before we settle down but I think it's fun. We're awfully well fixed here, tho! Let's hope for luck in AM.

It's <u>beautiful</u> here now. The trees are lovely. Lots of apple trees here on the hill. The birds are screaming around for mates - glad I've got one.

<u>Loved</u> pictures of Gene. We bought a swell camera from one of Shaw's buddies here (Photostat maker). We got it secondhand. This photographer says we are crazy to buy a new one. Taking pictures right away which he will develop for us, so we'll send them on.

Three more wedding presents! Pair of Japanese trays, silver vegetable dish (!) This one uncovered + vegetables etched on it, + another chop platter silver!

Tell dad to see Frank Buck's animal picture. Many elephants.

Mr. Bingham asked me right in front of Shaw if I'd be his partner in mixed foursome!

Finishing notes by tomorrow. Thank heavens! Had run out of paper.

---

10   Egbert D. Case was the Vice President of the Pitometer Company.

Hope you're out in yard every day.

Much love,
Wannie

1 Cent Postcard

Apr 27, 1934 - 1 PM
Beaver Falls, PA

To: Mrs. H.E. Getchell
        205 Prospect St.
        Woonsocket
        Rhode Island

Friday

Dearest –

    Everything swell. Have been cooking some very fancy meals. Smothered pork chops wonderful. Will send recipe. Pit. District manager dropped in for lunch the other day. Thank heaven for waffle iron! Harry Ingersol, Pit man on this job, has been having dinner with us this week. He can't believe I never cooked before! Mr. Casal told manager <u>not</u> to look for jobs - they have more than they can handle now! Won't let myself be gay until I finish thank you notes. My landlady is a <u>character</u> – she's kind of a bully + ever so nice to me. Tonight we're going out to dinner with Harry. Wonderful movies here. Last night I darned Shaw's socks + we got in gales of laughter because I didn't even know how to find the end of the thread on a new ball of cotton! Would love to send you flowers on Mother's Sunday but you understand how much I love you without them.
    Joan

Shaw brought home flowers on our first anniversary.

Letter from Joan to her family

April 30, 1934

Dearests -

Whaddya think - we're moving nearer you! Last evening, Shaw received wire from his father - "Be prepared for shift to Amsterdam, NY soon"! We figure "soon" will be this weekend since Harry was here and said they usually tell you to report on a Monday. Soooo - as Edwyn would say - I must get busy. I must rush through my ironing this morning, finish up my thank yous this afternoon, and start getting things together.

We're so comfy here that I hate in a way to have to leave, but I am very excited about another new place. Who knows what's just around the corner? We may find a mansion in Amsterdam. I think our biggest regret is leaving our next door golf course!

I think the town is between Syracuse and Schenectady (not sure) and is about the size of Woonsocket. It's quite near Saratoga.

I hate to leave my landlady - she's been so nice to us, and we've made some awfully nice friends - including the Caprons. We went over Sunday night and had a fine time with them.

I don't know what to say about our mail. I guess you better not write until you hear from me and then send our mail general delivery to N.Y.

Harry says it's a joke among the engineers that if you're told you'll go to Amsterdam the chances are that at the last minute you'll be sent somewhere else. So, we really aren't certain yet. However, I'll let you know as soon as I do.

I just looked at the map and found we are only about three hours from Northampton. So we're going to be real near you and hope to see you soon.

In great haste! Much love,
Wanie

Tell Mack I had planned to write her a three page letter today but can't

Letter from Joan to her family

May 4, 1934 - Saturday afternoon

Dear Each + Every One -

Shaw is out on the golf course playing a foursome in the club opening tournament. I am being positively heroic by staying home + writing my last ten thank you notes. If any more presents come - don't accept them! I rather enjoy the actual writing of them but it's the time I begrudge. However - it's the least I can do for the people who sent me the gifts.

Enclosed is our first attempt - which isn't so good. I hope to get a picture of the entire house, + one of the views from the bluff looking down into the valley - in fact we took one which didn't come out. I hiked way out to the seventh hole (and that's a long way when you aren't playing) with my camera slung over my shoulder, feeling like a German tourist. When I finally reached the point from which I wanted the view, I went to open the camera + carefully took off the wrong side + exposed the film! Could you save these for me because I'm going to start an album soon + will need them.

In fact, Harry Ingersoll says we ought to keep the letters we write home. It's an easy way of keeping a memory book + I'm no good at writing a diary, so would one of you mothers take it upon yourselves to collect them for me? I hope to be able to keep quite an extensive account of our nomadic life in that way.

We are quite sought after this weekend. Tonight, we are playing bridge with Mr. Garver and our golf buddy. They asked us for golf tomorrow but we're going to the Ingersoll's in Pittsburgh for dinner. Fred Ingraham also asked us for dinner + golf. So you see we didn't lack for company.

Last night, Harry, Shaw, + I drove out to Zenopole, a town near here, which boasts a country hotel with famous food. The country was beautiful - many rolling hills + fruit trees in bloom. Zenopole is the only town we've seen so far with any atmosphere. There were a couple of houses which actually looked old and clean, and two "antique" signs fairly made us homesick. The hotel was a typical country affair - many wicker chairs + spittoons + gents peaking over the local paper with toothpicks in their mouths. The food was delish and the china thick. Harry paid the bill after a heated argument, but he eats with us so much that he wanted to give us a party.

The main street is a sight today. Being Sat aft + warm, all of the local stores are doing a land office business. Many very homely girls are roaming up and down in last year's sun backed dresses and new finger waves. There is a very tired looking carnival at the bottom of the hill which looks as if it's made about twenty cents to date, but I suppose tonight the Merry Go Round will squeak around now + then. All of these towns look very passé to me, but I suppose it's because I'm not used to seeing so much dirt. I wish you people had Fanny Farmers[11] so I could suggest some of the recipes to you that I have found successful. This noon I fixed some eggs in such a fancy manner that the mother hen would have been thrilled to death.

And then I found a ham recipe that glorifies the pig something terrific. Shaw thinks I'm the smartest thing in the world so I'm careful not to let him read the cook book + find out how simple it all is.

My coffee tasted pretty bad yesterday + when I went to wash the pot I found I'd cooked a piece of my rubber glove along with it! I call it coffee a la Firestone.

No word has come from Case about moving yet so we just go blithely on. We can pack up in half a day so there's not much point in getting ready in advance.

Silvia LaVeen continues to amuse me beyond words! Her telephone conversations are fit for Cornelia Otis Skinner[12]. She talks for at

---

11 Fanny Farmer was the author of *Boston Cooking - School Cookbook*.
12 Cornelia Otis Skinner was an American author & actress. Her writing style was sometimes described as "monologue dramas".

least half an hour, and then sticks in an "are you busy?" + keeps right on going without stopping. She recites every detail of her day to each one who calls + if she gets any break at all she goes right on to what she's going to do tomorrow! Whenever she goes out she calls into me - "Well, here goes nothing!" And whenever she accomplishes anything she says "Well, that baby's born". She confided in me that she thinks it's really a terrible expression but that it just pops out. I had never known her to call the store without telling the man just how she's going to cook what she is ordering! Really, she amuses me most to death and I talk to her for the sheer fun of hearing her go on + on. Wash days are a feel day - we get so intimate over the tubs.

Forgot to say that Shaw bumped into a fraternity brother of his at an intersection in the road during our drive last evening!

Shaw brought me home some beautiful spring violets last night. He's a model groom all right + we get on like two peas in a pod.

We have become so attached to our flat. The wallpaper seems to have toned down, the jaundiced colored furniture + wood work had assumed the hue of a rare old grain + the grey hulking rocking chairs look very kind + receptive. I guess it's all because our eyes are happy and our hearts are hugging each other.

Who knows this may be the last carbon copy from Beaver Falls. "A.K. Beaver Falls - on to Amsterdam" - as W. Winchell says.

Guess I'll whip up an angel cake + some chicken mousse for supper - or in other words, stick the plug in the waffle iron!

Much love
Joan + Shaw in spirit

Got a screaming note from Charlie Cook in answer to my letter.

We'll probably send home some winter clothes. Half cleaned as stated + send me the bill.

Can't wait to see Chestnut fence. Take a picture of it when it's up.

Have a sneaking feeling Shaw may go to Hanover for a fifth reunion - I come home for three months reunion!

Terribly hot here but our living room lovingly cool. Blizzard next week probably!

Where are all the magazines I subscribe to? I'm desperate for reading material. About to take up palm reading!

Did yellow camel dress come from Gladdings? Hold until we hit Amsterdam.

How do you feel E.?

Dad - my golf swell. Shaw's also.

Write us a round robin when Coles are at 205.

Again I say we are <u>so</u> comfortable. AM. N.Y. sounds clean so I can't wait. People's hands perpetually dirty.

<u>Much much much</u> love,
Wanie

Early Married Years

A poem written from Joan to her mother, Edith Getchell

For Mother's Day, 1934

To Edie from Joan[13]

I love you, Edie, whom I've known for years;
You, who brought me laughter and dried my tears.
They say, "Spare the rod and spoil the child."
You spared the child for your rod was mild;
For, through stages of callow youth
Your rod was love and patience and truth
Great pals we were when we traveled wide,
You, the pocket-book, I – the guide.
For twenty-six years I've seen into your mind
And found much that is pure and good and kind
But – the last two years surpass all others
For I've glimpsed your soul, my wonderful mother.
Maybe the Lord had this purpose in view –
He strengthened me by weakening you.

---

13 *(Note from Aunt Marion Gilbert, Edie's sister, on the back of this which she sent me March 15, 1956)* "Your mother wrote this for her mother, your Grandmother Getchell – you know she was ill with "T.B." which finally ended her life. I think the poem is so sweet – sorry it is not in your mother's interesting handwriting, but I copied it and I have no idea where the original is."

Letter from Joan to her family

May 4, 1934

"GETCH-COLE"

Dearests -

Life goes on very smoothly. Shaw's working at night is very demoralizing because there is no alarm to wake me up. This morning I slept until 10:30!

This week I added "apple pie" and salmon soufflé to my repertoire and both worked! I'm <u>so</u> proud of myself when the right thing happens to what I mix. I've cut the food bills down quite a lot this month. So far we've eaten on sixty cents a day - I suppose Mart eats on about 40!

Last night, Harry, Shaw and I went out in the country for dinner with Mr. and Mrs. Bernie (head of the H_2O Co.) We drove to somewhere in Ohio - I feel so cosmopolitan when we step over into another state. We arrived at a country inn in a crossroads town and my heart sank when I saw the interior. A musty old place full of half dead lilacs, paper flowers, and rummage sale looking objects d'art. One room had been modernized with an unknown object in view. The walls were frescoed with bent looking people in some native costume or other standing flat against a few crooked vistas. From the rafters hung the weirdest collection of fauna you can imagine. A very crumby balloon fish, a pair of wide open jaws, a coconut, and a huge sized starfish which had shrunken decidedly from its strange new habitat. I think one of the locals must have travelled far and wide to the Atlantic seaboard and decided that the proof of his travels would be most widely advertised if strung up in the local inn. Anyway, the effect was anything but appetizing and I was more than surprised when a white coated server appeared + served us the most delicious chicken dinner possible, with all of the fixins. They served maple syrup with the baking powder biscuits - better try that dad, it's sweet!

And <u>what</u> by the way, takes you to New York dad? An event such as that should be more fully explained in your letters!

Glad Mother's Day was so successfully weepy! I cried when I wrote the poem so it's unanimous! Would <u>love</u> Harpers + a bird book of some kind in Genie's room. There are some beauties here that I'd like to identify. Did yellow dress come from Gladdings?[14]

---

14 There is likely more to this letter but it is missing.

Letter from Shaw to his Mother Mary Cole for Mother's Day

May 13, 1934 - Sunday
Beaver Falls, PA

Mother dear,

Today is the day set aside for you but in the interest of economy I refrained from sending you a vase of flowers - I figured perhaps you would think yourself a better mother if you saw that your son had really learned some of the lessons you tried to teach him.

I'm so sorry you changed your plans and had to miss Joan's presents to the two mothers - she cooked a delicious batch of brownies (all I got was a crumb or two) and wrote poetry to go along with them. Perhaps they will save you some of them for they were delicious.

This has been a beautiful day so far, although a little rough on Joan. Even now she's finishing up after dinner, but I will help her with the dishes.

This morning I played golf in a foursome and had a wonderful game. We were all pretty evenly matched + had a see saw battle up to the last shot. After golf I came back for Joan and went downtown to start a test going.

Then a bath and a delicious dinner, Joan's first Sunday attempt - fried chicken, rice, string beans, gravy, jelly and for dessert, apple tarts and coffee. Doesn't that sound good? It was better than it sounds. While we were in the middle of dinner the Caprons (young couple from Beaver) dropped in and chatted while we ate. Before long I'm going to go downtown, and look at my test and then join the Caprons for a short ride to Economy.

Perhaps you know of the Economites - they are one of the interesting sects which seem to have been very instrumental in settling this part of the country. We've been learning of the Mennonites or Amish Dutch, the Covenant Reformed Presbyterians, and now we're after the

Economites. They were Germans who settled near here or Ambridge to be more accurate, and who became very wealthy. They were around most of this valley besides other things. It seems they did not believe in marriage and they have died out now. Their meeting house is being restored and it is that which we want to see this evening.

You will be interested to hear that Joan is a full fledged Pitometer engineer - Friday night she went out with me and stuck till the bitter end. She couldn't have had a duller time of it because I was in a section where nobody knows much about the valves and connections. As a result we worked all night without getting more than a couple of shutouts. She's seen the worst of it now though and should be able to join me on any conversation that has to do with the Pitometer.

I've been very lax in letter writing but the truth is I've been working pretty hard. I'm awfully interested in the work for it's never dull and although there are some tough nuts to crack it's quite an exciting game to crack them. This last week I've been on nights and will continue for another week at least. The program is pretty much as follows - Up at 3:30 PM. 4 - Breakfast, then down to the office for about an hour - then Harry for dinner - after the dishes we have time for a bull session (usually technical), and then down to the office by 10 PM. We work till 6 in the morning + I'm usually in bed by 7. We've varied the program slightly with a picnic on the banks of the Ohio Wednesday and dinner on Harry in Newcastle on Friday.

I'm storing up questions and problems for Father and hope to write him soon.

Isn't it wonderful that the Stone House[15] is so nicely taken care of. You must be much relieved as well as pleased with the arrangement.

Do you really mean to say that you've got cousin David for the Sakonnet trip?

I'll be sorry to miss that excursion for I've enjoyed the others so

---

15 The Stone House was Grandmary Rockwell Cole's family homestead in Norwich, CT. It was a stopping place in the Underground Railroad where slaves fled to their freedom from the South to the North.

much but then this time you'll have him all to yourselves.

I wish I could tell you how much we have enjoyed your letters + Father's.

You've both been so good to us in so many ways and you continue to be so with your bits of news.

Regardless of the poems and other canned sentiments you are the most wonderful mother in the world and I love and appreciate all that means more and more as time goes on.

Always your loving son,
Shaw

Excerpt from her Scrapbook

May, 1934

En route from Beaver Falls to Amsterdam by way of Montclair – in which our impedimenta meets up with a clipper ship

Having planned to leave at 9 A.M. we took off at 12:00, after Silvia had treated us to a hasty farewell banquet in her kitchen – custard + cinnamon buns, laid on her best cotton linen, and served with her sterling silver which she surreptitiously unearthed from their fells and quickly polished. Her parting conversation was typical. Upon inquiring most anxiously of Shaw about the Essex Memorial Cemetery in New Jersey, and finding him completely blank on the subject, she told us that <u>much</u> against her hunch, she had sold some of her Chrysler stock to purchase some shares in the cemetery – which she had never seen. Her cousin-on-her-husband's side Annie assured her it was a good thing. Doubt assailed her the other day when she received a <u>personal</u> letter from the Board of Directors saying that her stock had matured, and would she like any preference in the location of the several lots to which her stock entitles her? "What do I want with graves! I thought I was buying some dividends!" Well, sir – she thought she'd just take a drive up to that part of the country this summer and see about that! (Other evidence of her faith in humanity was a group of 3 Oriental rugs which she purchased from a native-in-costume who called at her front door.)

Our car being stuffed to the gills we climbed in – I with a parting gift of a jar of Silva's piccalilli (plus the recipe) – and waved goodbye to our first, and I'm sure funniest landlady!

Hoping to arrive in Montclair before midnight we did not loiter by the way. Just before Harrisburg it came Shaw's turn at the wheel, but the good road had just begun so I insisted on continuing awhile. We were speeding along an almost trafficless road when an oncoming car approached and clink! The other car sped on, considerately dragging our luggage rack + contents with it. To the sound of awful thuds + scrapes I slowed down and stopped the car. I looked back, and through the car window I saw my trousseau spread all over the highway for seemingly miles. It suddenly dawned on us that either I, or the other driver, had been driving too close to the center of the road and his bumper had clipped our luggage rack. (I have always been glad he didn't stop, for I'm fairly sure it was my fault, but in continuing on he assumed the blame!) Jittery from the realization that our shave was a close one, we got out of the car to reap the highway of its sudden harvest. Countless urchins appeared and started to collect those articles of my wardrobe which wouldn't occasion a blush as they stooped. One small boy was apparently very sensitive, for after wading around among the wreckage he chose to select a pincushion which he presented to me with an I've-found-the-Holy-Grail expression on his face. I walked hurriedly along, scooping up my lingerie + other unmentionables while the small boys nudged each other knowingly. Our arms full, we hid behind the car away from the pop-eyed youths. My handsome new tweed suitcase, though demolished, was stuffed with goods + tied together, as was Shaw's pigskin bag. Everything was crowded into the front of the car along with ourselves, and, clasping hip bones, we drove on to Montclair, after reviving ourselves with a gob or two of Silver's piccalilli.

Letter from Joan to her mother-in-law, Mrs. Cole
"Love Among the Ruins"

Friday (no date)

My dear Mrs. Cole –

We did have such a charming weekend at your interesting country seat. Compton is such a quaint little spot, and it did us both so much good to enjoy a restful weekend in the midst of our hectic main line gaieties.

And now to get back to normal: We had a heck of a ride home! The traffic between New Haven & New York was like one long parade, but from then on we had no difficulty. However, the ride was made most enjoyable by frequent raidings of our very deluxe lunch. It was more than adequate and the two peaches we didn't eat were served for dessert the following day.

Our new quarters looked anything but hospitable. Everything was piled up in the "foyer", the water had not been turned on as ordered, & if the Coles[16] had not been kind enough to bring over a dishpan full, I don't know what we'd have done. They received us with open arms – Shaw tore off to work, poor boy, and I tore the newspapers off the bed, threw on a couple of sheets & crawled in. Wednesday was devoted to cleaning, & Shaw to sleeping, so now we are all settled in again for no one knows how long.

I shall entitle this chapter "Love Among the Ruins", for all of the walls are covered with framed remains of the glory that was Greece. As I sit at this desk the headless Victory of Samothrace in plaster is about to take off from the edge of the bookcase in front; two of the "Three Fates" are lounging against the wall, a framed print of "The Boy with the Thorn" is to my left, and some Grecian weaver in bronze is having an awful time trying to thread her shuttle. Everywhere are framed

---
16   These Coles were cousins of Shaw.

ruins of the Forum, Erectheum, Palatine & Parthenon and as I pass them I instinctively duck for fear a stone will fall on my head. The walls in this room are lined with books but I have joined a lending library nevertheless, for here is a sample of her library: "Poets of the Augustan Age", "Homer to Theocritus", "Discourses of Epictetus" etc. etc! I feel positively out of place without a toga for I feel that all of these ancients look down on my Hoover apron with scorn. I wouldn't know just how to classify the interior decoration of this house – maybe the Greeks had a word for it – I haven't.

Will finish this in the morning for it is getting chilly down here & my cold is so much better I don't want to take any chances.

Friday

Shaw pulled in at 4:00 A.M. due to inclement weather. It simply poured for 12 hours & everything outside & in is soaking wet. Last night was the first time since we've been married that Shaw has been rained out – a pretty good record, I think.

Yesterday I had a very classy day in town with Aunt Bertha. We drove in about 12:30 through the beautiful parkway, having first gone to a wonderful Scotch wool shop to help her select her fall costume. Incidentally, if any Getchells or Coles are looking for some fall tweeds, Vermont Native Industries has some stunners at 4.00 per yd. which are 56" wide.

We went directly to Rittenhouse Sq. which as you probably know is the Beacon Place of Philadelphia. She knows the history and genealogies of all the first families so our sightseeing walk thereabouts was most interesting. We lunched at the Barclay and the Square was oh so catish! Then we strolled down to a famous auction house where I placed a bid on a stunning brass tray which will make a good wedding present. (Mother – I received an invitation to Kitty Miller & Fowler Hamilton's wedding.) A cloudburst descended so we headed for Wanamakers & browsed around the furniture department where I learned much about woods & periods from her. It was all loads of fun & I consider myself lucky to have such a person show me around.

Shaw and I agree that this was our most satisfactory visit at Sakonnet. For we saw lots of each family. The Getchell-Cole buffet was a splendid thought, & should be an annual institution I think. Finding you so gay, Edie, was alone worth the 325 mile drive. Shawsie & I think we've done a very smart thing to join two such splendid families.

Mrs. Cole – thanks for sending our leavings, and particularly Shaw's coat. It came just in time for this rainy damp weather.

This aft we are going to the art museum; tonight to Bud Maucks, and tomorrow to the Cole's for dinner; so you see we really are very gay!

Celie – I've written Aunt Alice, so would you send the picture along?

I feel terribly that we didn't remember Mary's 21st birthday on time! I'm sending wee giftees to her & Genie which they may interchange if they wish.

Hope you are all having a nice rest after the hectic weekend. I do nothing but sleep.

Mother, get "Nijinsky." I think you'd like it.

Much love from both
Joan

1 Cent Postcard

May 28, 1934 - 1 AM
Beaver Falls, PA

To: Mrs. H. Eugene Getchell
      205 Prospect St.
      Woonsocket
      R. I.

Dearests –

What a life! One minute we're to go + the next we're to stay. Have been busy as a bee cleaning house all day as <u>well</u> as packing. Last night we drove over to Youngstown for a <u>wonderful</u> lobster dinner with the Bernies & tonight we all ate at their house. They are <u>swell</u> people + will never have such attractive employees again I understand. Sorry to leave all of our new friends but look forward to meeting more. This is a wonderful life banging around from place to place. Hope to phone you tomorrow night if we get in early enough. Very cold out so it will be nice driving – got your special M. Thanks.

Loads of love to Mrs. Bixby & you all,
Wannie

Letter from Joan to family

Monday (no date)

Dearests -

    This has been <u>such</u> a gay weekend! Sat. night we went square dancing - or rather "spectator square dancing" up in the Dutch country nearby with Bud Mauck + Kitty Summer (relative of Shaw's - Alfred Summer's sister). It was truly an experience! Most of the older people spoke Dutch and we felt as if we were in a foreign land. Everybody, old and young, joined in the dancing and we were amazed at the intricate steps involved in their dances. The man who called the steps worked himself up into a frenzy and the dancers became so excited they looked more like holy rollers than good stolid Dutchmen.

    Sunday noon we had dinner at the Coles + had a nice time with them. Later on we went to Jenkintown to call on Joe Tracey, one of the Pit engineers. He has a darling wife + two beautiful little children, both born on surveys! After supper at their house we went to Media to see Helen Choff and Bill West, a boy who was in Kentucky. Then this morning I had a washing bee with Aunt Mary and Uncle Arthur. She washed in the machine, I wrung, and Uncle Arthur hung them on the line - some system. After a quick lunch Shaw + I drove in to a baseball game - Phillies versus the Cardinals - which was loads of fun. The bleachers were full of squirming youngsters with visors on, which had evidently been passed out as ads, because on the rim in bright red print was "Double Bubble - The Gum For Fun". Several youngsters were blowing great balloons which were stuck all over their faces.

    We stopped for supper on the way home, + luckily Shaw made me buy twice as much spinach as I wanted to because it certainly did lose itself as it cooked! While I got supper he read a whaling book to me - this being inspired by Shaw's perusal of J. Cole's whaling log which Uncle Arthur has lent us. It is a most fascinating account and I would love to quote it at length but I'm sure you'll all have a chance for it at some time.

This week will also be gay for tomorrow night we are going to the Summers for dinner. Mrs. Cole - I will write you more in detail about them after our date. Kitty and Mr. Summers were at Bud's for dinner Sat. night. He is terribly attractive. Dianna is apparently ill + in a sanatorium. Will get the dope. Kitty is also attractive - says she may visit the Taylors over the races. Then Wed. Grace + I are going to town to an auction and Sat. we're going to Maucks for dinner followed by Guy Lombardo somewhere.

Forgot to say that we started the weekend well by doing <u>some</u> of the art gallery Sat. aft. A magnificent building - sorry you didn't see it Celie, because the facades + piezo on the outside are all done in polychromes as was the Parthenon (CF. Art22!) in the old days.

Took Aunt Bertha out for dinner Thursday to a place she'd never been. We were <u>so</u> pleased.

Expect Dad is up to his neck in golf at Rye - hope you are being lazy mother.

Our unseen landlady arrives soon. Our plans are nil until we see her. The Greecian influence is due to her deceased husband who was a Greek professor. Believe me, his memory lives on!

Much <u>much</u> love to all,
Joan

Happy Birthday - Mary, Genie, Mrs. Cole

Letter from Joan to family
"Love in a Garret on Garret Road"

September 19, 1934, Tuesday

Dearests all -

Where to begin! For we've moved again. We're now on the attic floor of a gate house to a 65 acre estate! It's in the town of Rosemont which is less than a mile away from our other two residences. Our house is on the corner of Lancaster pike and Garret Road but our post office address is merely Rosemont PA. For there is only the box system.

We moved for 3 reasons. 1 - Our past landlady, who's name by the way is <u>Mertie Gay</u> Baker, turned out to be secretary of the Quakers Association. 2 - She always keeps her house at about 50 degrees in the winter and the heat isn't turned on until a certain date regardless of the weather - a'la Paris, France. 3 - Consequently, she is always sick in the fall and is annually too grateful to all of the neighbors for sending over her meals. Naturally I wasn't crazy about paying to be her trained nurse. All of this was confided to me on the day of her arrival by Aunt Mary, who thought she better warn me, so I quickly woke Shaw and said "C'mon we're going a-hunting." We looked around at various towns near Phil. + found so-so places and one good apartment at $65.00 a month, which we thought we might have to take. One very seedy 70 year old real estate dealer confided in us that he was John Wannamaker's nephew and that John had done his utmost to get him a job in the store! Finally we got sick of it so we came home + dropped in at the Cole's. Mertie Gay was there + she turned out to be a rosy cheek jolly piece, weighing at least 400. She was more than nice to us the few days we were there so Grace claims we made a hit. We refrained from cigarettes and I played the Quaker maid, so you may believe we were some glad to get out. Grace tipped us off to this place, and we liked it immediately. It sounds very impressive to say we reside on the converse estate but our quarters are not so impressive. A relative of the Converse's lives here + teaches at Balwin school. Also two other school teachers. It's a very well built house and large. We have living room, bedroom and bath on the third floor. There is a 4th room besides two store rooms but we said they could rent it if it would reduce our rent. The price is 35.00 including everything. The living room is up under the eaves. It has a fireplace and two big French windows which lead out into space. Everything is very Victorian. They had recently discovered that the walls are pine with cherry trimming so someone is scraping it. One side of the wall is all scraped and is very pretty. Another is partially scraped, another has some battleship grey paint here and there, and the fourth side has bits of blue flowered wallpaper still stuck on! The furniture is a conglomeration of every period + in our bedroom there are two very elaborate worn out brocaded Louis XVI chairs which obviously used to be in the "big house". Our bedroom has little closet space but lots of old fashioned bureau drawers. The lighting system is rather poor. Therefore, the many chords from the center fixture form a cat's cradle. Our dining room is the pantry on the first floor. I have a separate sink and back stairs. I am not allowed in the kitchen when they are using it so our dinner cannot begin until 7:30 but we don't mind that. My ice box is in the laundry and has no drain so it has to be emptied twice a day, and since a four months old Irish terrier is kept there, all doors must be kept closed leading to it. There are six! This description sounds as if it were awful but it isn't at <u>all</u>. We really love it. It's nice and cozy here up under the eves and our fireplace will prove a great joy.

We moved in yesterday and when we got sick of working we left everything and went into town to the movies and dinner. Movie - *Count of Monte Cristo* - You <u>all must</u> see it. We came back just in time for Shaw to get to work, so I settled things somewhat and decided to retire - when I found our blankets missing. So I made the bed with all of our coats and slept very comfortably until suddenly I was awakened and found myself all in a heap with Shaw on the floor! When he had climbed in, the slats had given way. We unmade the bed, readjusted the slats, climbed in again, and boom! On the floor again. Just my side went down. I was so sleepy I didn't care, and he was so tired he didn't either. So we gave it up and slept at a 45 degree angle from then on. Why I didn't dream of climbing the Matterhorn I don't know! When I awoke I felt exactly like Sarah Crewe - lying in a broken bed in an attic bedroom without any blankets. Luckily, it struck us both as being funny and it will make a nice chapter in my "book"!

Nighttime -

I got even with them for giving us a bum bed - for tonight I broke their stove. I'm not sure that I was to blame, but the oven door broke while I was using it so I'm incriminated.

I can't remember when I last wrote so I don't know what I told you. Did I mention the wonderful auction house in town which is just full of interesting things? Aunt Bertha took me in one day and I have haunted the place ever since. The first floor is junk, the second floor slightly better, and the third floor like Christy's in London. I took Grace in last week and I fell for a stunning copper chafing dish whose feet are three big lobsters. It's very solid and well put together + will prove very useful here in our attic. I made up my mind I wouldn't pay over $3.00 for it, and I was lucky, for my competitor stopped when I got there. Every time I go in town I drop in and see countless things I want in the way of furniture. Lots of lovely brass + copper things + every time I go in I want to buy a lot of the stuff and open a "Brass + Copper" shop. Aunt Bertha has bought lots of lovely paintings there and Uncle Ross restores them.

Uncle Ross by the way, had a burglar in his hotel room who took his wallet. He lost only $30.00 but many identification papers, license etc. and blank checks.

We went to her house for a luscious dinner the other night. Also we went to town together for lunch and movies.

Sat. we went to the Maucks for the weekend. In the evening we drove out to the largest dance hall in the country to hear Guy Lombardo. There were over 2,000 people there, which proves his popularity! Sunday it poured so we just sat around in this lovely house. Mr. Summer + Kitty came out and told Harriet that "Di" is no better. I am so sorry for them. The Mauck children are <u>darling</u>. When Ward first saw me I had on a long dress and he said – "Hello, where did you get that pretty dress?" But Toddy said – "Where did you get that <u>big</u> dress?" Not quite so flattering!

Today I was purchasing towel racks etc. in a 10c store where a college friend of mine accosted me. She was also stocking up, for she has been married only a week and lives nearby. I didn't know her very well but she was most cordial and is going to invite us over when her apartment is ready.

I suppose you saw the pictures of Woonsocket. On the front page of the Herald Tribune? My, but that fracas was terrible. Shaw has been kidding me about all of the smug New Englanders who told him in Sakonnet that nothing would come of the proposed strike.

Here's a teaser for you Mr. Cole – I bought your Christmas present the other day and had to go to six stores before finding it. It will take from now until Christmas, I'm sure, to complete it. Can you guess what it is?

Thanks for your nice letters. Celie – be sure to write about N.Y. Tell Vee I'm dying to have her visit me – we have a cot in the living room which is dying to be christened.

We call this chapter "Love in a Garret on Garrett Road."

Much love to all,

Joan

Mrs. Cole, describe the scene of the races to us in your next.

Sorry you didn't get to the golf, Dad.

Mother – I would know by the length of your letters how much better you feel. <u>Please</u> don't write too much.

Letter from Joan to family

Dearests -

I have my girlfriend drying my dishes with me now, so everything is under control!

Picture me at this setting - in a cool white screened in porch furnished with white and green painted furniture, looking out on a cute little lawn completely enclosed by lilacs at the rear + trellised grape vines at the side and a little bird bath in the center. Shaw sleeps upstairs in a room with 3 big windows and a doorway into a sleeping porch. Side of our bedroom is a nice <u>white</u> bathroom - a joy after Beaver Falls' brownish, yellowish, greyish one.

The only catch is the stove which has no regulator + is fairly old. I suppose I'll catch on soon. I have never seen so many kitchen utensils in all my life - all sizes + shapes, many of which are Greek to me.

Mrs. Donnan proves to be very nice. To tell the truth I think she is tickled to have us here because she was so lonesome and rattled around in this house. She comes out on the porch + has a cigarette and chats with me quite often but she is away the best part of every day. Our meals are at such odd hours that we haven't conflicted in the kitchen as yet. I have to be very careful because I think she is spitten' neat. She has no garbage pan in the sink + not a waste basket in sight + all of the utensils are spotless. All in all it's perfectly swell and I'm afraid it's going to spoil us! It's so comfortable on this porch that it's an effort to move off it and we're positively going native. I'm glad we don't know anybody here + we're having such fun together that I hesitate to look up the Smith girls here. The boy next door called last evening. He has a twin who was Dartmouth '33 but Shaw didn't know him.

While we're here we hope to drive to Saratoga and Lake George, the country is so lovely around here.

I'm sending you a description of the Sanford home - now the city hall. It is magnificent and I was lucky enough to go through the whole place with the night watchmen the other night. Mrs. Donnan has lived here all her life + she's said she's never had a chance to go over it that thoroughly!

I have started a huge diary scrapbook of our travels and I am anxious to get Beaver Falls complete so would love the pictures + letters (which contained descriptions of our apartment). I thought I'd just copy them into the book. It's so much easier than writing it all over again. Mr. Cole - you'll be glad to know I've devoted 3 pages to Silvia LaVeen!

Living around like this gives us lots of good ideas about the house we're going to build sometime. The porch is item 1 in our plan!

Will write individually from now on.

Dad - your letters send us into <u>gales</u> of laughter. You haven't the faintest idea how funny you are - and <u>newsy</u>.

The pictures you sent were a complete success. Your hair wave makes you look much fatter mother and the fence looks very idle hour farmish. We will take pictures soon.

My statement came and I almost swooned when I looked upon my first balance containing now cashed checks. I have spent .79 on clothes in two months - that on a pair of sneakers. Not that I wasn't stocked up or anything! Dad sometimes I hope to get around to my wedding budget statement. Tackling our own budget seems to be all I can manage so far.

Answer <u>this</u> - is the *House Beautiful* you sent the only magazine received so far addressed to me? I subscribed to *Good Housekeeping*, *Harper's Bazaar* + *Cosmopolitan* also and I want to kick.

When does Genie finish? Did Jennie have a good time? I'm glad Mrs. Bixby worked out well. How is Charlie Cook? When does Celie finish? Did our bushes bloom? Have you found Barbra Royce's sheets? I will have to look up how many I bought her - I can't remember.

It will be <u>such</u> fun to see you all soon.

Much love
Joan

EARLY MARRIED YEARS

Letter from Joan to family

1934, Tuesday - 7:30 A.M.
WHITEHALL
Haverford, Pennsylvania

Dearest Mother and everybody –

Enfin! We are the proud tenants of an honest-to-goodness-no-landlady apartment. It is such a joy to have what space we live in actually belong to us. I have just this minute moved in and everything is topsy turvey, except that I have placed our two orientals on the floor and they look exquis.

This is an apartment hotel, and <u>so</u> Spanish in feeling that I feel lost without a rose between my teeth. The name "Whitehall" is strangely incongruous but I've decided that the present owner & manager – Major L. Stanley Stanford changed the name when he came into possession for some of the silver & plates in the dining room bear the name "Casa del Rey". This Major Stanford is a very nice American gentleman but his taste is execrable. His office is also his living room apparently, and the four walls are lined with not too good pictures. One side is literally covered with sporting prints & the other with Venetian boat scenes so I guess his wife owns one side & he the other. He must have fallen heir to some castle furniture for it is massive & oh so ornate. I am anxious to find out more about him for I'm sure he'll prove to be an interesting character.

To write in chronological order – we encountered <u>no</u> traffic on the way to Montclair, so arrived in plenty of time for dinner. We stayed on and on & even had supper before we left. (Dad, a very dear friend of Mrs. Cole's was there, who had been suffering acutely from arthritis for years. She was a patient of Dr. Burbank who is <u>the</u> arthritis man in N.Y.C. but was becoming steadily worse. She went to Locke twice, was helped the first time but not the second. Then she went to Dr. Swains & is <u>swiftly</u> recovering.) We arrived here about 10:30 & came straight to this hotel, and also went straight to sleep! Yesterday morning we arose at 7:00 & I drove over to Lansdowne with Shaw who reported to work only to find that the engineer in charge granted him a holiday in which to get settled. So we came back & I laid out a house hunting program while Shaw went to the manager to see what he could do for us. I had been here before but his price was 65.00 & a long lease. Shaw came back with the good news that we could have one for 55.00 and a weekly clause in our lease. We figured that it was worth it for many reasons. When we shared the kitchen in our gate house we ate out so much that we easily ate up the difference in rent. Also there is all kinds of service here. The dining room will be a great convenience for Shaw when I go up to Vee's wedding & we have ample room for guests. So we decided it was worth the difference & I promptly, and with great pleasure called up our past landlady.

We are on Lancaster Pike, as before, we are near enough Shaw's office so that in a pinch he can walk, we are only a block from the Coles and also from Aunt Bertha (who comes home Thursday). There is a garage with the hotel which we will need now that winter is coming. In fact everything is quite perfect. The apartment was unfurnished and for some reason or other the Major couldn't rent us a so called furnished apartment, but he rented us the apt. and is lending us the furniture. We have kitchen, living room, bedroom, tiled bath with shower & <u>huge</u> closet space. It is laid out thusly –

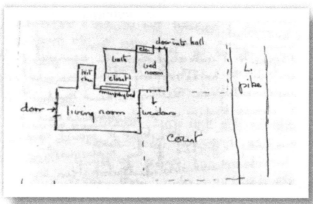

Early Married Years

We have a double bed & the one that comes out of the wall in the living room is also a double, so we can sleep four people easily. Our furniture is somewhat sketchy but comfortable. We have a big suite in the living room; couch + 2 chairs, very massive & grey (thank goodness). As yet we have too few little tables but hope to inveigle 2 more. We must furnish our own kitchen utensils & dishes so I shall raid the 10¢ store for bare necessities. We have Genie's & Mary's dishes in Montclair which we will get, & shall try to borrow some stuff from Aunt Mary. Celie, may have to ask you to send me a few things but I'll wait and see.

After we settled our housing situation with the Major we went into the University of Penn. where Shaw has some Pitometer business & rather than sit in the car and wait for him, guess where I went? – Freeman's auction house! My but it seemed good to be back at my old haunt! They were having an exhibition of beautiful old silver, miniatures, & rare prints which I enjoyed tremendously. On returning to get Shaw I saw a big poster advertising a food fair nearby which I couldn't resist, so I collected Shaw & we went. It was a 40 ring circus & I collected enough samples to start in housekeeping. There was one supersalesman selling a new kind of mouse trap – a bottle arrangement with a hole in the top, which trapped but didn't kill the mice. It would have been very effective if the mice with which he demonstrated hadn't been so well trained, but whenever he placed the bottle among the mice they just scampered in & there wasn't even any bait in the bottle. They could hardly wait to get in the bottle. However, we didn't feel that the mice we knew would be so inclined, so refrained from buying. I had lots of fun listening to the salesmen and seeing the pretty displays but Shaw was enchanted with a lady who could read your mind & the serial numbers on your bills. With great control he refrained from purchasing a horoscope but I finally broke down & bought the well known set of utensils (which I have watched work at countless fairs) which enable one to cut vegetables in pretty shapes.

We then came home, ate supper & went straight to bed. Pretty soon I am about to run over to the Coles for a minute & then come back & settle ourselves. When I have my "flat" arranged I will describe in more detail.

Much Love,
Wanie

I wrote Bud, Celie.
Send trunk to address on paper. Better say Lancaster Pike.

Early Married Years

Letter from Joan to family

Wednesday, Fall, 1934

Dearests –

Being only 11:00 P.M. I am about to do some ironing and clean the living room, but thought I'd write you all a little hello first. I never go to bed until 2:00 A.M. and arise at 10:30 A.M., so you see most of my work is done from 8:45 on – after Shaw leaves.

I hope you are all established in your city home. I still can't think of 205 Prospect St. other than when it was all full of wedding excitement and festivity. I shall be interested in hearing about the new wall paper. To my mind, Thibault's is the worst place in the world to look for any because there are so <u>many</u> kinds, I should never be able to choose.

I have had lots of fun fixing up our little pine living room. I bought some maroon colored theatrical gauze and made (or rather cut it into) some curtains. Then I used 2 of my bright checked Italian doilies for tie-backs, placed the others on the various tables. My copper chafing dish is a great success here. One part, a lovely big bowl, I have on the fireplace mantel full of bright gay flowers, which my husband supplies. Then the chafing dish part is full of lovely bittersweet set off by a red tray in back of it. Then I've set the cover of it upside down on the stand & keep it full of bright colored fruit. So, except for the fact that we lack a comfortable chair, all is very cozy.

Dad, you would have envied us the other night, for we went to see vaudeville in town and it was Thurston the Magician. We sat in the second row from the front and marveled at his cleverness. When he was about to do the "cut the lady in two" act, he invited anyone who wished to come up on the stage & witness it from there. So I, along with the rest of the five year olds, went. I was not only interested in seeing that act up close – I also wanted to take a look up into the ceiling to see how many wires were suspended and snooped around the wings

& noted <u>many</u> hinges on the various contraptions used in the different acts. I also caught on as to how the trick was done.

Another day I went into my auction house to watch a sale of very fine orientals. I learned <u>much</u> from a person side of me whom I pumped when I found she knew her stuff. Shaw & I are going to invest in one or two small ones if there is another while here. Some <u>beautiful</u> old ones went for less than $1.00 a foot. We shall enlist Aunt Bertha's critical eye & taste.

Shaw & I went there for dinner Sunday. Had a <u>wonderful</u> meal & a very nice afternoon with her.

Sat. we are going to the famous Jersey shore for overnight. One of the other engineers & wife & 2 small children were offered a cottage by their landlady and asked us. To tell the truth I'm <u>anything</u> but enthusiastic about it because the boys will sleep most of the time and we'll take care of the babies and cook. Also I have a rough idea of what the landlady's house will be like. But I wouldn't offend them for the world and it will give me a chance to see the famous Jersey coast.

I'm <u>so</u> tickled Vee is coming Monday. We'll have such a good time together, and I'm anxious to show her Phil. Celie, I'm just <u>sick</u> to think you didn't see the beautiful park. It's just like the Bois – statues & all. It's a cinch to go into Phil. that way. Remember the <u>awful</u> time we had.

Auntie Bertha is so good to us, & such fun. When she goes out to see Uncle Ross she's going to give me her symphony ticket – a very swell box seat.

Celie there was a debut in the Dupont's greenhouse last Sat. Fancy that!

Harry Ingersoll, the engineer in charge is coming here & we're both very tickled, because he's much fun.

Mother has your neuritis completely disappeared? I can <u>certainly</u> sympathize with you for yesterday I had a crick in my arm from sleeping on it wrong and it was <u>so</u> weak and sore. I think you're <u>very</u> smart not to have caught a cold amongst so many. Are you eating better?

Now that the fall bracing weather is coming on I'm sure your appetite will increase. Now you must continue your darned old routine of porching & you mustn't exercise – I think you should eat downstairs once in a while for I know it does you good, but why not set a definite rule – like eating there just Wednesdays and Sundays. Then you can look forward to it regularly. Also, don't forget your bedtime hour will you? I hate all these don'ts but it is so <u>natural</u> to want to do too much. Just remember how much happier you are this fall than you were in 1932 about now – that alone sets me way up. It is so wonderful to be able to think of you without that awful unhappy feeling. I wish you'd write me how you do feel & how your temp. is. I think of you all <u>so</u> often. Shaw & I have decided that marriage has made us both want so much to be with our families when we're visiting – instead of out gadding, or wishing you'd all go to bed so we could kiss.

Dad, would you possibly visit me here? Or would you rather wait until we're shifted to Blackstone or Uxbridge? I know you hate to travel but I'm always afraid the next place will be farther away. And Doc & Mart – <u>how</u> we'd love that. If only they could leave on the midnight Friday & return on same Sunday. Tell them I'll pay their fare one way as a Christmas present to all three.

Shaw & I went to another ball game Monday. Connie Mac's boys made 2 home runs which won both games. <u>Very</u> thrilling.

Well, goodnight. I love you all <u>very</u> much. Take good care of each other. My love to Jen & Theresa.

Bestest love,
Wanie.

Letter from Joan to family from new apartment

Monday –

Dearests,

It was such fun to come home to a nice, light, private apartment! It's just peachy to be independent of any land lady and to be able to do as we wish without interference. Everything is in order now except that I still lack any kitchen utensils, but I buy them as I need them, + it is surprising how easily one can get on with a few tools. Our first meal was screaming! I had bought two plates, two cups and saucers and one frying pan (and a kitchen fork which I lost on the way home). We had no pillows the first night and lacked many other small things which I find I had always taken for granted. I've raided the 10 cent store so now we are almost equipped. The furniture isn't bad at all, and my curtains look <u>exquis</u>. Needless to say, they are just pinned. Our two Orientals add greatly, + my chafing dish + various table colors, also my horse + my French prints lend an air. We are so divinely comfortable that I hope we stay here a while.

That may not be, however, for Shaw had a talk with Mr. Cole yesterday and it seems that Mr. Case is all excited about Worcester work + wants him to do some more! So we may be back on your hands one of these days.

I am anxious to get in on Vee's excitement. If you tell me how much to spend I will scout around a present for you. I am going to hunt for some antique after dinner coffee spoons.

I plan to drive home with Uncle John the day after Thanksgiving. Isn't it lucky I'm getting a ride! Shaw won't miss me as cook for there is a very good dining room here.

We had <u>such</u> a good time with Bud and Ceile, he's just like a kid about next weekend! Incidentally, the Sat. night party is very informal - just what we wear to the game. Sunday aft. we're all going to the

Moyers' which will be fun - silk dresses I suppose. You have some good press agent for Johnny Phillips can't wait to meet "the Getch". Bud brought us some <u>wonderful</u> apples - stamen wine saps from Virginia.

Mother, I'll send you A. Bulthas bag address real soon, will call her in the morning.

Bumped into another Kentucky house party girl today. She is working in Bests's.

I think we're coming to Montclair this Thursday so Shaw can do some work in New York office. In that event we'll see you soon Ceile. Bring ruby + rhinestone clips.

Hope everything is going smoothly. I'll see you all soon, and Ceile even sooner.

Thanks for sending trunk. Expect it soon.

We're <u>so</u> happy.

Much love

Dodo

Letter from Joan after a visit with Vivian

Tuesday (no date)

Dears -

Such a homecoming as I had! I am sure Vee didn't enjoy her Sunday one bit more than I! Shaw met me at the train with a corsage of gardenias. Then we stopped at a fancy place en route back here for a bite to eat. When I walked into our little apartment a beautiful plant greeted me with a welcome home message on it. The table was all set for breakfast and the rooms spotless - even clean sheets. We were hardly in the door when Judy Tracey called up to say she had a light supper waiting for us in her apartment and while I was talking to her Harry Ingersol dropped in to welcome me back. I was so thrilled at seeing my darling Shaw again and everybody contributed into making me feel like a bride. I vow to have the most considerate, wonderful, <u>affectionate</u> husband possible, and I don't envy a soul in the world.

It is fairly certain that we'll be on your hands again soon, for Mr. Cole wants Shaw to do some tests in Worcester in connection with his paper which must be done around Christmas. He will not let Shaw go unless it is certain that he could return to this job so at present we have no definite answer. I should imagine, however, that it will be around the 20th of Dec. if we come. Isn't that peachy? Our expenses will all be on the company so our trip up will be free.

Send me the bill for the cretonne which I must have left in my room somewhere. I am sorry not to have paid it when at home but didn't have a check.

Yesterday my voice completely left me, but I didn't feel tired at all. I did spend most of the day relaxing and thinking over what a success my visit had been.

What size slipper does Mart wear? I'll send you Shaw's when I ask him.

Lots and lots of love to all my <u>dear</u> family -

Joan

Letter from Eugene H. Getchell, Joan's father

October 17, 1934

Dear Joan -

Perhaps Mama forwarded my scribble to her describing my first look see of Williamsburg and the side show.

But in a few words I arrived at 5 P.M, finding at least 500 ahead of me. After waiting an hour it was announced that the doctor would not come out again that day.

I decided to beat the game so after a shave in the coldest and hardest water I ever used I was on the spot (I had to go six miles to get a sleeping place) at 7:30 A.M. finding 400 ahead of me and the M.D. on the job.

I do not know how many he had treated before I arrived but I was 30 from the throne and there were 14 lines; three lines of wheelchairs and 11 of other suckers.

Anyway I had to stick it out so I danced around until 10:15 when I arrived at the center. Wasn't it cold. When I got through at 10:15 there were at least 550 people in line? He must be "handling" from 150 to 2000 people a day. A girl (sloppy looking) follows right after him and gently twists your hands. She just squeezed mine. Then you are supposed to enter a shed and get your legs pulled by one girl, your arms by another and your neck by a third. I did not even peek into that place. These imitation osteopaths do do some good at times for they break an adhesion in a stiff elbow or arm once in a while, whether from skill or luck I do not know which.

I went up there with the intention of giving him all the credit I could and meet him halfway in everything but after I saw him treat about 40 people for I was near enough during that time and saw him do practically the same thing to cripples, malformed feet, young and old and perfect feet like me, I was convinced he has the best racket since bootlegging went out.

He could do it with his eyes shut as far as any examination is concerned as he simply grasps your heel and gives a rather gentle twist to each foot. At no time did he use any strength or pressure and it simply amounted to a laying on of hands and the look in the faces of some of the gullible reminded me of the expression on the faces in some of the old pictures depicting adoration.

Rather a crummy lot of people but some well-dressed and evidently wealthy. Place full of boarding houses all little cottages needing paint badly, ramps instead of front steps, restaurants or rather hot dog stands galore.

He cannot possibly help a person except by getting them to wear shoes with supports but I will say he did seem to be pushing the purchasing of shoes unduly. He makes no remarks and asks no questions but will answer if called upon. I asked him if my shoes were suitable and he said yes.

It is needless to say, I started for Hanover and got there at 7 P.M. that day. I drove 270 miles to Woodstock Inn for dinner as it is a very high class hotel and I wanted to get with some nice people for a change. This is one time I would have gone to the Waldorf (Astoria) had it been available. I drank my cocktail and ate the whole bill of fare, strutted around the lobby and collected myself for the trip to Hanover twenty miles away.

Sunday I met Molly in Keene, changed cars and got back to Woonsocket well satisfied with a most interesting experience. It seems to be the local sentiment that Rex Beach and the shoe company have much in common. Beach's last article sent droves of customers. Dr. Locke had treated as many as 2500 in one day which seems impossible but we timed him as he turns them out at the rate of fourteen in five minutes, stopping once in a while to unwind his swivel chair and empty his overflowing pockets.

Give me 1,000 people with their confidence and belief and I will make some remarkable cures.

There are a thousand things I could and will tell you but one of the funniest and saddest sights was to see the wheelchair boys racing down the street hell bent for election getting their charges to the line and then running back for others. It was just like a movie where they get some imitation cripple in a wheelchair and turn him loose downhill.

I played golf with Dr. John last week and today he and his foursome are coming to the R.I.C.C. to play with me. Won't we have fun?

Your last letter is skating round the country somewhere as Mama told Genie to forward it to Canada. Let me say that Mama is in complete accord with my feelings about the miracle man of Canada.[17]

Doc and I are making the New Haven trip this weekend and I am sure Shaw will visualize us stopping at the Taft.

---

17   (*As written on the plaque put up for him in the town of Williamsburg, Ontario, CA.*) Dr. Mahlon W. Locke (1880-1942) Born in nearby Matilda Township, Locke studied medicine at Queen's University and in Scotland. In 1908 he opened his medical office in this house. Interested in arthritis, which he believed was caused principally by fallen arches, he treated many arthritics in the following year by manual manipulation of their feet. Large numbers of his patients claimed to be cured or relieved by this method and his reputation spread throughout North America and overseas. From 1928 onwards thousands of the sick visited Dr. Locke in Williamsburg where he reportedly treated hundreds of persons daily. During the depression years this enormous influx brought significant prosperity to the region.

Letter from Joan to family
Camay Soap Contest

Fall, 1934, Saturday

Dearests –

Welcome to your city house! Isn't it fun to see the beautiful trees again, Mother? We have no lovely foliage out here and I find I miss it more than I thought I would.

I have been frothing at the mouth (literally) over the Camay Soap contest. Shaw looked up from his book the other evening to see me lapping it! I was trying to get some ideas by tasting it. Have you entered it? You better hurry cause it ends the last day of September & it has to be mailed by midnight. The first prize is $1,000.00 a year for life – eemagine! I've sent in 6 slogans which means I now own 21 cakes of soap. I decided they might be very careful not to award it to one so young, so I signed my name Mrs. E.S. Cole, 133 Belleview Ave. If they choose to check up, they'll find that Momma Cole is no callow youth. The award is to be made Christmas day. Of course, I won't win it, but it's worth a try. I should never have won that Marlboro contest! It will cost me more than $50.00 in the end. Here are the slogans I submitted. Tell me the one you think best.

"Your skin will achieve the softness of its suds."
"Even a beast worshipped beauty."
"Camay claims only to make you clean – but beautifully clean."
"Outward beauty brings inner poise."
"The soap that brings beauty as deep as skin."
"Fair and clearer with Camay."

Be sure to write me which one you like.

My husband seems to be growing what <u>he</u> calls new stomach muscles, but I think such a growth is commonly diagnosed as a bay window. He certainly gets enough exercise climbing in & out of manholes so it must be my delicious food.

By the way we had company for dinner the other night and I served what I think is a very fancy meal. Here is the menu. Believe me it took all day and all my strength. First, May Ballou's tomato juice cocktail recipe, or sherry, plus hors d'oeuvres. Next, roast lamb & roast potatoes, gravy & mint sauce, Brussel sprouts & hollandaise, popovers, salad, & homemade meringues with whipped cream & chocolate sauce. Isn't that something?

Mother there are the darlingest pair of colorful Swedish woolen gloves in the curio store which I know Genie would adore for college – or Celie in Wenatchee. They cost $3.50. Can I buy them for you to give for Christmas? <u>Answer.</u>

Jane Arnold, friend of Genie's & Mary's in Sessions House called on me the other day & two days later gave me a luncheon for twelve! Debby phoned me and I saw her & lots of other friends of Genie's there. They are all <u>darling</u> girls.

As for my secret, Mother, you can tell Dad. It's coming along but I have to wait for days when I'm inspired. It's <u>so</u> long, and will take lots of going over before I can ever send it to anyone. I'll send you a copy when it's ready for the press.

Shaw and I are <u>so</u> happy together. Really there is nothing lacking in him. He appreciates me <u>so</u>. We do have such a good time together. This life enables us to enjoy each other's company more than most married people do because we are together alone so much, and we find ourselves preferring to do things alone than with others. We want to have children but we don't feel we want one badly enough yet to put up with the sacrifices that we'd have to undergo to manage one in this racket. So forgive us for not presenting you with Ellis Rockwell Cole for a while yet.

I hope you aren't worrying yourself about this moving. It's been done for 25 years - & what <u>of</u> it if the rugs aren't straight in the front room? Every once in a while just say to yourself, "Oh what the hell anyway!"

Much love to you Poppa & Mamma -
Your potential thousand dollar a year heiress – Joan

Written down the top margin the following note to Aunt Genie from "Mother" – (Grandmother Edith Ellis Getchell);

Dearest G.G.
So awful to say Good-bye to you. Dick has just gone - says you are fine. He took Ford to Providence. Brother's wife trailed him here this morning. You are very precious to your father & mother. Take care of yourself. Have a happy time but try to think things out. I go to Boston tomorrow. Shall be thinking of you lovely. What a wonderful family I have to think about though separated from you all. So hot here & I know it's lovely there –
Love
Mother
Wed.

My Book of Happy Memories

Entry from Scrapbook about Blizzard Drive

1935

 Our main line sojourn was abruptly terminated by the customary telegram and the customary bedlam ensued. Two tins of salmon found a comfortable niche 'mongst my Paris underwear and a leftover Christmas plum pudding was packed with the shoes. The bulging trunks, cartons, + suitcases were stamped closed at 3:30 and by 4:00 I was encased in the Plymouth. As usual, the heavy baggage was fitted into the rear compt. But this time we found many many leftovers... the bed pillows, for instance; which were placed under us; an enormous laundry tied up in our last night's sheets. Why does soiled laundry occupy so much more space than washed? "It was jammed between me and the door"; all of our periodicals were under foot, and my inevitable tapestry bag crammed with everything from my last look around the apartment gathered up. My pocket was stuffed with two nut Hershey's, the other with receipted bills which Shaw cautioned me to pull from the waste basket. Never before had we resembled quite so completely a traveling chautauqua, but we were to be grateful for these remnants of a hasty packing e'er long.

 Now, while we had been hurling things into our trunks, Mother Nature had been hurling great flakes of heavy snow onto this Earth, and by the time of our departure, this blizzard had already become front page news. Had we purchased an evening paper we could have seen that it had already become headlines: in fact, already, it was "the blizzard of 35" + already loyal defenders of "the blizzard of 88" were scuffing at it - though snow bound.

 The sun was shining brightly on the snow as we drove toward Morristown and the wind was being very playful. We amused ourselves by imagining how such a blizzard must have crippled activity "when father was a boy" and decided that drifts in those days merely looked higher when seen from a low seated sleigh. We mentioned how much more beautiful this back way was. After a storm one could really appreciate seeing the isolation of the farmhouses - when we sighted three stopped cars ahead of us on the route up a hill. Engine trouble I said, as we approached, waited a few minutes, then Shaw got out and went up ahead to look the situation over. "It's really quite windy" I thought to myself, and turned up the car heater another notch. Shaw came back fairly frost bitten. It seemed there was an open meadow, a big drift, and cars floundering so we must go back a ways and take the Allentown route. Well, maybe we were a trifle optimistic, but if we hurried we could still get to Montclair for a 7:30 dinner. The Allentown route was plowed, cleaned-two wide lanes, until we suddenly found the plowing ended, a huge drift and a batch of cars. Again we stopped and again Shaw got out. Really, this big two lane road can't be impassable I thought, but it was. There we were in a "cul de sac." The only route left was the four lane Roosevelt Boulevard highway, the main Phil. NY road, that necessitated going back to Phil and starting over again, yet that was what we had to do. About now we began to realize that possibly we should've gone that way the first time.

Letter from Joan to her in-laws while staying at their house
A dinner party with Vee and Craig and an icy trip to the city

Jan 8, 1935, Friday
133 Bellevue Ave, Montclair, N.J.

Dearests,

Another blizzard rages outside, but all is easy in our nice, warm, country home. We think of you constantly and wonder if you can <u>possibly</u> be too hot!

I feel <u>terribly</u> about missing the first mail date. Somehow I got it in my head that the 12th was the first chance for us to get in touch with you. We were in Woonsocket at the time and my mind ceases to function concerning outside affairs when I am in the bosom of my family.

All is well at home and I was awfully glad to be home long enough to get caught up on local news. Dad seems to be in much better spirits but continues to have no great love for Mr. F.D.. Mart + the baby were here all week and Genie came home for the weekend – so, since all the family were assembled, we (as usual) got the "family group picture jag" on. I will send you the results when developed.

Shaw was at Hoops each night but returned Friday evening at 1:00 A.M so we drove down Sat. starting after lunch. The sight of the Pickwick Arms in Greenwich made us very hungry, so we dropped in for a very sumptuous meal, served with all the flourishes. Since our return Shaw has been alternating between the office and Passaic, and since Mr. Case heartily approves of accuracy tests, we expect to return to Worcester Monday. I say "we expect" – but, of course anything might happen between now and Monday!

Peg[18] and I have been having a perfectly lovely time together. We sit by the hour and argue Chippendale versus Hepplewhite, Englebecks

---

18 Peg was Shaw's sister-in-law, married to Shaw's brother John. For a short time in 1935 the two couples were living together in Montclair, NJ while GrandMary and Grandpa Cole were travelling.

Early Married Years

versus A + P. and so on. We feel like the Mrs.' Millionbucks with a servant at our command, and we wrack our brains in search of new quaint recipes with which to charm our Husbands. We keep the <u>most</u> detailed accounts of our expeditions so that we may divide them evenly when our visit is terminated, and you would laugh to see how careful we are not to gyp each other! When I came I announced to her that I hoped she would act as boss, but she is so sweet about not wanting to seem dictatorial that we both bow and scrape when we make suggestions! Everything works out beautifully and we both wish this arrangement might go on indefinitely.

Our entertaining this week has been confined to a very swell meal for Vee + Craig, who came out Wednesday to stay overnight. Peg + John cleared the guest room for them, and it was <u>pathetic</u> to see Vee enjoy the sun + stars. She left the shades way up at night so she could watch the stars, and just reveled in the sunshine which fell on her as she lay in bed in the morning. They had just decided to continue living in the city but one night in the country wrecked all their plans + they are all for the suburbs now.

Maybe you'd like to know what our collation consisted of. Poor Isabelle[19] was probably a nervous wreck by the time dinner was over because all three of us were in the kitchen preparing our own specialties! She moped around doing her darndest not to show the slightest interest + whenever she did deign to glance at what we were doing she had a that-won't-turn-out-right look on her face. However, she did all of the dirty work and made an excellent prune whip. I made some very classy hors d'oeuvres and when I finished them I made Isabelle eat one. She said, "Those are alright - just cream cheese." To which I remarked laughingly, "Isabelle Cherry - don't kid me. They're the best things you ever ate." I was rewarded by a very, very faint suggestion of a smile. It must be agony for that girl to smile because the corners of her mouth have to travel so far in order for them to get up where they ought to be.

---

19   Isabelle was Grandmary Cole's cook.

Peg made the main dish - a baked stuffed halibut with parsley cream sauce, which was exquise. Baked potatoes and those little french peas accompanied that, followed by one of my heterogeneous salads, served in Peg's big silver bowl from Aunt Alice + the salad spoon + fork from the Alvords. Craig ate three helpings of the prune whip, followed by coffee in the living room and the rest of the evening was spent discussing the Hautmann Case. Shaw unfortunately, didn't get home until 8:30 so missed our classy meal.

Tomorrow night Peg works at the two hundred club show, and Shaw, John, and I watch from the balcony. Yesterday I called on Jean Strait to find that they leave for 3 years on March 6th. They are sent over on the company in great style - a suite plus a nurse who will accompany them. They are then put up in a hotel until they find a house. All of this plus a very good raise in salary. Harold is to be in charge of the bond department of the London Office. All of Jean's relatives are in London or thereabouts + her maid who is going with her is Scottish and dying with joy at the prospect. Mrs. McWaddy will live on in the Summit Ave house but hopes to come over this summer. Doesn't that sound like the grandest opportunity? <u>What</u> a chance for a real book!

Mrs. Holliday has taken a house in back of Mrs. Chase for next summer. Besides that I know of no more Sakonnet news.

Peg and I had a wild day in New York Tuesday. We decided to drive in and window shop for furniture, linens, china, silver etc. It was snowing a little, but I took the car just the same because some of our shopping was to be way up town. The minute we drove out onto Bellevue Ave, we realized that it was going to be terribly slippery for there was a glaze of ice under the snow. We realized it even more fully when we almost collided with a truck down by the Church on lower Bellevue. I avoided the truck but went sliding into a few big rocks which bent the rail under the mudguard. That should have been a warning to me, but oh no! I was determined not to be a sissy + turn back, so from then on we drove about 10 miles an hour and were

Early Married Years

simply <u>miserable</u>. N.Y.C. was a sheet of ice. I have never driven on anything so treacherous, so we did most of our running around on foot after all. We quickly called our husbands - Shaw was out, but we got in touch with John, and in honeytones suggested that instead of going out on the dirty old train, wouldn't he like to drive out with us? As soon as he got behind the wheel he realized he'd been double-crossed and we were both in disgrace for two days. Anyway, we did get a lot of good dope and saw many stunning things and we tried to convince Shaw + John that we did it all for them.

I imagine someone from New England has written you of the awful conditions due to the blizzard. Macky + Junie were forced to sit up in the Biltmore lobby all night along with hosts of others. The management passed around robes + hot coffee to the overflow + there wasn't a hotel room available in all Providence. Many theatres stayed open all night, as well as schools. There were many sad cases of women unable to get to maternity hospitals, etc. For three days Prospect St. was unsullied by silver plow or auto. I think it a <u>terrible</u> reflection on Rhode Island politicians. With all their graft they couldn't even get the Main Sts. cleared.

A letter from Mary this morning gives us the details of the exciting fire in Sessions[20]. We read of it in the paper but didn't call Mary because it did not sound serious at all. Thank <u>goodness</u> it was so well managed. I think it is a tribute to the college - and the girls. Mary looked fine last weekend + seemed in the best of spirits. She said she was awfully glad to come home and find that she had lots of loving family on this side of the Atlantic. Peg insisted she have breakfast in bed and we drove her in to the train Sunday.

I am gradually running down. Of course we eagerly await first news of you. There are millions of questions I would like to ask about "my old haunts," Madeira, "Gib" and Algiers. You are in beautiful Palermo today. I hope the sun shines on you. We are all so glad for you that this

---

20 Mary Cole (Jordan) is Shaw and John's little sister. Sessions is a dorm at Smith College.

trip is possible. You both were due a nice, long spree and we're all so happy to think of you carefree and alone together. I expect your little finger to be <u>worn</u> out by your return[21].

I shall leave off here for Shaw to continue. Au revoir for now. Try not to worry, for I assure you, we will all look after each other.

Much much love to you -

Joan

---

21 "Little finger" is related to an old family saying where you can feel someone thinking good thoughts about you in your little finger.

Letter from Joan to Shaw's parents
Trip through Pennsylvania Dutch Country

February 23, 1935
Shippensburg, Penn

Dearests,

At the moment of writing, I see by the itinerary that you have left Nag Hammadi, and are passing through Seshneh about now. Well, that's just peachy I suppose, but it sounds like hieroglyphics to me!

We were <u>so</u> glad to get your first letter + cards, and find that everything is living up to your expectations. Now <u>do</u> not spend all of your time at a writing desk. Just remember everything and give us an illustrated picture when you get home.

We too are on a trip – and what a hick town this is! My "Shouts from the Shelter Box" came due yesterday! So I wrote an account of our stay here, and entitled it "Oh For a Ship Out of Shippensburg!" We arrived Monday afternoon and I don't know when we're leaving, for poor Shaw is having a tough time of it. Snow, and mud, and air in the pipe are adding their share to the complications of a new type of work for him. If he gets on well today, we will drive to Phil. tomorrow, since he wants a session with Mr. S. Logan, and, after dinner at his house, we will return so that Shaw may finish up here. Our immediate plans are unknown, but in 2 or 3 weeks we will be sent to Cambridge. That, of course, sounds simply splendid, for we have many friends around there, and it will be nice to be so near home. As for the housing problem, I imagine Aunt Alice will generously offer her third floor – but !!!??? However, we shall see what will transpire.

Now for the highlights of this little sojourn. The route, by way of Harrisburg, took us through the Penn. Dutch country, which consisted of one farm after another. The farms were ornamented with huge brilliantly painted geometric figures, which proved to be "hex" signs.

Also, life-sized cows, pigs, and horses were painted thereon. Every third barn convinced me that I was missing most in life by not chewing "silver cup tobacco", but a stick of Beechnut gum appeased my watering mouth. Many of the houses were decorated with large iron X's and stars, further precautions against the evil spirits. I began to get the willies and closed the car windows, lest a witch fly in.

After leaving Harrisburg, the towns became smaller + smaller + smaller, until finally we saw about three lights in the distance among the hills. That was Shippensburg. The hotel problem promised to be acute, but, to our amazement, we found not one poor hotel, but <u>three</u>. A view of four, very fat, sloppy, google-eyed men spreading all over the so-called lobby queered the first one. The same four have been in the same chairs each time I've passed. Could it be a wax works, do you suppose? The second hotel boasted no lobby. The cashier's desk in the dining room was apparently the headquarters. One glance at the bathless room queered that. I could never have lived among such floral profusion. Room with a bath sold us to this one, even though our room is directly over the saloon (which unbeknownst to us, was raided for slot machines the other evening). It is a lovely room with tin furniture overlooking the lumber yard. The landlord looks exactly like Pancho-Villa, so I kept my door firmly bolted at first. He proves to be a harmless soul who spends all of his time gazing out of the lobby window. The window, by the way, is decorated with a big branch up which four stuffed squirrels climb!

There seems to be one restaurant in town suitable for ladies who joyfully advertises "a dinner for $.25." Every combination offers "Lionized potatoes." Fried eggs and bacon prove to be their forte. A box of Crax and a bottle of ripe olives in my room provide the necessary roughage + vitamins.

My recreation consists of absorbing culture from the State Teachers College on the hill. When not reading, I watch the students flirting with each other over reference books. I brought along some college books of my own, my tapestry, and Thomas Hardy's "Far From the Madding Crowd." Little did I realize how appropriate is that title for this locale!

The highlight so far was being interviewed by the local reporter during dinner at the second hotel mentioned. Here we bravely ordered a Porterhouse steak, which proved to be a mass of sinews which only a rotary saw could sever. Dinner music was provided by the country Rotarians who were bursting with pep on the above floor.

The paper came out yesterday, so I arose early and tore down to the newsstand to secure a copy. I quickly grabbed one and scanned the headlines and there, sure enough, my hero's name was emblazoned in large size print on the front page – "E. Shaw Cole Makes Tests Water Main – Research Specialist." Nearly bursting with pride, I magnanimously glanced at the other front page articles, and found – in equally large print – in the bracket side of Shaw's, the following, "Increase in Egg Hatching This Season. Calvin Martin says busy season coming"! I reflected – who was more insulted? Mrs. Calvin Martin or Mrs. Shaw Cole?

The above account is almost verbatim of what I put in the Downstream Orifice, as nearly as I can remember. So if you do not receive one, you have at least read my page.

We had a very pleasant weekend at the John R. Coles. Celie drove down with us for the weekend, driving back with another friend Monday. Bud is up there this weekend, and I would send glad tidings to you concerning them if I could, Poppa Cole, but the fact that Bud is going to the West Coast in April to be gone a year at least may throw a monkey wrench in the works. He is to be placed in charge of an office near Seattle, and though I know for a fact (entre nous) that he would like her to go with him, I'm afraid it is a little sudden for her.

Peg gave a very swell buffet supper Sunday night, to which Bud, Celie, Shaw + I were invited. She will probably tell you all about it, but she may be too modest to tell of its success. Her guests were most entertaining, and we spent most of the evening in the playroom singing. Shades of a like evening you spent there last spring!

Well, dears, I guess I've said my say for now. You would not believe it, but I am busy as a bee in this little room of mine. The time does not lag in the least and I am very grateful to this little sojourn, for it has proved to me that I can never be bored!

I haven't cooked for so long that I shall have to get acquainted with Fanny Farmer all over again!

Loads + loads of love to you both. <u>Don't</u> worry about any of us, for, should anything go wrong, there are five Coles and four Rockwells who would immediately put it right.

Have lots of good times,
Joan

Shaw just came in with your card from Naples. Glad your good weather continues.

THE NEWS-CHRONICLE

Entered as Second Class Matter at the Shippensburg, Pa. Post Office

"YOU CAN'T DO TOO MUCH FOR SHIPPENSBURG"

TUESDAY, FEBRUARY 19, 1935

INCREASE IN EGG HATCHING THIS SEASON

Calvin Martin Says Price Is Better; 5000 Chicks Hatched Each Week

Busy Season Coming

E. SHAW COLE MAKES TESTS WATER MAIN

Head Pressure, Velocity And Friction Coefficient Are Determined

Research Specialist

E. Shaw Cole, research specialist for the Pitometer company in New York, has been in Shippensburg since Monday conducting a research survey on the basis of tests made on the Roxbury-Shippensburg water line. These tests deal with water pressure, velocity and the coefficient of friction in the main. Mr. Cole states that the local water line is an ideal system on which to make tests, for the water in either of the town mains can be shut off and the other supply brought into service. In this way the standard pressure of either main when not in use can be ascertained.

In an interview with Mr. Cole, it was learned that the given pressure at any point on the main will vary depending upon the rate of flow. That is, if the pressure were 2,000 pounds at a point near Lurgan when the main was closed, it may drop to 1,800 pounds when the water is turned on. In order to determine the pressure, velocity and the coefficient of friction in the line at any point, a corporation cock is tapped and the pressure guage attached. To determine the velocity of the water a pitometer is attached at the same aperture but in a different manner. The pitometer tube fits into a sort of sleeve that is entirely closed when the test is registered. The part of the pitometer that operates within the main consists mainly of an orifice that faces up stream to measure the velocity and another that faces down stream to measure suction.

STAR ROUTE

The highest cow at this sale brought $98.50 and the highest horse $188.00. A tractor plow brought $44.00 and a mower brought $76.00. A hammer mill that had been used one year sold for $78.00. According to Sam Rosenberry, one of his calves, a young bull, got loose and ran out over a neighboring field. This bull brought $30.00 "on the run." One cow was not sold at all. She got loose while being led out for auction and was chased across several fields and fences and was last seen disappearing into the wilds of Bear valley.

Fur Taking Decreases But Prices Go Higher

According to records just compiled by the State Game Commission there have been fewer pelts taken during the 1933-34 season. However, the value increased considerably over the previous year. During the 1932-33 season, 1,121,967 pelts were reported, having a value of $525,867. Last season 1,683,328 pelts were reported with a value of $934,154.

The total included 377,654 muskrats, 343,753 skunks, 206,546 opossums, 88,578 weasels, 30,732 raccoons, 12,444 minks, 9,337 grey foxes, 7,590 red foxes, 195 wild cats and 6,499 beaver.

E. Shaw Cole Makes Tests

(Continued from page one).

the pressure, velocity, elevation and length of the line, the percentage of or coefficient of friction is figured.

The loss of head pressure from the source to the point where it is distributed to the individual users on any particular line could be determined if the water were turned off for a certain length of time while the test is being made; but in some cases this is nearly impossible. For this reason surveys made on water lines, such as the local system, are useful in computing available head pressures for various kinds of pipe in other localities where a change of pipe or a new source is being contemplated. This information is

---

BURKHART'S RESTAURANT

FAMOUS FOR OUR 25¢ DINNER

SHIPPENSBURG, PENNSYLVANIA

"Shaw breaks into print alongside the hens!"

Letter from Joan on their arrival in Dunkirk

THE WHITE INN
MURRAY HILL BARTLEY. PROP.
FREDONIA. N. Y.
"On The Great Lakes Tours"

April 6th, 1935, Tuesday

Dearests -

We aren't here, but we were last night and couldn't get out quick enough. It's a summer hotel and much *too* summery for this snow storm weather we've bumped into.

We arrived in Dunkirk at 5 o'clock in the midst of a sleet storm. One glance at the town, + we named it Dumpkirk. It's plop on the edge of Lake Erie, which I suppose is lovely on a hot summer day, but last night it looked very large and very cold. We got in touch with Ted Storey, the Pit. Engineer that we are replacing as soon as Buffalo (thirty miles from here) comes through and his tale of house hunting was very discouraging. They spent four days looking, + finally some man in town let them have his summer cottage on the lake. They've only been here two weeks + are not charmed at the prospect of moving again so soon. Ted suggested we come and stay with them till they leave and then continue to occupy the cottage. That seems to be the only solution so we have accepted. I have yet to see the cottage and our hostess for the next week or two! We're going there for dinner tonight so can write you more details of our future home later.

In case we need blankets we will need those in a hurry so I'll give you our trunk address now in case we wire. It's simply Dunkirk N.Y. care of Pit. c/o Pitometer Engineer - Dunkirk Water + Light Co. Also I may find that I'll have to have my winter bathrobe, for there is only fireplace heat. It is in my attic bedroom closet in one of the dress cases.

The brown monogrammed woolen bathrobe. You'll have to send that in a separate box for we have the trunk keys. Send both trunks.

We are located for tonight in a tourist house somewhere between Fredonia and Dunkirk. I don't even know our landlady's name - in fact all I know is we are on route twenty. It's a very comfy house and oh so cheerful. I can just hear the landlady shopping for chintz + wallpaper, "Yes - it's pretty, but not gay enough." It's very clean and cozy though and so much better than the hotel.

I find I have lots of friends in Buffalo - many Smith girls, and since we're only thirty-one miles away I guess I'll write some of them.

I'm still a touch dazed from all of these wild changes of plans. Thank goodness it wasn't Cincinnati. That sounded *so* far away.

I'll write you soon a new chapter for my book - "A Little Cottage On Lake Erie - in April."

Write to me, Edy, and tell me how everything is.

Much love,
Joan

Letter from Joan to family

1935, Friday
Haverford, PA

Dearests all –

Many thanks for sending the trunks on so promptly. We were greatly in need of blankets, but not in any hurry for some of the other things, such as evening clothes and summer finery.

Now for a description of our locale. First, picture a small town made up of about 15 Arnold + River Sts. Then follow a road out of Dunkirk along Lake Erie for about four miles. Then you see a muddy road to the right – take it + continue until you would land in the lake if you didn't bump into a group of cottages all very "juxtaposed". Imagine the scrawniest you've seen in the way of Island Park-a-bide-a-wee-stop-a-bit-you-need-a-long-nest cottages, and there you have our happy home - with one exception - the plumbing doesn't trickle down the front porch beams into the bathing beach like Island Park, but wherever it trickles to, I don't know. I do know that you can't trickle at all in this house without sounding as if all the roof gutters were leaking. It sounds so loudly we, who are all downstairs, all but duck when we hear the refrain.

Enter the kitchen door, and if you are dusty and tired from traveling, just strip and enter the shower bath, conveniently located within arm's reach of the stove. Then proceed to the living-dining room + pause to note the gigantic iceless ice box which decorates the dining side of the living room. Bow reverently to all of the crucifixes, sacred palms etc. which, before their removal, vied with a large sized framed picture of the Dem. National Convention, 1929, which spreads itself out over the fireplace. Now, pull in all of your protruding members and wirm up the stairway into the bath. Should you take either a left or a right in time, you will land in the 2 bedrooms, adequately equipped with 4 tremendous double beds, but nary a closet.

The Storeys, plus one incorrigible 3 year old, occupy one, we, the other. Both rooms are flagstoned with trunks, suitcases, and trunk drawers. Happily for us, our room is equipped with a sort of a piece of furniture. It is a po-po commode, but instead of living normally on the floor, it is nailed half way up the wall. Maybe their idea was to make it easier to dust mop under it, but they failed to realize that it would look less gravity defying if they had sawed off the legs + casters which simply dangle in thin air.

The Storeys are very nice, if a touch crude in ways. For instance Ted said last night, "I'm certainly glad you people are what you are. There are very few people we'd care to live with," all during which statement, he was picking his teeth. They are very interesting, however - she is a very good musician, which of course affords a common bond between us.

Although the fireplace + stove are our only sources of heat, we are very comfortable. The lake is literally our front yard and when it gets a bit warmer it will be just lovely here. There are many assets to living here even if there is no style, and I have no kick coming at all. There are two deck chairs out in front + when good weather comes, and the Storeys leave, I expect we'll spend most of our time outside.

So we are all hail and hearty here together – even to the Hail Mary who hails Al Smith + the rest of the convention on the other side of the wall.

Will write you about our landlord next - Mike O'Laughlin, one of the N.Y. state electors, who has never missed a Dem. Convention, but whose wife serves him tomato juice when she serves the rest with wine, cause she doesn't think he ought to take liquor!

Much love,
Joan

Letter to family from Dunkirk

Monday – 2:30 P.M.

Dearest Mother –

By the time Celie's nice letter arrived this noon, you had already gone through the ordeal you so dreaded. All weekend I've been thinking of you and wondering if you were perishing of dread. Now, it wasn't as bad as you thought it was going to be, was it? So let that be a lesson to yez and cease to worry about your store teeth. As far as your new ones are concerned, maybe you could arrange to have them centered correctly. Your front ones never did match the end of your nose!

We are all getting on <u>just</u> beautifully. The Storeys are awfully good eggs and ever so nice to live with. The baby proves to be very winning, and now that the dog has had a gay weekend in Buffalo with his lady friends he's very docile + unbothersome. The Storey's are due to leave us next Monday to go on a survey in Buffalo. That will leave Shaw in charge so we won't be moved until the job is finished, which probably will be somewhere around the end of June. We're so <u>lucky</u> to have this cottage which only costs $20.00 a month! The lake is beautiful + there are many trees around us which will give us more seclusion when they come out, and when the other cottagers arrive. So far, we are monarchs of all we survey, for there is no one living on this point but us.

The weather has been terrible so far and today is the nearest approach to hurricane weather I've ever known. The Lake is foaming + about 15 yards nearer our "sea wall" than normally. It almost looks as if there was a tide but I suppose that's due to the wind.

The Storeys went to Buffalo for the weekend so Shaw + I had our first meal "en famille" since early in January - lamb chops, cauliflower with Hollandaise, baked potatoes + avocado pear salad. Sunday we spent in front of the fire. I reading the Sunday papers + writing my Downstream Orifice, Shaw composing a report on his Worcester work. The Storeys came back in time for a waffle + sausage supper, supplemented by fried chicken for Shaw and me, since we hadn't had any dinner.

We keep perfectly warm here. The fireplace sends out all of the heat we need in the living room + in the morning we light the gas oven to warm up the kitchen. I haven't had to wear a coat once in the house, so you can see it's very comfortable. I <u>did</u> appreciate my winter bathrobe though, for the first leap out of bed is a little startling as yet. Many thanks.

Write me a penny postcard Mother + tell me how you feel. I <u>hope</u> it's better, except for the discomfort involved. Did you let Mrs. Guerin know about Mary, the waitress? She might still be looking for someone.

I forgot to mention the very nice looking golf course less than a ½ mile from here. There are exactly two nice houses in town so I guess they aren't very fussy about the membership. Shaw and I will enjoy playing after he comes home from work.

Our phone number is Dunkirk 810F22 (!) in case you want to get in touch with me.

I wish I could have been home to help you grin and bear it, but I know that Celie did all that was necessary. Please <u>always</u> remember that I understand your mental sufferings.

Much love,

Joan

Love to Poppa, Mart, Doc, & Gene. The Coles are spending 2 days in Capri + will be either in Florence or Rome for Easter.

Letter to family from Dunkirk

April, 1935
Tues. Eve

Dearests -

Shaw has departed for night work so I am monarch of all I survey - which includes all of Lake Erie and five empty cottages. I am not the least bit afraid of staying here alone, and I'm very cozy here in front of the fire, munching on a big Hershey bar.

The Storeys left Saturday, praise be! Gladys is a perfect peach and ever so nice to live with but Ted, her husband, has an idea that he is God's gift to mankind - which idea, Shaw + I do not share. His judgement and knowledge on any subject is supreme and all embracing - especially on the child raising topic. Their daughter June Eve is being reared strictly according to government bulletins and the new psychology and more than once I ached to supplement the new psychology with a smart spank on the bottom. For instance, she was completely attached to a filthy old woolen shawl which she carried with her from dawn until dark - and then slept with it. I asked her mother one day if she had been born wrapped up in it, but it seems that this is her second. She had dragged the first one to shreds. Well, come when Gladys + I would prepare the meals, out would come June Eve, + the shawl plus 3 balloons (Mickey Mouse and two of the three pigs) plus a miniature gas station toy, + any other toy which she felt sure would take up the most room. From then on, getting a meal became an obstacle race. My feet would get constantly tangled in the shawl and the balloons would hover around whatever I was mixing. One day I saw to it that Mickey Mouse hovered near a paring knife, but alas, he was replaced before nightfall. After a few days of hopping and leaping around I could have replaced Nijinsky at a moment's notice. I became thoroughly adjusted + ceased to mind it after a while, but I never did get used to one strange habit of Blinky's - the Boston bull. For some unknown reason, all percussion instruments caused him apparently terrific agony. There is a large-sized parlor clock on the mantel which strikes very slowly + very mournfully, and whenever it struck, the dog would simply screech with pain. Twelve o'clock, either A.M. or P.M. was his Gethsemane and my Anathema!! I would gladly have stopped the clock and relied on my astronomical knowledge for the time but no - Ted wound it religiously every night.

So - as you may be able to conclude - we are delighted that they have departed. The weekend was a blessed and a noiseless one. All of the inconveniences in our little cottage seem to have departed with our host and hostess and we find it ideal. We look forward to many sunbaths on our front and back porches, and you may visualize us basking in the two chairs in the photograph.

Sat. night in the town of Dunkirk was <u>something.</u> It was the first warm evening, besides being Easter Eve. We laughed at ourselves, going into town Saturday evening to do our marketing and "take in a show" with the rest of the farmers! The whole world seemed to be on Main St. and I could see that some of the town lassies just couldn't wait until the next day before putting on their new rigs. One white pink ensemble gave me a case of chilblains on the spot.

Shaw will probably work nights during most of our stay and we're both glad in a way, for it will give us more chance to play golf and lie in the sun. He will get up about two o'clock and we will go into town together. I'll do my shopping + he his office work + from then till 9:45 he'll be free.

There is an emporium in town which boasts the following sign:

Pictures + Frames
Electric Refrigerators
Funeral Directors

Thanks for your two letters mother. As I have said before, <u>please</u> write penny postcards.

A card from Celie today listed her activities for the week. What a whirl! Shaw + I are <u>so</u> happy about them.

I didn't realize my first letter to you was particularly humorous. If so, send it back and I'll copy it into my book. First impressions are what I want and I've forgotten what I said. Also return these pictures and save Mrs. Cole's letter. There will be more pictures soon.

Lots + lots of love to you + Dad. Everytime you two think of us you should beam with joy to realize how happy we are. Everything is A-I, 100% perfect with us.

Joan

The Coles stayed in our hotel in Rome. Found it fine.

Entry from Scrapbook about their "acute garbage trouble"

April, 1935
Dunkirk N.Y.

This is dedicated to the lowly hog.
May he always be hungry for what I don't want!

We have been having garbage trouble – but <u>acute</u> garbage trouble. Situated, as we are, on the very brink of Lake Erie, one might suppose that the lake would solve our problem, but alas – there is no tide! During a great storm last week we tossed a great accumulation to the waves wondering, half guiltily, if it would eventually mar some romantic couple's vision of Niagara Falls. Our altruistic worries were unfounded, however, for next morning we were to find the harried remains still nearer our front lawn, to the delight of the sea gulls who were fairly picking their teeth on the porch steps.

So the problem became greater, and so did the garbage. It soon spilled over the refuse can into various cartons, thence into shirt boxes, and thence into paper bags. Wild and domestic animals came to know of it, and shouted with glee to their feathered friends that, at the end of a lonely dirt road off toward the lake, a veritable feast awaited them. Each subsequent morning I formed a tableau fit for the brush of Millet – "Reaping the Garbage at SunUp." True, my collection of leftovers was somewhat purged, but not greatly reduced in quantity.

Now, during this fretful period, there was a garbage man in our employ. Once he came in a broken down wagon, and gathered up the remains for his pigs, and was seen no more. We were told that this Italian will o' the wisp was probably emerging from an overdose of fermented grapes. We gave him a week in which to recover, and then set out to make him a friendly call. His place was a jumbled collection of segments of shacks, wagons, slays, fences and livestock. In the yard sat also a segment of a man. Shaw approached him with the air of a Canadian royal mounted police, his eye gleaming with an 'I've got my man' look. But no, this man could neither understand what Shaw was saying nor make him understand that he didn't understand, but he finally succeeded in directing Shaw's attention toward another shack. An old apple tree of a man, with a peninsula nose and an isthmus neck, hobbled toward him, and Shaw made a great stride as if to ask him before he died if he was Andy the garbage man. He wasn't, of course, and couldn't possibly have been, for the first step of a wagon would have seemed an insurmountable height to one grown so horizontal from age. Shaw found his powers of reception still intact, so delivered a message for Andy, to which the aged one grunted and stumbled on up the steps of the outhouse.

Call number one brought no response. Nor did call number two. Meantime, the days were growing warmer, and the garbage was growing not only bigger, but also warmer. A neighbor, who had come down to the adjacent cottage for the day, said we might cart it over to his garden & deposit it therein, since it was to be plowed under shortly. That suggestion set us out, all the more determined, on call number three.

As we approached that final resting place of all junk known as Andy's Place, we were suddenly startled by a series of violent shrieks and squeals. Oh, good! Thought we. Andy must be home today, for who else would dare beat his wife? We drove gleefully into the yard, hoping to spare the wife and solve our problem at one fell swoop, but to our amazement, there, midst the wreckage was Mike O'Loughlin, our landlord, bending over and clutching a very animated burlap bag. The two gentlemen of previous acquaintance were also surveying the writhing object, which turned out to be a young pig, who was strenuously objecting to being thus enclosed. Hence the squeals — so Andy's wife was still intact. In fact, as usual, Andy wasn't there.

How, asked Shaw of Mike the landlord, was he ever going to get ahold of Andy? "Well," said Mike the landlord, "I'll tell you. I'm buying this pig from Andy for five dollars. I'll give you the money. Andy is bound to come & collect his five dollars, and when he comes to collect you can get him to take the garbage."

So, I now hold the five dollars. I also hold the garbage, but I don't expect to long. And I have a plan which will ensure five collections, at least. The five dollar bill has been changed into the same number of ones. I shall bait him. One dollar he shall get for five consecutive visits. After the fifth call, another scheme must be worked out – in the meantime, I shall pray that he will have formed the habit.

Shouts from the Shelter Box[22]

Letter of transmittal.

Dear Editor,

Please accept this brief attempt. I realize it is far too short to fill a whole page, but a steak picnic seems to have filled up all those places in me where inspiration might lurk.

Anyway, you probably need the rest of the page for trunk survey information. (Wonder where she got that idea? - ed.) I permit you to use it - since I seem to have exclusive control over it!

With the above came a poem – no less!

PITOMETER WIFE'S GREETING TO HER HUSBAND
AFTER A DAY OF MAN-HOLE MANIPULATION.

Blessings on thee, little man,
Grim boy, with dirty pan!
Thy Sears and Roebuck pantaloons,
I see, today have met their doom,
And thy work shirt is worse off still,
Before I've even paid the bill.
As bride I glowed with deepest joy,
Beholding such a handsome boy.
Thou art not now – thou'at but a bum.
So cold, so dirty, tired and numb.

Yet the top hat dandies preen,
There's more to thee than can be seen.
I love thy brain and brawn, stout feller,
BUT TAKE THOSE THINGS OFF IN THE CELLAR.

---

22 "Shouts from the Shelter Box", in the Downstream Orifice, was likely a publication of sorts that Joan controlled entirely by herself. She would put little notes at the top to the other writers or to the editors (both herself).

Shouts from the Shelter Box

Edited by the Forgotten Woman

You can give this poem a title to suit yourself.

Behind him lay the record sheet,
    Which pictured a deflection great;
Before him a long city street,
    Before him a two million rate.

The driver said, "I gotta clue!
    By gees, I hear a funny drone!
Hey, Pito man, what do I do?"
    "Why, boob, hand me the aquaphone."

"My gang grows scornful day by day;
    They think this is a wild goose chase."
The noise had faded soon; the ray
    Of hope soon left his frost bit face.

"What'll you do, Pito man, say,
    If you don't find this leak by dawn?"
"If I don't get this leak by day
    The water board will say 'so long'!"

They looked and listened along the curb,
    Until at last the poor man sobbed,
"Gee, Ed Case sure had his nerve
    To guarantee this lousy job."

"It would be on this noisy street
    I'd have to use an aquaphone.
These damn curb stops are sure a treat.
    Why won't kids leave these things alone!"

They yanked, they wrenched. Then spoke the gang,
    "Say, boss, it's cold here in the fog.
Let's let this service box go hang -
    How's for a hamburg and some grog?"

"We got a long time yet to hunt.
    At least let's get our bellies warm."
The boss gave a discouraged grunt,
    "Guess I'll listen on this one. You guys go on."

Then, pale and worn, he dug the dirt,
    And peered through darkness. Ah, the squeak
Of shovel hitting brass! And then a spurt -
    A leak! A leak! A leak! A leak!

It grew, a geyser bursted forth!
    The gang returned and stood agog;
Then shouted through lips rimmed with froth
    In awestruck voices: "God! What grog!"

Shouts from the Shelter Box

The Zero Hour

Between the dark and the daylight,
    When the sun is commencing to tower,
Comes a pause in my peaceful slumber,
    Which is known as Pitometer Hour.

I hear on the pavement beneath me,
    The clumping of big heavy feet,
The door of a truck slammed wide open,
    And voices raucous and deep.

From my bedroom I see in the dim light,
    Three hoodlums ascending the walk,
I'd be frightened to death if I hadn't heard
    My husband's voice midst the talk.

A few short minutes of silence,
    I close my poor, sleepy eyes,
When the elevator door crashes open,
    MORE noise - what considerate guys:

A sudden jab at the keyhole,
    A clattering shove and a boom,
Through a door which now must be splintered,
    They burst to the living room.

They race out into the kitchen,
    Stumbling o'er every chair,
I slide down under the covers,
    But I hear them from everywhere.

I imagine them stripping the chicken,
    Which I'd planned to warm up for tonight.
Oh, why won't you pick on the meat balls!
    Of them I am sick of the sight.

Do you think, you blustering bandit,
    Because you've just finished your work,
That it's tea for the rest of the outfit,
    And the sun and moon gone berserk?

In the future take tea in the lunch cart,
    Along with the rest of the bums,
For they don't care how you revel,
    As long as the business still comes.

Please leave the homes unmolested,
    For those who know night from the day,
Else some fine morn when you stomp in
    Your wife will have flitted away.

Letter to family from Dunkirk

May 1, 1935
Dunkirk, NY

Dearests -

This has been a very gay weekend, for the Hoopers have been with us. They arrived Sat. eve and departed Tuesday morning for the West coast by car. As I may have told you, Hoop (Wor. Lab.) was awarded the Freeman scholarship - Prov. Freeman - which enables him to go all over this country inspecting various plants and labs. It is Edith Hooper's first trip out of New England, so you can imagine how thrilled she is. Edith, by the way, is the eighth generation to be born in their farm near Millbury, and her tales of the old homestead are very interesting.

Shaw has stayed with them so often that we were very anxious to do well by them. Sunday dinner did do well by them, for we had cocktails and canapes, two tremendous porterhouse steaks, mushroom sauce, French fried potatoes, popovers, asparagus with hollandaise, endive salad, fresh strawberries with whipped cream and coffee. Isn't that something? The weather was horrible so we stuck close to the fire, but I guess they were glad of a little relaxation.

Now that Shaw is working nights I am back on my twelve hour sleeping periods. It is so quiet here, and since there is nothing pressing, I sleep on and on. I must have a marvelous constitution, for whether I sleep five or twelve hours I always seem fit. I usually write some letters after Shaw goes, then hop in bed with a good book - read for a while, fall asleep, wake up a couple of hours later to put out the light, and then I'm off again for a long stretch. I partially wake up when Shaw comes in but don't show much interest.

I've just read "Shining And Free" by G.B. Stern, which I think you'd like, mother. Also, I think Priestley's "The Good Companions" - a great and wonderful tome. If you should read it, mother, you will come to know Joe Silvia better, through the guise of a little Yorkshire character.

Our garbage problem and solution has been a scream. Since I am writing it up for the Downstream Orifice I won't relate it here, but we'll send you a copy.

The other evening Mr. Beckwith, a district manager, stopped here on one of his trips. Since Mike O' Laughlin, our landlord, is head of the water board in Fredonia, three miles away, he and Shaw paid him a call and received the dope on the situation in Fredonia. Thus, he got the chance to go to a council meeting that evening to present the various benefits of a Pit. survey. Shaw and I went along + received a liberal education in selling. The meeting took place in a lawyer's office in the city hall, which is also the movie theatre. One of the council said, "When you hear the singing in the church next door cease, let me know, cause that'll mean my wife is waiting for me and I'll have to go." This being a private meeting, there were only six present, + needless to say, I was the only female. After Beck had the floor, I felt that all of the cities who hadn't had <u>one</u> survey at least were going towards a rapid decay. Beck thinks the selling in this town would be a cinch but he's afraid the water Co. is too good + therefore there aren't many leaks.

Celie, your service sounds exquis. Isn't it exactly like Mrs. French's? What's the table cloth like? - + the wedding ring. And what was Mrs. Rathbun's luncheon like? Take some snapshots of you in your two coats + send me for my book. How was Cabrant?

Did you know Lib Thorndike had a baby girl Sunday? Her name is to be June, I think. It came just when they were expecting it.

Mother, dear, I hope you are getting used to the idea of having a good looking set of teeth.

Lots + lots of love to Poppa, Celie, Mamma, Jenny, Theresa, Mike and the flowering shrubs. Are they flowering? Spring has hardly begun here.

Joan

Early Married Years

Letter from Joan to her in-laws, Grandmary and Grandpa Cole, upon their return from travelling abroad

May 7, 1935

Dearests –

Welcome home! – and oh how sorry we are that it is impossible to be able to say that in person. Had we been near enough New York to make such a plan feasible, I for one, would have been standing on the dock (for hours probably!) with outstretched arms.

It is going to feel so good to know that you are both near at hand again. Not that we worried about you while you were gone – goodness knows you are seasoned travelers – but it's a cozy feeling to have you back just the same.

I take it for granted that you received our last letter sent to England, so will not redescribe our present abode. The forthcoming "Shouts from the Shelter Box" will suggest our locale and if you missed the letter I shall remember all of the highlights to tell you.

Letters from home indicate that Mother is weak and nervous. Whereas there was no direct plea for my presence I read between the lines and have decided to go home next Tuesday until after the wedding. This decision entailed quite a mental struggle on my part, but in the end I decided that I could indirectly help five people by going home. I <u>hate</u> leaving Shaw here by himself – my only consolation being, that since he only sees me three out of the twenty-four hours, he can't miss me too much.

I am hoping, Pappa Cole, that you will yearn for a nice long weekend of "coefficient" and "one percent error" palavers with Shaw, so I have an extra bed all made up for you, and a nice muffin recipe marked in Fanny Farmer. You may have a private porch overlooking Lake Erie in case you haven't seen enough water and Shaw can lull you to sleep by reciting your paper by heart.

We shall think of you this weekend and envy those present at the family reunion. I imagine Aunt Alice will be down by plane. Please don't get unwound before we see you, which I imagine will be at the wedding, or even sooner, if possible. I'm only too sorry my train home takes me through Albany instead of N.Y.C.

We hope to phone you Friday eve, if we can get the dope on your boat. Our address by the way is c/o Water Supt., Dunkirk, N.Y. + our mail is always sent there.

Loads and loads of love to our cosmopolitan family!

Joan + Shaw

Letter from Joan to family just before Celie's Wedding

Monday

Dearests all -

Over the weekend I had a definite presentiment - "205 needs shining up a bit"- something kept telling me. You were all on my mind so, that by today I felt absolutely certain that a certain elan and joie de vivre is lacking in the old homestead. Therefore, thot I, next week I should put on my clown costume, grab a dust mop, oil my efficiency cog and whisk myself homeward. First, I shall crack mother's nut open + dust out all of the worries. Next, I shall become the good housekeeping institute and relieve Celie of the domestic duties which she will soon be assuming for good. And lastly, I shall set up an office in the front hall which shall be a clearing house for all frowns, sighs, complaints + confidences. In fact, I shall be a Godsend.

Now in preparation for this taking the citadel by storm, I request one thing of you, mother, which is: never be without a pad and pencil, day + night. Write down <u>every</u> idea + worry that comes into your head. <u>Please</u>. Then, when you read them over next day you may erase the 75 percent which were unfounded, and save the 25 percent for my inspiration.

Next, Celie - make up your little attic bed, for I insist you sleep there. It's so cozy and way-offish – and I expect you to rest there every day for a few minutes. You aren't to answer the phone or go to the door, and maybe I won't even let you read your own mail. And while you are up there resting, you are to realize that this wedding is going to be <u>fun.</u> Shaw and I are spending a lot of good money in car fare + I'm going to make it worthwhile. Also, you're going to sit down and invite all the out of town friends of yours + Bud's that you want and can think of, and Shaw and I will see that they are entertained. Doubtless, Mrs. Cole will have Colecot open by then which will mean lots of room. Leave out some of the Harry Dele Barrers if you want, but don't leave out <u>any</u> of your pals because you're going to look some cute in that wedding dress and you'll only wear it this once.

And say, if it's not too late to change - how about having the wedding about 7 or 6 or 6:30 or sometime like that? Then after you and Bud left, Shaw + I and Mart + Doc + Genie could continue the reception after you left. I'll bet Vee or Mackie would give a breakfast for the leftovers next morning - or we could give it with the leftovers!

Dad, all you have to do is keep that swell grin of yours turned on, and start making the punch.

I shall arrive in Worcester sometime Tuesday - so gird up your loins one + all!

Best love
Wannie

Photographs from Celie's Wedding in June, 1935

Home is Where We Hang Our Hats

June, 1935

I have been married fifteen months, and we have moved fifteen times. Lest our monthly vacations arouse suspicion, let it be quickly known that my husband is not a piker - he is an engineer. Not the nice sane kind who drives a train and always gets back to his starting place, my husband is an engineer-in-the-field, and we have neither starting nor stopping place. Our length of stay in any one place seems to depend solely on the whim of our general manager, and he has many whims. Apparently, he sits in his office with a map in one hand and a Western Union blank in the other. With each glance at the map he dispatches a telegram, and recently, the following message is supposed to have been received: "Proceed at once to __ arriving not later than last Wednesday."

Consequently, we have been the poignant regret of many a rental agent and obviously we are never considered the most desirable tenants. Hence, our many abodes have seldom been the objects of our choice. Take, for instance, the garret in the gatehouse (of which more later), and the unheated cottage on Lake Erie during an icy March, or the two weeks sojourn in a creaky hotel room over the saloon. Oh, but I am amused when I listen to my sedentary friends discuss house hunting, "I wouldn't consider that house on Glen Row. Why, both living and dining rooms have northerly exposure! Exposure, ye Gods!" All I ask for is a window that opens without the aid of an icepick. And the various appraisals of closet space; why, if I ever had a closet large enough to hold even the few things we carry, I'd plug in a bridge lamp and label it "the study." Tea time debates concerning Chippendale versus Hepplewhite find me silent, for I could not discuss the merits of fake Renaissance three piece suits, upholstered in that prickly stuff, or describe one very orchid and pea-green bedroom we had which didn't make me appear as feminine as was its intent. Certainly made my husband appear hideous.

No, we can't be the least bit fussy as to details. All we ask for is an apartment on the right side of the tracks, furnished with house-keeping facilities, including a bed which doesn't have to be coaxed down off the wall - and no lease. It is always my "Of course you don't require a lease", uttered with false assurance, which raises havoc with our hopes. Heretofore the prospective landlord was the effusive salesman, but now he becomes the overbearing warlord, and we must cringe. Actually, a lease can be gotten around in many different methods, but we prefer to be honest about it, so, though we're clean living Christians and prepared to pay well, we must place ourselves in the hands of Fate when we are suddenly plunked down in an unfamiliar town; but let me tell you that this elusive gentleman doesn't welcome us at the city's gates as the Rotary Clubs do. There is a definite procedure by which we track him down, and the routine never varies, be it a town of five thousand or a city of half a million.

There are three avenues of approach. First, a tour of the residential section may reveal empty dwelling places; second, the classified ads hold possibilities; and third, a real estate dealer may solve our problem. So far, the first method has proved futile, but still it's worth a try, so I embark on my quest by driving up and down the residential streets vainly searching for a "For Rent - Furnished - No Lease" sign. There are many "For Rent", or "For Sale" signs, countless offers of "Room and Board", and loads of people needing fifty pounds of ice this morning, but since these prospects are out of the question, I procure the latest local paper and scan the real estate section. Of course, none of these offers state our requirements in black and white, but usually one or two sound possible. And may I inject a hint to future advertisers; never use the words "Cozy" or "Den" in your descriptions; or "Running water", or "Refined". "Cozy" may always be interpreted to mean "too small for comfort". "Den" always summons up visions of worn out Morris chairs, souvenir ashtrays, and pipe racks. "Running water" implies that there's not much else, and as for insisting that the tenants be refined, who would ever look at such an ad and say, "No, Sadie, we can't take that. We're not refined." Having read countless descriptions of "desirable" vacancies, I have attained a certain proficiency in spotting flaws, and thus a little close study usually saves me many a futile visit.

Should the latest edition be sold out, as sometimes happens when the paper is a bi-weekly, I seek out a real estate office. In small towns these are often combined with the fuel dealer, insurance agent, and "Giftee Shoppe" and in cities they are as thick as fleas. The agent beams on me until I mention the "no lease" requirement, whereupon he denounces me as utterly unreasonable. I'm perfectly willing to agree with him on that score, and after we've both admitted that I'm crazy, he takes me into every dwelling place on his list, glibly explaining to the landlady that though I can't sign a lease, the chances are that I'll be there forever. So far, I've double-crossed every agent by telling the truth, and my veracity has won over many a landlord. By evening of that first day I've said, "Yes, it does seem colder," to every custodian of every vacant dwelling in town. When I meet my husband for dinner, I drag endless notes out of my purse and we survey the situation. The evening is spent in revisiting the two or three, or sometimes only one possibility. During these calls we try desperately, but not always convincingly, to give the impression that the whole town is after us, and before we return to the hotel we usually have a home.

I say a "home", but very often it is part of someone else's home. I've shared kitchens with landladies, I've shared bathtubs with landladies, and I've shared laundry tubs with landladies; in fact, much of my knowledge of housekeeping has been gained through such associations. There was the very affable soul who taught me how to do my laundry. Such folksy Monday mornings we used to spend together; she never failed to apologize for her husband's taste in underwear, and she always saw to it that my monogrammed linen was hung facing the neighbors.

Among the many useful hints she gave me, I think the following impressed my inexperienced mind the most; "In summer I never iron my sheets," she said. "Really? Is it supposed to be cooler, or something?" I asked. "No," she answered, "But ironing them is supposed to take all the vitamins out."

Then there was the gatehouse where I shared the kitchen not only with the landlady, but also a collie dog, a Scotty, and a cat. I was given elaborate directions as to which doors were to remain closed to which pets, and when no one was home, I could scarcely restrain myself from thrusting open the five doors from the kitchen and pantry, standing up on the stove and yelling "Scram!" Since the rest of our living quarters were on the third floor, we were comparatively free from animal life up there. Our landlady (she'd faint at being called that!) was a poor relation of the folks who lived in the "big house", and not a day went by but what I was reminded of that somewhat distant connection. I was oh, so far beneath her as was evidenced by my taste in daily reading matter. "Why in the world do you subscribe to the New York Herald Tribune?" she asked, "Of course you know it's a notoriously poor paper!" It was fun to knock the wind out of her sails by being able to greet her every third day with the happy news that our bed had broken down during the night. In fact, it was worth the discomfort of sleeping at an eighty degree angle just to see the annoyed look on her face. My most gleeful moment occurred one evening when she entered the kitchen just after the stove had blown up. My husband and I were eating in the butler's pantry at the time, but even so, we were accused. Being totally ignorant of what causes stoves to explode, I couldn't deny that I might have been the remote cause, so, crossing my fingers, I agreed to pay for half the cost of repairs. Next day, I accosted the repair man, and asked him in rather loud tones how such an explosion could have occurred. "It occurred, Madame, because the stove was in such lousy condition. If you'd of been hit by that oven door, you could 'of sued 'em." It has been one of my deepest regrets that I wasn't hurt – just a little. Our living room was supposed to be quaint, but it was only quaint in spots, for though someone had attempted to scrape off the dirty flowered wallpaper, thus revealing the old pine wood, the point at which this venture proved bore-some was easily definable. Consequently, portions of the room lent a studio effect, while the rest was nothing but a dirty attic bedroom, and as I sat looking out of the window at the flock of sheep nibbling the spacious lawn which swept up to the terrace of the big house, I often thought the thoughts of Sarah Crewe.

Then there was the three days venture we called "Love Among the Ruins," for the house which we occupied was crowded with facsimiles and photographed remains of all the glories that were Greece. I look back in my diary and quote from my first entry written in that cultural surrounding; "As I sit at this desk, the headless Victory of Samothrace in plaster is about to take off from the edge of the bookcase facing me; two of the Three Fates are lounging against the wall; the Boy With the Thorn is bent over his work nearby, and to my left, a Grecian weaver in bronze is having difficulty threading her shuttle. Everywhere are framed ruins of the Forum, Erectheum, and Parthenon, and they create such a crumbly atmosphere that as I pass beneath them, I instinctively duck for fear a stone will fall on my head. I feel quite out of place without a toga, for I imagine these ancients looking down on my Hoover apron with scorn. The general effect is indescribable. Maybe the Greeks had a word for it – I haven't!"

The two weeks hibernation in a tiny Pennsylvania town was an interesting experiment in solitary confinement. A very chilly room in a two-story wooden hotel answered for home. The landlord made Pancho Villa seem gentle and sweet, and I was to find he ran the most popular saloon in town. There, my chief thrill of the day was a lingered-over breakfast in the town's only restaurant, whose menu offered many combinations of the same edibles under different names, each of which included "lionized potatoes." One morning on my way to breakfast, I was accosted by a very unhygienic looking man, and I confess I was a little perturbed until I heard his request. "Lady," he said, "It's not money I'm after. All I ask is that you take me across the street to that drugstore and buy me a cake of Life Buoy soap." Ignoring him, I hurried on but as I passed him there wasn't a shred of doubt in my mind as to his need. Back in my room I would lock, bar, and bolt the door and read the day through. A bottle of ripe olives provided both my noon repast and my exercise, for every three pages I would allow myself one juicy mouthful, after which I hurled the pit with a resounding plunk into the tin wastebasket across the room. "Far from the Madding Crowd" proved the most appropriate in title and length of the books I brought with me, and since the floor was hardly soundproof, Thomas Hardy's contribution to my culture was amply supplemented by various conversations arising from the saloon below.

My husband having been interviewed by a gentleman of the local press, I eagerly awaited the edition of the bi-weekly newspaper. Hastening to the newsstand the morning it was issued, I purchased a copy and quickly scanned the headlines. Sure enough, there was his name in large print, "Research Specialist Tests Water Main." Feeling somewhat self-conscious at this sudden prominence I casually glanced at the other front page articles and beheld in equally large print, right alongside my husband's bracket the following; "Increase in Egg Hatching; Calvin Nortin Says Busy Season Coming." My pride suffered a decided drop, but further perusal of the paper opened up a whole new field of recreation to me, for the society columns provided delightful entertainment that I culled the choicest items and filled a clipping book. Here are a few of the ones I've preserved; "Mrs. Emma Snoke and stepdaughter called Wednesday on Mrs. Roy Aument to see her large lily." – "Milton Powell and Amy Nye spent a couple of hours in the home of Mrs. J.R. Morgan." – "Elmer Shoop purchased a new car last week."

I must cease with this description of our various homes, for I am anxious to assure you how carefree is our existence. Though we have our hectic moments, the role of housekeeper is a simple one. It goes without saying that we do not transport furniture, but those of you who have ever rented furnished apartments know that the equipment is meagre at best. Experience has taught us what we must expect to provide, and I look back on preparations for our initial adventure with a great deal of amusement. On that first packing day I remember standing in the middle of the room surveying our generous wedding loot. Seeing my eye light on articles both cumbersome and breakable, my husband shot me a meaningful glance which warned me to be practical rather than artistic in my selection. Alright then, the toaster we must take, of course. That sounded practical and unbreakable. Next we selected the Mixmaster, for though I had never beaten an egg, the folder convinced me that eggs just shouldn't be beaten any other way. I meekly suggested including the French Onion soup bowls but my husband averred that his mother had kept house for thirty years without them and so he guessed I could. My flat silver was taken for granted and I was allowed room for a silver platter, vegetable dish, and a gravy boat. After dinner coffee cups sounded essential at the time, so of course, an appropriate tray accompanied them. A small set of Adams china was selected for its adaptability to any environment, and lastly, we decided on taking a card table, a collapsible drink table and a pair of framed flower prints. These things, plus linen and our clothing, comprised our impediments. At the date of writing almost everything has been junked or sent home to the attic. I have found it possible to prepare a meal without the aid of a Mixmaster and the glass bowls have a tendency to sever. The Adams china set grew smaller each move and the only imported china I have had since bears the label "Made in Japan". My silver has stayed with us, but the after dinner coffee spoons are only excess baggage for the cups proved all too fragile for their mission in life. I gave up hoping for a fitting background for my flower prints, and the card table stayed with us until we realized that Culbertson could be just as effective over the dining room table. And the worst of it is that no matter how much we discard, each time we pack there is always more than the last time. There was the lovely copper chafing dish (most impossible to collapse) which I couldn't resist bidding on at an auction, as well as a Bokar rug. Also the radio which we thought we ought to purchase since we were able to get it wholesale, and a Seltzer bottle which we couldn't help winning in a mixed foursome. It is perhaps significant that aside from my husband's engineering books, the dictionary, the Bible and the Book of Facts, the only other book I carry with me is entitled "The A B C of Collecting".

You may imagine that our method of packing would horrify the "tissue paper between each fold" school. When the upheaving telegram arrives, we immediately explode into action. Scooping up everything in sight we fairly dump things into the ever-ready trunks, I hurriedly fitting things into their accustomed niches. My two stewpans make lovely nests for socks and stiff collars, and the Worcestershire sauce goes alongside of the cleansing cream. The full dress suit has been buttoned over my silver tray much oftener than around my husband's middle. The soiled laundry is always a problem and I've never understood why dirty clothes are so much bulkier than clean ones. Since I can't bear to leave good staple groceries behind, I must resemble an alchemist as I pour things from one container to another in an attempt to reduce their bulk. There is an unwritten law that nothing goes into the trunk of the car, consequently the remainder of our energy is spent in stuffing everything into our luggage compartment. There is always one carton too many, of course, and every time we're faced with this problem we swear we'll buy a trailer.

Yet, in spite of these hectic moments, my role as housekeeper is a simple one, for I'm gadget free. You ladies look around sometime and notice the countless special duty tools and utensils you have to take care of. Take the kitchen, for example. A New York store recently advertised a complete set of kitchen tools for $65.00. My equipment is about one tenth as inclusive, costs one tenth as much, therefore there is one tenth as much to keep clean and orderly. I have everything from butter curlers to razor blade holders at home in the attic, but since necessity has forced me, I have learned to manage minus the frills. For instance, my biscuit dough is rolled thin with the aid of a milk bottle, and I cut canape rounds with the open end of an orange juice glass. Nuts are chopped by rolling them up in a dish towel and batting them with a quart bottle of ginger ale. I've made casseroles in cake tins and I've roasted a chicken on a cookie sheet. Many's the time I've washed clothes in the bathtub and ironed them on the back of a bureau drawer. Once I planned a meal too ambitious for my equipment, and found it necessary to cook the eggs in a coffee tin. The water seemed to boil just as furiously as in a Lewis and Conger stream lined stew pan – and I could throw the can away. The cardboards from my husband's newly laundered shirts can be bent into an excellent dustpan, and they go along to the rubbish with the floor sweepings. In case you're thinking we're slovenly tightwads, let me remind you that everything we acquire must be packed and unpacked on the average of at least once a month, and it would seem foolishly extravagant to leave so much good equipment behind. And besides, it is the very lack of these various gadgets which makes housekeeping so simple.

How do I like this nomadic life? I love it! – and these are the reasons why: my husband and I enjoy complete intellectual independence; through enforced isolation we have gained a true sense of companionship; and lastly, we've discovered that happiness does not depend upon the extent of one's possessions.

We glory in our independence. Now that sounds self-centered and smug I know, but don't misunderstand me. I was born and brought up in a small town and thus fully realize the benefits of being part of a community. Working with and being a part of a group has many satisfactions, and not being able to ally ourselves with any civic activity is one of the drawbacks that comes with this sort of existence. So it's not that sort of isolation we delight in; rather it's the mental independence.

Ever-changing environment brings us in contact with widely diversified personalities and their viewpoints are a constant stimulus. We have such an opportunity for gathering in the outlooks of different groups, sorting them out and formulating our own opinions that we are bound to become increasingly tolerant. And then there is the social independence which we thoroughly enjoy, for we are free from the pettiness which seems so prevalent in a small social clique. So many of my friends seem to me to degrade themselves in order to appear loftier socially, and the lofty ones seem so ruthlessly unkind in their attempt to remain lofty. There is so much superficial criticism and snobbery among "polite society" that I honestly am glad that we can never become identified with any one group. One's activities and behavior so easily become patterned by crowd feeling that we find it a pleasure to be at liberty to choose our own friends and our own form of recreation.

My husband and I have grown to be completely self-sufficient, and I doubt if we would be had we settled down in a town immediately after our marriage. He would have formed his associations, I mine and naturally most of our evening and weekend recreation would have included others. But we have more or less been forced to enjoy each other's company exclusively, and as a result we have become perfect companions. That, I find, is a relationship somewhat rare among couples yet I'm convinced that if young husbands and wives spent more of their leisure alone together they would be more contented at present and much less bereft in the future when their children marry and leave them to their own resources again. I don't envy my friends their constant social whirl, for I think it is much healthier to be able to look forward to going out of an evening than to yearn for a chance to stay in. You couples who have been married one or two years, try doing nothing together for two or three weeks. You'll be surprised how much closer you'll feel toward each other, and incidentally how much money you will have saved. In all probability we would not have been thrown on our own resources had we commenced married life in our own home town, so this is decidedly a benefit accruing from this mode of living.

And, oh, we can be so carefree! At first, when people came to call I could hardly restrain myself from saying, "I have loads of beautiful things at home." For a bride our lodgings looked pretty crude and barren and I did yearn for the things packed away in the attic, but gradually I began to realize how deliciously irresponsible I could afford to be. No cream colored carpets to despair over, no eggshell china to weep over when smashed, no expensive draperies waving on the rain-soaked sill. In fact nothing that couldn't be replaced at a small expense. I don't doubt that the pleasure gained from living in choice surroundings is worth the care and worry, for I'm sure it is, but I'm gladder than glad to have found that such possessions are not indispensable to a happy home, for we are sublimely happy and we've had some pretty queer homes. And so I won't be bitterly disappointed if we never possess the ideal house most young couples look forward to building someday, and I shall never envy the people who live in those sumptuous houses. All I always wanted to be sure of having is a home, and I'm sure that will never be denied us, for home is where we hang our hats.

Letter to family

Monday Night, during Total eclipse of moon.

Dearests,

I am perforce writing with pencil, for the only lamp downstairs doesn't happen to be anywhere near the desk.

Shaw has just left for night work + I must say I'm not sorry for him for it is perfectly beautiful out, lovely and cool, + a beautiful full moon which is now almost completely eclipsed and giving off a beautiful orange hue.

This weekend was like something I've had to go to the movies to know about heretofore. It was so exquis and here it is - move by move. Sat. afternoon Shaw played golf so Prule and I drove over to lake Minnetonka. This lake is outside of Minneapolis and oh so <u>Newporty</u>. The shore is lined with great estates, mostly Minn. people, all of which are beautiful. We went to a flower show over there, which to my mind was an example to all garden clubs. They had some very interesting classes and oh <u>such</u> tables. Each table featured something different; for instance, glass, wood, silver, china, pottery, copper etc. The linens, flower vases + plates were all choice. Another interesting class was one in which flowers were chosen and arranged to express moods such as; grandeur, simplicity, harmony, discord, grief, contentment, gaiety. The contentment arrangement consisted of a pair of white pottery swans on a large mirror. The backs were hollow and from them spread beautiful white stock, which formed the swan tails. Simply lovely. There were loads more fascinating classes but I must get on with the weekend.

From there we drove to one of the lakeside clubs with some friends. We went through the club, sauntered out on the swimming pool terrace + phoned back to the club for some iced coffee which we enjoyed sitting on the pool edge. From there we called on an Aunt of Polis + met some of the most charming people. Her house was a gem - right on the lake. We sat on the terrace and sipped iced tea and watched a yacht race while a house boy arranged pillows on the sand in case we wanted to relax on the shore!

I "ohed" and "ahed" to Prule all the way home, then changed into a dinner dress and drove out to White Bear Lake. This Lake is the St. Paul resort + they claim it is very informal and not swell like Minnetonka, but it's alright with me. K. + B. Fobes (landlord) had about twelve people over to meet us before dinner then we all went to the yacht and golf club for Dutch treat dinner dance which was much fun. During the dance, one of the boys came up to me and said "would you like to go for a little ride?" - I was about to say "say what's the idea?" - when Shaw whispered in my ear "speed boat". I fairly shouted <u>sure</u>. We walked out on the dock + Shaw + I climbed into the backseat and enjoyed the most wonderful spin in the moonlight. Joan Crawford would have been jealous at the sight of me.

We stayed with Bob + Kay overnight and Shaw and he played golf next morning, + we called on people. That afternoon we played golf in a mixed two ball foursome and <u>won</u>. I got a $7.00 bag which I changed for a bathing suit today, and Shaw a thing that makes soda water. My golf was pretty good for the first attempt since Beaver Falls. In fact, a college friend of mine is head of the team + is urging me to join so I can play on the team. That means playing all of the neighboring courses free so I think I shall. We came home + hopped into bed at 9:00 PM, tired but happy.

Today was George Dean's birthday so we gave him a picnic tonight. Twelve of us and lots of fun.

The people here are so <u>natural</u> + friendly. Many of them have oodles of money, but though they have lovely homes they don't put on the dog a bit. It's the kind of place where if you say you can't afford such + such they think more of you for admitting it. In fact, I guess you gather by now that we love it.

I have one request. When Jennie goes home next could she go over to the house + collect all my evening clothes. I finally gave up carrying them around and oh how I need them now. Jennie - they are in 2 bags in the arcade closet - there is my brown and yellow one, a green one, a black one, + a blue and red chiffon. There are a couple of pairs of evening shoes in a black patent leather hatbox side of the big bed in the front attic room. My silver service is in the bottom. Honestly, I hate to ask you but I really need them terribly.

I'm taking in the most wonderful free lecture course on the appreciation of literature at the university. The last two lectures have been on Shakespeare. She has recited pages and pages from the different plays and her ability is so remarkable she seemed to see each character and setting, and completely forgot that she was just one person speaking from a lecture platform.

Mary I <u>hope</u> you are beyond the acute suffering stage. Is it consoling to feel you never have to have them filled?

Mother, Shaw + I dote on the Sunday section. Send them always will you, or tell Celie to forward them. I got such a long letter from you, also one by way of Celie, that I felt over sure you must be better.

Mrs. Cole, my tapestry stuff is being sent so forward it pronto and I'll get it started and return it to you.

Well. Goodie night all. Even though I'm being swell I still love you folks back on the farm.

Papa Getchell and Papa Cole, we loved your letters. You both fulfill your paternal duties more than adequately!

Much Love,
Joan

Letter to family after a golf tournament

July, 1935
Wednesday

Dearest,

Such a flood of letters arrived this morning! I get so confused when I open a letter from Wenatchee + see Mother's handwriting and then a Sakonnet postman brings one from Celie. You are all doing much too well by me - don't strain yourselves cause even if I don't hear from you I know you love us. Genie has been particularly communicative. I shall write you a private letter soon, Genie.

Well, we have had one busy week. The high spot was the St. Paul open tournament which took place Thursday + drew all the big guys like Hagen, Sammy Parks, Richard Arlen etc. It is the custom here for the Jr. League to supply girls who score for each threesome so I was enlisted for Thursday + Friday. Of course we were all dying to draw the big bag + though I didn't get Hague I did get two wonderful threesomes. First day I drew one of the visiting Japanese, a charming man + beautiful golfer, + the second day I drew a threesome of very timed players all of whom shot par and under. One, Jim Newnan, a ranking player from Chicago, got seven birdies + an eagle! It was lots of fun for we walked right along with the players + chatted about each shot they took. There was a gallery, we were always inside the ropes + felt very important. At each open green a boy scout would come up to us, take the individual scores + phone them back to the club house. It was terrifyingly hot + quite hard work + as a result, most of us got burned to a crisp. One of my pals, who has recently moved here, drew Walter Hague + Richard Arlen. Arlen is a St. Paul lad + very popular so they paired him with Hague. Naturally, the gallery was tremendous, and Mary Jean had a whirl scoring for them. They were awfully nice to her but the gallery was disgusting. One woman came up to Arlen on the

3rd hole and said, "I'd like your ball for a souvenir and would you give it to me now cause I can't follow you for 18 holes?"!! And another one wanted the sweaty towel on which Arlen had wiped his face between shots!

I called Shaw from the Club Sat. noon to see if he was awake + wanted to come out. He greeted me with the words, "The Hoopers are coming tonight, stopping in on their way home." Gosh I had a fit because we didn't have an extra bed even and the house was filthy! I had been so busy at the tournament that I hadn't done a thing. Well, I raced home + lo!!! Shaw had procured a bed from our landlord. They had put it on top of the car, moved it here + set it up. Also my hero had <u>washed</u> the kitchen floor, both the bathroom floors, carpet swept, dust mopped and <u>dusted</u>!! If he isn't an angel. I nearly died of joy + surprise, because I was so hot and tired after golf that I dreaded cleaning the house. Well, they arrived at eight that evening + left yesterday morning. We had a very nice visit with them. Their trip has been most successful + even Edith has never been out of Mass. hardly, her reactions were interesting. She says she's just begun to realize how beautiful Mass. is.

This weekend we are going "up North" with Hank, Ed, another couple and Prule.

I'm still a little uncertain about our destination, but it's "up the Brule." Brule seems to be a beautiful river in Wisconsin and very wild. Many people go there for the summer from here. Women's state golf tournament is in Duluth this week. It ends Sat. + is followed by a big annual junior league ball, so we leave Sat., see the finals of the golf, then go to the ball, and afterwards drive on to the Brule where we will stay at Prule's grandmother's. Sunday we hire a guide + go up the river, returning home that night. I shall write you a complete account afterwards, for that is all I know so far. Thank heaven for White Bear Lake! The golf/yacht club is there + each day I drive out for a nice cool swim. It's so heavenly to be able to jump in the water + cool off. And speaking of golf - last Sunday morning Shaw played <u>wonderfully</u> in a tournament + got an 83 with an eight, and walked off with the prize. I wrote Mary Cook + asked her to visit me + she answered that she was dying to but was rehearsing for a ballet just now and couldn't till later. Also wanted all the dope on Romey Hill, is still crazy about him. He's in Paris + everyone here thinks he's nuts + it's too bad she's crazy about him because people say he'll never get hitched.

Mrs. Cole, what a <u>houseful</u> you had! I have the tapestry + as soon as the temp. goes down sufficiently so I can look at wool, I'll get to work.

Mother darling, I read between the lines of every letter hoping something will indicate that you are better. You <u>must</u> be better than when I left else you couldn't write such nice long letters. How I'm <u>hoping</u> for you.

So glad Dad has mailed my dresses for I'll need one this weekend.

Dearest love to all,
Joan

Mart's beach party sounded fun.
Mary's wisdom teeth <u>didn't</u>.

Trip on the Brule River

August, 1935
Wednesday

Dearest all,

Each morning, when I read the paper, I turn to the US weather chart and look at the Rhode Island and Seattle spots. According to the symbols, both places have been enjoying good weather over the weekend. I hope now that August is here, you will have nothing but sparkly Sakonnet days.

Now that I've been polite and commented on the weather may I start in and rave about our deluxe-exquis-superb weekend? Oh it was so much fun, + so different from anything Shaw and I have ever done.

Hank, Ed, Shaw and I left for Duluth Sat. at 10 o'clock, Shaw having had but a couple of hours of sleep. It was simply stifling in St. Paul and the prospect of the <u>cool</u> north sounded unbelievable. We drove 140 miles in what seemed about a minute (the roads are so wonderful), stopping en route for lunch and a wade. Shaw got some sleep on the way, + when we arrived in Duluth we went directly to the hotel where we had hired a room in which to dress. There we met the rest of our party + all had dinner together - about fifteen of us, + from there we went to the dance. Duluth, being on the lake, is always much cooler than St. Paul, but even so it was a touch hot for much lively stepping. It was a Jr. League dance + had a very cute floor show. Also a raffle + most of the boys in our party spent mints trying to win powerful flashlights with which to shine deer on the Brule. Shaw + I had brought ours with us. After the dance we all collected and started out for a forty mile drive to the river. Oh, I forgot to say that we saw Judy, Mary, and she almost <u>fainted</u> when she saw us. We had a nice chat with her and met her brother.

Now for a little geography lesson before I proceed. The Brule River is a fairly narrow, shallow river, which is very important, historically since it was the main water route connecting the Great Lakes with the Mississippi. Many Indians and missionaries from Canada traveled across Superior, up the Brule into the St. Croix River, which joins the Miss. and thence the South. It is beautiful wild country, therefore, excellent fishing and hunting. The government has stocked the Brule with countless trout so that they are as common as chaugies in Sak. Harbor. The shores are lined with magnificent virgin Norway yellow and white pine and countless century old cedars. I have never seen such stately trees, nor have I ever realized they grew to such heights. What grandeur they lend to the face of this Earth.

The "camps" on the Brule are all tremendous logged houses, + though they all fit beautifully into their setting, they lack none of the modern conveniences. Prule's, where we were, was built by her grandparents', as are most others. Those were the early days for this part of the country, + there were many Indians about when they first came there. Her house is right on the riverbank and I shall never forget how beautiful the world looked next morning when I stepped out into that cool woodsy smelling air + glimpsed the river winding among the pines. We all fairly lept to the bank for an early morning dip. It is the custom there to build logged bath houses out over the side of the bank with a hole in the floor, so that one may bathe as undressed as the trout who fairly tickle your sit down as you dip. The current is quite strong and the river spring fed, so it is icy cold and oh so stimulating. After repeated dips and sunnings we six went over to the next camp to join the other half of our group, guests of another girl and there we sat down to "brunch". There were about fifteen of us at one long horrible golden oak dining room table. This other camp was a <u>scream</u>. It was a gigantic house built by some more grandparents and it contained all of the cast off furniture of two generations - countless iron beds (four to a room), old hat trees, morris chairs and in the dining room was a combination gun closet-desk-bookcase just exactly like the one which used to live in our nursery, Mother! There also were countless old hats there, from fur to straw, and it was a rule of this camp that everyone had to wear a horrible hat all weekend. We all wore shorts and bathing suits and the combinations were ridiculous!

After breakfast we strolled over to see the Pierce estate nearby. A very eccentric man + his wife used to live there, but now it is unoccupied. It consists of a mere <u>4,000</u> acres of virgin wood, through which the Brule runs; various camps including one deluxe one equipped with an organ! Do you remember when Coolidge took a vacation in Wisconsin one summer? It was here, + what a tough time he must have had. Also, the supposedly largest trout hatchery in the world is on the estate + we had such an interesting time inspecting it. They had about 15 <u>albino</u> trout which were very weird looking.

After lolling about until four o'clock we got ready for our picnic trip "up river" by putting on all of the woolen clothing available. We met our guides and got settled in our canoes - two to each one. They were fitted out with low chairs and pillows and I'd give anything to have a picture of Shaw and me lolling in our canoe with our chauffeur guide polling in the stern. The day was calm + still save for the "laughing of the water" and we were beside ourselves with happiness as we were pushed along against the current with trout leaping around us and the little cedar wax birds chirping over each bug they had caught. Twice the river widened into quite large ponds + there's times we went through small sized rapids and finally after six miles, arrived at our picnic spot. Gradually the others came along and we all landed and lolled some more while the guide prepared our meal. A minor disappointment lay in the fact that the countless brook trout which had been brought along were packed in an air tight box and therefore had become a bit spoiled. I was sorry, both because Shaw has never had one, and because I wanted to watch the guides cook them. However, we had plenty to eat - cold chicken, fried potatoes, beans, eggs, bacon, coffee, bread etc. Just about dusk we left to go home down the river all equipped with flash lights, with which to shine the deer. The reflection of the shoreline and sky on the water was beautiful. We were the first canoe so we hoped to see many deer, but one of the guides in back of us had a good voice and <u>thought</u> he had a wonderful one, so he sang to us all the way down + consequently scared the deer off for miles around. The stars came out bright and clear and many of them shot through the sky and were reflected in the water. It was now very cold and we were all bundled up. What a thrill to wear woolen clothes when those back in Saint Paul were sweltering. One of the boys, apparently moved by the beauty of the scenery, turned around to kiss his wife, threw a canoe off balance, and had to jump overboard in order to save the canoe. Needless to say - he was frozen when we reached home. In fact, all of us enjoyed a roaring fire of birch logs, around which we all sat + listened to endless songs from the talented guide. Finally, we were all asleep on our feet so one of the boys tipped the guide, thinking he would take the hint - but he was overjoyed and said for such a generous tip, he'd be willing to sing all night. Eventually, two of the boys said in a loud tone that they would drive him home so he took the hint and departed.

Those of the party who had to be at work Monday morning arose at 5 am but luckily, Shaw was on nights so Ed, Hank, Shaw and I didn't leave until after a dip and breakfast. We drove down the Wisconsin side through beautiful country and spent the whole day enroute. Each mile South brought more heat, so every time we saw a lake, we hopped out behind the bushes, donned our suits, and went for a swim. We purchased some food in one of the countless lumber camp towns through which we passed, drove on to the next lake and picnicked. When we finally reached home, at about 5:30, it was so hot we stopped at the yacht club for another dip.

Thus ended a glorious, wonderful weekend. Shaw and I were so crazy about the country that, if we are "laid off" out here we hope to scrape our pennies together and take a short camping trip.

But I guess we won't be laid off, for it looks as if we move to

Minneapolis soon. They're almost sure of a trunk main survey there with the possibility of more work here later. I'll be sort of sorry to have to leave this house, but we will be so near Saint Paul that it won't make much difference. I shall try to sublet a house for August and then move when the owners return, because an apartment in this weather doesn't appeal.

Shaw received an invitation from Don Cruickshank to be his best man! He's marrying a Montreal girl - a skater we think - and she's having a large wedding there in October. Of course we'd love to go, but as usual it all depends where we are.

Mrs. Cole, <u>thank you</u> so much for my cute purse. You know how I love that woven material and you are also right about the color. Your package was a <u>very</u> pleasant "s'prise".

Dad, you sent the right clothes. How did you do it! Many thanks. There was a black evening dress among the others but I won't need that in a hurry, so don't send it until you have something else. I'm so glad you sent Shaw's suit, for he was going to have to buy one.

Mrs. Cole, I expect to finish "your" tapestry today + we'll send it post haste. I'm sorry I've been so slow but I had to pick the cool moments in which to do it.

Shaw won <u>18</u> golf balls in that tournament. I don't think we'll be very popular around here long!

Hank Dean had a very classy buffet supper last night + we were surprised to see a C.+G.[23] friend of Shaw's from Minneapolis. Honestly, I pity the Pito engineers who haven't had college educations. Even if I've forgotten every fact I thought I learned in college, I certainly am grateful for my four years of making friends there.

Would you send this to Celie? Celie, would you store this in your trunk drawer, because it should eventually go in "my book of happy memories". When the mail arrives I get <u>so</u> mixed up because letters postmarked Wenatchee contain letters from mother - and those sent

---

23   Joan is referring to *Casque & Gauntlet*, a society Shaw was a part of at Dartmouth College.

from Sakonnet contain Celie's!

Here is the most exquis potato dish. Take day old baked potatoes and cut them up without skins. Put in frying pan + add a jar of cream (it's cheap here!), lots of butter, salt and pepper and let them cook for a while. They thicken up and make the most <u>deluxe</u> creamed potatoes you ever tasted.

Mother, Mary B. Graham left me a note. A friend of Mrs. Parker's - would you tell her I haven't gotten in touch with her yet but hope to soon. I'm writing Mrs. Hopwood, Mrs. Cole.

Thank you Papa Cole and Papa Getchell for your nice long letters. Mart, send me a picture (recent) of baby Gene. Mama, your nice long letter arrived and I was so glad to hear from you. Did you know Helen Flemming was in Paris? I haven't the details from Prule yet.

Well I've practically disabled this right arm for life. When it regains strength I'll write again.

Lots + lots of love from us happy clams.

Mary I never mentioned the <u>tome</u> you wrote us. Have a few more teeth out if it will inspire another such.

Letter to family

Monday morn

Dearest all,

Another very gay weekend has ended and wash day is here. Did I tell you I have a screaming Swedish wash lady at 25 cents an hour? She's actually poor so I raised her to 30 cents, but don't consider that overly generous. I fuss around in the kitchen on purpose while she's doing the ironing because her Swedish accent is greater than anything you could hear on the stage. We became very "inty" last Wednesday and I got all her family history. She was one of 8 children back in Sweden, and, at the age of 16, four of them came to America to seek their fortunes. Shortly after she arrived here she met and wed a Mr. Olsen, who came over shortly before her and who lived 5 miles from her back home! When I told her I came from the East she asked, "Chicago?" I smiled to myself, for it wasn't so long ago that I considered Chicago the far west! She was overjoyed to find I came from near Boston, for that is where she landed. She spied Shaw's dinner pail one day, and after that I felt we had a great common bond, for she puts up one for her husband, too. Upon hearing that he worked on the night shift, she asked if he was an "Inginneer"- which I interpreted to mean engine ear. I found shortly that our conceptions of that profession differed, for she remarked she thought it must be wonderful to drive a train! I told her Shaw worked nights every other two weeks and she responded that that was just like the firemen do. So you see blue Mondays are hardly blue with her to entertain me.

We went out to White Bear Sat. aft and Shaw played golf while I swam and did some calling. We dressed at the Fobs (landlords) who had a cocktail party for 28. Dutch treat dinner dance at the club followed which was loads of fun. We hadn't planned to stay all night, but Anne and Colonel (Nickname) Griggs asked us to, so we accepted

Early Married Years

with great pleasure. They live in a darling little farmhouse on her aunt's estate, which includes a private pond. Next noon, we had for Sunday dinner - chicken, beans, corn, milk and cream - all picked from their garden and farm yard about ten minutes beforehand. The cream and milk weren't exactly "picked" - I guess they were "pushed"! This Aunt is fabulously wealthy, and must be Anne's fairy godmother, for when she became engaged, this Aunt gave her all her linen, which, among other things, included 36 monogrammed linen sheets and cases, four damask tablecloths, four dozen bath towels, special linen towels, for which she sent to Belgium, a dozen blanket covers, etc. etc. etc. - all monogrammed! Kind of fancy! Her two daughters had just left for Scotland the night before for a month of grouse shooting. Sometime remind me to tell you how one grouse shoots in Scotland. It's quite fascinating and accounts of it left me popeyed.

Shaw played golf in the morning, and we had a 2 ball foursome date in the afternoon which became a three ball sixsome. Then we went to supper at the O'Briens (our golf date) an awfully attractive couple, who were married five years and remained childless. They were about to adopt one when she had a little girl, and since then, in 3 ½ years - they have had four children, including a set of twins! That is a warning to Tom and Jane! There were 8 others at supper, none of whom we had met before so we added them to our countless list of new friends. We found another old pal of Shaw's at Hank's supper party last week - a C+G. at Dartmouth.

Everyone around here hunts in the fall. Colonel Griggs, with whom we stayed Sat. night, told us that just after he graduated he bumped into the father of one of his school pals. This man was president of some big New York bank, and before he left town, he offered this boy a job. Col. replied that he was very flattered, but couldn't possibly accept because there was no good hunting around New York City. The New York banker nearly fainted!

Shaw and Ro are packing the instruments this morning, for this job has ended. They have heard unofficially that the Minneapolis contract has gone through. We have had no instructions from the office, but, knowing what Monday mornings are like at 5o Church Street, we expect 3 or 4 wires before noon. If we are sent to Minneapolis, Ro assures us that we won't have to move over right away, so we shall stay in this nice, cool, house until the Fobes come back from the lake and then hunt for something over there.

This week promises to be very busy. Tomorrow I'm having some girls for lunch and we're going out for dinner with Mr. Parker's friend, who was very nice. Wednesday, we're going to the lake for dinner, and Thursday, to someone else's at the Lake. I wrote Mrs. Hopwood and she called this morning to make a date, but we had to put it off until the weekend for we couldn't get together. She sounded very cordial.

This afternoon I'm going to call on Prule's grandmother to thank her for our Brule Trip, and I shall be very interested to hear about the early days up on the river. It is such beautiful country.

Mother, your nice letter came this morning, and I'm so glad you've met Mr. Case and Aunt Mary and Uncle Arthur. The phone just rang - so I took pencil and paper being sure it was Western Union, but it was only my hero saying we were only going to Roe's for dinner tonight and that we had no news as yet. He was tickled pink that you had met the phantom Mr. Case.

I shall now deliver a eulogy on the Coolerator refrigerator! I am a good one to praise it for I've used eleven different ones since I was married - all kinds - and this tops them all. It is the ice box type, but all white and shiny, wonderfully insulated, and holds good old fashioned Yankee ice, which never seems to melt. My particular one costs about 50 dollars, and lasts much longer than an electric one. They are made in Duluth and are now being sold all over the country. A friend of ours sells them, and last Saturday, which was terrifically hot, he sold 14! It seems that extreme heat placed tricks on the electric unit in the frigid air type and the thing goes flewy. Really, if any of you ever get another box, buy a Coolerator. I am going to compose a testimonial for it when I leave town cause I'm so sold on them.

Shaw's one white suit and pair of white trousers should be constantly dizzy - for he wears one, then the other, after which I quickly call the laundry, put in a rush order so they'll be back for the next day and then they go through the same thing all over again. My ancient evening dresses are coming in very handy. The blue and red one I wore Saturday was bought for ten dollars at a Waterman sale in 1931 and worn all over Europe! I'm afraid I shall need the black one, mother but in no great hurry. Could you send my dish towels along with it?

I think it's so splendid about Tom and Jane! Shaw and I spread ourselves and sent them a Jensen silver baby spoon. I'm anxious to hear from them concerning the brain child. I also would like to see Jane washing diapers!

Did I tell you a little boy looked at me when I got out of my car the other day. He glanced at my license plate and asked in an awestruck voice "what's the country like where you come from?" I said, "It's all pretty and green with lots of seashore - and it's oh so cool!"

Lots and lots of love to you all.
Joannie and Shawsie

Letter to family about moving to Minneapolis

Wednesday

Dearests -

The fact that Minneapolis "came through" is probably old news to you by now. We received the news Friday, + they started work Monday morning. We also received the sad news that we must move pronto, so Monday + Tuesday were devoted to the great hunt for "inexpensive furnished apartment with no lease." And what a survey we made! Alva Queaneau went to the University, so knows Minn. like a book but she doesn't drive a car, so we joined forces – I provided the car and chauffeur service + she provided the brains. Monday, we started out with thousands of addresses culled from the Sunday paper + various real estate offices. Luckily, we were after entirely different types of places. They have the <u>most</u> gigantic, and most horribly, sniffy, smelly, drooly English bulldog which they idolize – named Algernon! Consequently, their whole aim is to find something nice for "dear little Algy", as they call him. They were seeking a 2 bedroom duplex, <u>not</u> newly furnished, not near the city, and enclosed back yard, and adjacent to a park so Algy could do his daily dozen undisturbed by nearby traffic. They found a perfectly swell place in a nice section, but since it was going to be all newly decorated, they wouldn't consider it. Imagine how crazy that sounded to the real estate woman! Alva and Ro are really awfully nice, and since they are unable to have children, I think their love for that dog is pathetic.

Well, I was after a one bedroom apt. fairly near town in a good apartment house. By yesterday noon we had looked at about 40, when I suddenly came upon an apartment house which looked very nice. There was no vacancy sign outside but I waltzed in nevertheless, + found just what we wanted. One bedroom with a Murphy bed for company, a good stove + fairly nicely furnished. It's $52.50 without garage and that seems to be the prevailing rent in this place. This is a heck of a time to find anything, for it's renting season, anyway, + due to the very <u>definite</u> boom out here, there are millions of people looking for places to live who will sign leases. This is rather a choosey apt. house – no dogs + no children + they want a 30 day clause in the lease. Shaw and I went over last evening + stated our case + we are waiting to hear the result. Mrs. Lee, the rental agent, was the wife of a civil engineer + went through our same racket, so we played on her sympathies + hope it worked. She concluded the discussion by stating that she'd do what she could with the business manager, because she was a pretty good judge of character etc. etc. + thanked us for stating the case so frankly. So around 4 o'clock I'll know whether honesty is the best policy or not.

If honesty is the best policy, we'll move to 2809 Park Ave. Minn. Sunday. I shall get my lovely Swedish Annie to help me clean, so it should be very easy. Much as we hate to leave 600 Summit, I think it will be fun to get to know Minn., + now that the worst of the heat is over I shall be sort of glad to have less space to neglect cleaning.

Yesterday I also hied myself over to the Univ. to see if I could be a college girl again and get my degree. They have quarterly semesters so I thought I'd take a chance on being here for all of the first quarter + enroll. But, as usual, the whole senior year has to be in residence, so that is that. I shall try to take some courses, however.

Genie – this is <u>important</u>. Send me Debbie's address, will you? I can't find it, + I'd love to look her up.

Mother, don't bother to send my black dress, for when cooler weather comes I'm going to have to have some other things so they can all come together. Do I get your silver fox this fall?

We had a nice letter from Jane telling us of her pride + joy, + also suggesting that we visit them. Maybe she'll rue her words when I write her today + tell her we'd love to come for over Labor Day!

Shaw is all excited about the football season + we shall get season tickets immediately. If we are transferred we can easily turn them in.

You may remember that Minnesota was undefeated last year.

We seem to follow all of the exciting events! The National Women's Golf is in Minn. Soon, + Glerma Coletto is going to enter. Also the Minn. State Fair is the first week in Sept. and that will be most interesting.

I am <u>so</u> sorry about Jenny. How do you exist without her? Tell her for me that if she's learning to drive a car – I'm glad I'm out in the far west!

I'll let you know our address as soon as I do.

Lots + Lots of love,
Joan

Letter to Edward S. & Mary Cole, Joan's Mother & Father in-law, when Joan rushed home to Woonsocket to be with her Mother who suffered from tuberculosis

Fall, 1935 - Tuesday 1:00 P.M.
Near Elkhart, Indiana

Dearests -

You will be surprised to find I am en route to Woon. (Woonsocket) by train. A telegram from dad yesterday summons me home on account of Mother. I know nothing of the details for I left before his following letter reached me. His telegram stated "no emergency" but to please come home at once to help solve the servant problem etc. for Mother was coming home. I can only conclude that she has had a sudden definite turn for the worse for my last letter from Mother showed me how great her hope & faith was in Uncle John & said she realized the nursing home was the place for her temporarily. Knowing that Dad would underestimate the situation in his wire so as not to worry me, I immediately wired back stating how soon I could arrive by plane, to which he replied "No hurry. Take Train."

So I am very much in the dark, but greatly fear that the telegram I have unconsciously dreaded ever since I've been married has arrived. Consequently I am speeding home to do everything in my power to make Mother happy & ease Dad's worry.

Poor Shaw has been left to his own resources. If he wasn't an angel of good naturedness I should worry more about him. I am so glad he is with Alva & Ro Queneau on this job for they will prove to be true friends I am sure. Alva has asked him to eat dinner with them & she has arranged to go over to the apartment & clean things up occasionally.

Not knowing how long I am to be home, we spent yesterday packing the things Shaw wouldn't need in the event that I cannot return before the job is over.

I will write you more in detail when I reach home. Possibly you know more than I already.

I arrive in Worcester at 8:45 tomorrow (Wed.) morning. I am sorry I couldn't go through N.Y. & catch a glimpse of you, but this was way quicker.

Much love-
Joan

Fall 1935 - Thursday night

Dearest Mother Cole & Father Cole,

Pardon the pencil but I'm all snuggled in bed & Mother never allows "ink in bed."

I imagine you realized I couldn't talk freely over the phone. Dad was right there, and I couldn't say what I wanted to. I'm afraid I sounded very formal, but believe me, I was glad to hear your two loving voices.

The fact is – I was never more needed in my life, for Dad has temporarily lost his grip. The four years' strain is finally telling on him and his nerves are shot to pieces. He is by no means having a real nervous breakdown, but he definitely needed someone to talk to and take some of the responsibility. Thank goodness I can be "it".

True, Mother is coming home Saturday because she has had all the necessary tests, & the noise of Beacon St. does her more harm than good. However, she is far from well. Besides her T.B. she has anemia, is terribly nervous (as you know), and has a certain amount of cardiac trouble for her heart has undergone great strain in her effort to breathe. She is taking something which is certain to ease the strain on her heart, and as for the injection made from her sputum, we can only hope. Uncle John says quite frankly that the next six weeks are all important. If she improves, it will be wonderful, otherwise we must face the facts.

Because of Dad's condition & his knowledge of the case, it is a tremendous emotional strain on him to be with Mother, so I have my work cut out for me. I shall try to entertain Mother by reading to her etc. and make it easier for Dad. He yearns to find a hobby which would interest Mother so this evening we have been going over "The Leisure League of America" publications, hoping to find something which would interest him.

As far as Mother is concerned, she must have a great deal of rest, and no nervous strain. And most important of all, she needs hopeful thoughts, so I shall spend my time trying to make her look forward to the future. I don't think she realizes how important the next six weeks are. I hope not.

So poor darling Shaw is having to sacrifice for the good of the whole. He is the soul of goodness and I am so glad I don't have to worry about him. Mother and Dad are upset beyond words to think I should be called away from him, but I feel it is right – for we have the whole future ahead of us, and Mother and Dad have not.

As for N.Y. next week. Dad has to come down on business and if the practical nurse works out I may feel free to come. I will let you know. If it would relieve him for me to be here, I will stay, but I do want to see you both so much.

As for me, I am "in the pink." Two years ago this situation would have simply floored me. But I seem to have gained an inner strength. My excellent health is a great asset and if I can only retain the sense of calmness I have at the present I shall be very grateful.

Dad's wire was misquoted when delivered to me. Instead of reading a "change of <u>help</u> imminent", it read "a change of <u>health</u> imminent." Thus, someone's carelessness was responsible for my very uncomfortable train trip. I hoped it meant "help", but under the pressure of worry one is never optimistic.

My dearest love to you. I will keep you posted.

Joan.

Fall 1935

Dearest Mrs. Cole -

Just a quick note to tell you that Mother is safely home. We went to Boston Friday, had dinner & went to "The Great Waltz" with Uncle John & Aunt Alice & stayed over night with them. I had a long conference with Uncle John & then we drove Mother home Sat. noon.

We had hired a nurse to come yesterday, <u>much</u> against Mother's wishes, & she arrived about four. I spent the rest of the day showing & telling her things. Then this morning at 7:30 someone phoned her to come home immediately!! And she went. Now I can't believe it was a put up job – for goodness knows she would have it soft here. She claimed she didn't know what it was all about, but would phone me later in the day. So I'm waiting to hear.

Now in the meantime, I wonder if you could tell me what Orlie is doing? Could you find out once again for me what her program is? If you could gather the information without her suspecting it – any way you can think of – I'd be very grateful. Could you let me know as soon as possible? Dad has to go to N.Y.C. Thursday – expects to go on the boat & be there only for the day – but if this girl isn't coming back, he might be able to arrange an appointment with Orlie for Thursday. If that couldn't be worked out, I don't think one is really necessary. I haven't mentioned this to Dad or Mother because I think one more tentative plan would drive them nuts. So if you'd just send me a special delivery instead of a wire, I think it could be more easily explained. If she is not busy I shall probably phone you for further "orders." You might enclose her address when you write.

You can't possibly realize how much your loving attention meant to Mother this summer. Whenever she mentions it her eyes fill with tears.

I just missed Mary in Boston. She was planning some weekend. Aunt Alice was included in a cocktail party after the game. She could talk of nothing else while I was there – she was <u>so</u> thrilled.

Much <u>much</u> love
Joan

(written along the side) I can't make N.Y. this time. See you soon, though.

Letter from Joan's mother Edith, 3 days before she passed away

November 7, 1935
Thursday A.M.

Darling Joan,

You did so much for all of us, but - I am truly glad you have gone to live your own life now. But just where is that to be? Thought of you on your way + in Macy's etc. - but did little but doze yesterday after my "shots in the morning". Dr. King met the nurse and agreed they would study my case & try to get an appetite for me somehow. Dr. also found me better in many ways. Orlie is getting used to the routine and I might just give up being so New Englandish about my room etc. I know you and Dad went off more happily knowing she was here. Papa invited the Rockwells for Thanksgiving & The Coles if they will be in Boston and Mary of course. It's just a joy to be your mother, I will try to do as you wish - love to the Coles.

Mother

Woonsocket Call

Tuesday November 12, 1935

Edith E. Getchell Dies At Her Home
Wife of Business Executive Was Interested In Many Charities

Edith (Ellis) Getchell, wife of H. Eugene Getchell, president of Getchell and Son, Inc. died Sunday morning at 7:30 at her home, 205 Prospect Street. She had been ill three years.

She was born in Woonsocket, November 3, 1879, the daughter of the late John W. and Mary (Howe) Ellis. All her life she lived in Woonsocket, graduating from Woonsocket High School in 1895, and from Smith College in 1899. She was married to Mr. Getchell on June 6, 1905.

Mrs. Getchell until her serious illness had been active in club and welfare work in Woonsocket, her especial interest being the Girl Scouts, of which she had been commissioner. She was a member of the Olla Podrida Club and the O.M.S.C., and had been active in the Woonsocket Public Health Nursing Association, the Woonsocket Day Nursery and Children's Home, the Woonsocket Hospital Aid Association, the Woonsocket Alliance of Universalist Women, and other local welfare organizations. She had been a member of the Woonsocket Fortnightly Club and the Providence Plantations Club.

In addition to her husband, she leaves a sister, Mrs. Marion Ellis Gilbert of Hanover, N.H., four daughters, Martha, wife of W. Roland Harrall of Providence, Joan, wife of E. Shaw Cole of Upper Montclair, N.J., Mary Lucile, wife of G. Warren French of Wenatchee, Wash., and Edith Eugenia, a student at Smith College, and one grandson, H. Eugene Harrall.

The funeral will take place Wednesday at 2 p.m. at her home, 205 Prospect Street. Rev. E. Dean Ellenwood of the First Universalist

Church will officiate. Burial will be in Union Cemetery.

It was suggested by members of Mrs. Getchell's family that, in accordance with her wishes, no flowers be sent. Her wish was that the equivalent of the flowers which her friends might be prompted to send be given to some of the charities in which she was interested.

Edith Ellis Getchell
1879 - 1935

Letter to Edward & Mary Cole, Joan's parents-in-law

On or after Nov. 10, 1935
The day Joan's mother, Edith Ellis Getchell died

Dearests -

The porter is making up my berth so I am writing this note in the ladies room.

Oh, but how glad I was to see you two loving people waiting for me. I was in need of diversion & added information as you both well understood.

Also, I was so glad to be able to talk calmly with you both for I know I shall break down sadly when I go into our home. Somehow, being away from the scene made it possible for me to assume a somewhat detached attitude, and I can't help but feel that distance will do much to assuage Celie's grief. I can't hope to remain as calm as I have been, for home without my beautiful Mother there will be a sad place. However, Mother would want us to be brave & helpful to Dad after all, he will suffer the most. So I shall try to swallow my grief in the hope that all of us girls can help him through this inevitable period of suffering.

Thank you <u>so</u> much for your wonderful help to me. I did want you to know that this hectic day of yours was worth the trouble you went to for me.

A great deal of love -
Joan

Letter from Shaw to Joan

December 1935, Wednesday
Frackville, PA

My darling,

Your note did a lot to brighten up this dreary day. I've been thinking of you constantly since I left you Sunday - and even dreamed of you the other night (with no disastrous results).

Isn't that wonderful news about Celie and Bud? I can't wait to see them.

The drive back Sunday was pretty bad as there was fog all the way - got to bed by 11 & had felt fine all week. Cold almost gone & everything. Fortunately the weather has been fairly warm, so the work has gone fine, and in spite of being rained out last night I should finish subdivision tonight. Thus, giving me a chance to get back on the day schedule and leave here at noon Saturday.

I'm worried about the guarantee here - I only have two decent rates and I went over them superficially this afternoon with no results. But perhaps something will show up when I go over the services.

I'm changing my mind about this town - it's really better than Shippensburg except for food and room and there are some nice homes - a couple. You may be disappointed in your local color.

All my love to you darling,
Shaw

Will you get license & registration from Hanks at Valley Road garage[24] so we can fill them out and have the applications in?

---

24 Joan was in Montclair, N.J. when Shaw wrote this letter.

Early Married Years

Letter to family after their move to Toledo

Sat. April 25th, 1936
Toledo, Ohio

Dearest Everybody -

Should Shaw and I ever achieve George Washington's fame, we would be far and away ahead of him regarding "beds we have slept in" signs, for tonight we shall crawl into our sixth in six nights. The sixth, we hope will be as comfortable as the others, for it promises to be our permanent one during our stay here.

The first of our six was by far the most artistic, it being the four poster at 133 Belleview[25]. The second was in Harrisburg, at the Penn-Harris Hotel, a welcome haven after our drive through a prolonged cloudburst. The picnic lunch made the trip much less monotonous and I must confess we pounced on it long before supper time. Shaw and I had eyed it furtively since Verona and by Allentown we had both agreed that it might get stale if we waited too long.

The next day was beautiful and our drive across Penn. took us along much of the flooded territory. The realization of how horrifying it must have been dawned on us as we came upon toppled over houses, washed out bridges + trees who's tops were full of debris. The roads were being reconditioned + we were forced to take a detour here and there, but on the whole we lost very little time and made Akron by dinner time. Akron turned out to be a horribly dirty, smoky city full of Goodyear, Goodrich, and Firestone rubber mills - very different from Polly Curtis' description, though I realized that she lives in very different surroundings from the ones we saw. I had planned to phone her, but there were so <u>many</u> Firestone phone numbers that I was at a loss. I don't think that she is there now, anyway. We spent the evening relaxing in our nice hotel room, and departed bright and early next

---

[25] This was the address of Grandmary and Grandpa Cole, Joan's in-laws, in Upper Montclair, N.J.

morning so that Shaw might get here by noon.

We went straight to the Hillcrest (an apartment hotel) as directed by my E. Orange friend and Shaw went to the office, while I spent the afternoon going through the usual routine - scanning the ad section of the local paper, driving around the residential sections in search of "Apartment For Rent" signs and seeing a real estate man. The Hillcrest was out from the start, for being expensive, it included hotel service, and why, please, should I sit in a two room apartment and watch a maid do the work!

Toledo, let it be known, is a Pitometer wife's <u>delight</u>, for it abounds in furnished apartments requiring no leases - the only drawback being the fact that they are cram jam full of occupants. I cannot understand why there are so many such accommodations, for the real estate people claim that this population is not a transient type.

It seems that the big boy to see around here is Sam Davis, a man of many businesses, including a chain of furnished apartments. In search of his office, I became hopelessly confused and asked his whereabouts of a motorcycle cop. "Why, lady, I'll take you to Sam Davis." And, lady, he did, right down to the main streets under police escort. I thought it was very impressive, but Shaw said it looked as if we'd been pinched. Having dropped Shaw on route, I went into a gigantic warehouse, which looked more like a Ford plant than the customary real estate office, but upon inquiry I was assured that this was the right place. Alright then, could I see someone about a furnished apartment? "Unfortunately, our real estate man is out just now." Feeling a little cocky as a result of my recent police attention, I said that really I simply couldn't wait on his return - that there must be someone who could take care of me. Whereupon a deep voice boomed forth from an adjoining office + I was ushered into the presence of Sam himself. Now Sam is a great, big, florid, raucous voiced hooked nose, I'll do you a favor, cigar-in-his-mouth Jew, and as I entered he flashed a golden smile on me + told me to sit down. "Madam, whatever you want - we've got it." Oh yeah, I thought, remembering past experiences, but I launched forth. "I want a furnished, one bedroom apartment in a nice neighborhood, preferably in the outskirts of town," whereupon he picked up the phone and asked into space, "Is 318 in the Ina vacant? When will you know? O.K." Then to me, "Well, that's the only one in 7 apartment houses that may be vacant soon. When do you want it?" "Tonight," I said, gulping. "Well, you can't have that tonight, but I'll take care of you in the meantime." "Where, and for how much?" ask I. "In the same apartment house, for nothing, and we'll do all the moving. I'm putting you in a more expensive one that's vacant right now. You start your regular rent today and if we can't fix you up in a cheaper one, you can keep the better one at the lower price." I couldn't see any flaw in that, but now I launched the bomb shell. "I can't sign a lease, not even a monthly one." "That's okay with me lady, as soon as you go out somebody else will move in." "Will you put your signature on that?" "I will." "O.K., then I'll take both the signature and the apartment, but the signature first."

In Memoriam

Herbert Eugene Getchell
1872 - 1936

Trustee of Woonsocket Universalist Society for a quarter of a century. Member of the church, since April 5, 1917. Faithful to its every interest, and zealous for its progress. Devoted lover of family, friends and community.

> "No earnest cause appealed to him in vain,
> That hoped to lead the old earth up and on.
> Yet Love will dream, and Faith will trust,
> Since He who knows our need is just,
> That somehow, somewhere, meet we must."
> (From "Snowbound", his favorite poem)

May 3rd, 1936. Woon. Universalist Church

Herbert Eugene Getchell
1872 - 1936

Article from a Woonsocket Newspaper

April 25, 1936

H.E. GETCHELL. 63, IN BUSINESS FOR MANY YEARS, DEAD
Prominent Woonsocket Citizen Takes Own Life While Hospital Patient

Wife Died Recently

Deceased Long Identified With Civic Movements; Active In Golf Clubs

H. Eugene Getchell, 63, of 205 Prospect Street, one of the most beloved of Woonsocket's prominent citizens, was found dead by his own hand this morning in the Woonsocket Hospital, where he had been a patient for several days.

Mr. Getchell, whose wife died last November, had recently returned from a trip to the Pacific coast, and Tuesday of this week he entered the hospital for treatment of a throat ailment. Thursday he underwent a minor operation and was presumably on the way to complete recovery.

Last night about 10:30 o'clock he retired in his room at the hospital, and the nurse closed the door. This morning at 6 o'clock, she entered the room and found Mr. Getchell had left his bed. Half an hour later, finding he was still in the bathroom, with the door locked, she called for assistance. The door was opened with a master key, and Mr. Getchell was found dead on the floor, his throat cut with a razor.

Leaves Note For Family

Mr. Getchell left a note to his family in which he said he could no longer suffer the mental torture. Expressing confidence that his family would understand, and that the children were well cared for, he indicated that he wished to join his wife in death.

Dr. Edward L. Myers, medical examiner, said death may have occurred even before midnight. He gave permission for removal of the body, which was taken in charge by Undertaker Edgar L. Spaulding.

Herbert Eugene Getchell was born in Woonsocket, Dec 21, 1872, a son of the late Seth Sherman and Martha J. (Bamford) Getchell. He was educated in the public schools of the city and at the Mowry & Goff School in Providence. He then went to work with his father in the sheet metal business, and the firm name became S.S. Getchell & Son. The business was then located off Bernon Street. Later it was moved to Island Place, where it is still located.[26]

When the late Seth S. Getchell retired from active business, the son carried on as head of the firm. The elder Mr. Getchell died in 1912. A few years ago, the concern was incorporated. Mr. Getchell, as president and treasurer, continued as active head of the business until the time of his death.

Home-Loving Man

Mr. Getchell was essentially a home-loving man, devoted to his family. He was active in all civic affairs, took a prominent part in philanthropic activities, and belonged to numerous golf clubs.

On June 7, 1905, Mr. Getchell and Miss Edith Ellis, daughter of the late John W. and Mary (Howe) Ellis, were united in marriage at a home wedding. The couple had been devoted to each other, and the death of Mrs. Getchell last November 10 was a blow from which Mr. Getchell never fully recovered. Last February, Mr. Getchell and his daughter Edith Eugenia, went to the Pacific coast to visit another daughter, Mrs. G. Warren French, and also made a side trip to Alaska. They returned to Woonsocket April 8.

Mr. Getchell is survived by a sister, Mrs. Blanche G. Robinson, widow of A.M. Robinson: four daughters, Martha, wife of W. Roland Harrall of Providence; Joan Ellis, wife of E. Shaw Cole, of Upper

---

26 Getchell & Son Inc. is now located on Route 7 in Smithfield, R.I. www.getchell.com

Montclair, N. J.; Mary Lucile, wife of G. Warren French, formerly of Wenatchee, Wash., and now of Upper Montclair, N.J., and Miss Edith Eugenia Getchell of this city. He also leaves a grandson, H. Eugene Harrall.

Member of Masonic Bodies

Mr. Getchell was a member of the board of managers of the Woonsocket office of the Rhode Island Hospital Trust Company, a director of the Morris Plan Company of Rhode Island, a trustee of First Universalist Church, a trustee and for many years a member of the executive committee of the Woonsocket Hospital, a trustee and member of numerous committees of the Union Cemetery Corporation, a member of the Woonsocket Chamber of Commerce, City Club, Cumberland Golf Club, Winnesuket Country Club, Ironstone Country Club, Rhode Island Golf Club, New England Golf Seniors, Sakonnet Golf Club, and all the local Masonic bodies, including Morning Star Lodge, F.&A.M.; Union Chapter, R.A.M.; Woonsocket Council, R.&S.M.; Woonsocket Commandery, Knights Templars, and of Palestine Temple of Shriners in Providence.

During the World War he served as Federal coal commissioner in Northern Rhode Island. Before these banks were absorbed by the Rhode Island Hospital Trust Company, Mr. Getchell served as a member of the board of trustees of the Mechanics Savings Bank and as director of the National Globe Bank.

The funeral will be held Monday afternoon at 2 o'clock with services in the home at 205 Prospect Street. Rev. E. Dean Ellenwood, pastor of the First Universalist Church, will officiate. Burial will be in Union cemetery.

Letter from Joan to Vee (Vivian) Craig and her husband

Saturday - late May 1936

Your <u>nice</u> letters deserve a much longer answer.

Dearest Craigs,

    This, as you may imagine, will be a tinsey weensey note, for we are at last getting under way in answering all of the letters we've received.

    So it's really just a very unflowery thank you for the many nice thoughts you sent in the way of flowers, telegram + both of your letters.

    We're all getting on ever so well. At first we were just numbed, but for some reason or other we've come to without any theatrics. It seems so logical for Dad to be with Mother and we all understand his act so well.

    Celie arrives around Tuesday and then we will start making a few decisions. I hope to get back to Shaw sometime in the near future. If I go via N.Y.C. <u>let's</u> have a long knit together.

    I really am getting huge. Mart says I'm much too big for only 4 months but I've gained very little. She has great morning trouble. Be <u>sure</u> to wire her when your heir arrives.

    We all had the <u>best</u> time at your house for dinner Thursday. It was the first time we'd been out since Dad died + it seemed <u>so</u> good.

Dearest love,
Wanie

Articles in the Woonsocket Call concerning the Wills of Edith Ellis Getchell and Eugene H. Getchell following their passing

Fall of 1935

Getchell Estate Is Set At $95,000 In Will Offered

Husband Refuses Trust As Executor And Nominates R.I. Company

The personality in the estate of Mrs. Edith Ellis Getchell, prominent in social and philanthropic work in Woonsocket for many years, who died last week, following a long illness, is estimated at $95,000, according to a petition to prove the will with an accompanying two weeks' order of notice, filed with the local probate court today. Judge Olivia Lambert presided at the session.

The petition names her husband, H. Eugene Getchell, and four daughters, Mrs. Joan E.G. Cole, of Upper Montclair, N.J., Mrs. Mary Lucille G. French, of Wenatchee, Wash., Mrs. Martha G. Harrall, of Providence and Miss Edith Eugenia Getchell, of this city, as the heirs-at-law.

Following the payment of just debts and funeral expenses, the will directs that the residue of the estate be bequeathed to the husband, "trusting that my said husband, the said H. Eugene Getchell, will make suitable provision for my children."

The document recommends that Mr. Getchell be named executor, but was declined. When the matter faces the court again, in two weeks, the Rhode Island Hospital Trust Company will be appointed administrator c.t.a., at the suggestion of the nominated executor.

Spring of 1936

THE WOONSOCKET CALL, TUESDAY
Daughters To Get Getchell Property

Become Beneficiaries As Will Bequeaths Estate To His Late Wife.

The will of H. Eugene Getchell who died last Saturday, was filed today with the city clerk for submission to the Probate Court next Tuesday.

The will, dated Jan. 13, 1932, bequeaths all property, real and personal, to Mrs. Edith (Ellis) Getchell. Because Mr. Getchell's wife died last November, the property will be divided equally among the four daughters, Mrs. E. Roland Harrall of Providence, Mrs. G. Warren French and Mrs. E. Shaw Cole of Upper Montclair, N.J., and Miss Edith Eugenia Getchell of this city.

Mr. Getchell requests in his will that the Rhode Island Hospital Trust Company and Mrs. Getchell be the executors. Because of Mrs. Getchell's death, it is presumed that the court will appoint the bank only.

The will was drawn by Attorney James H. Rickard and filed by him today. There is no estimate of the amount of the estate.

Excerpt from Joan's Scrapbook, Summer 1936

We break up our Woonsocket home, which Mother entered as a bride from her own home across the street.

A house beloved by all of us, who were allowed to live fully and freely in it - a house whose lighted windows formed a smiling face.

Part IV
Motherhood

Motherhood

After her parents passed away, my mother's life, as life often does, went on without slowing down. She and Shaw continued to travel for his work, and on October 9, 1936, I, Joan Shaw Cole (Pixie), was born while my parents were living in Montclair, New Jersey. Getchell Brewster Cole (Bruce) joined us on August 29, 1938 in Fall River, Massachusetts, 22 days before the 1938 hurricane. We moved to our first permanent house on Wildwood Ave in Montclair, New Jersey, and my father began working in the New York office of the Pitometer Company.

On November 27th, 1943, our baby sister Heather Dunclee Cole was born in Montclair, New Jersey.

Though the letters and scrapbook entries become less frequent with her new bundles of joy to take care of, my mother's sense of humor and excitement for every new thing in her life is unfailing. It's bittersweet to hear her speak of me and my siblings and the life she had planned for us all.

We were a wildly happy family for a short 23 days after Heather was born before losing my mother suddenly and shockingly to a pulmonary embolism, but through all she left of her voice, we keep her close to us.

Joan and Pixie

Shaw and Pixie

The Getchell girls and their husbands: Doc, Martha, Shaw, Joan, Celie, Bud, Genie, and Richie

3 Getchell sisters and their children: Celie & Wayne, Martha & Lee, and Joan & Pixie

*Cousin Gene with his mother Martha (pregnant with Lee),
Joan (pregnant with Pixie), Celie (pregnant with Wayne), and Genie*

Bruce, Joan, and Pixie

"Wildwood Ave. Our house is small but it's fun to have a home at last."

Pixie and Bruce

Birthday Party in Sakonnet, R.I.: Joan and Mart and the children, Lee, Bruce, Pixie, Wayne, and Gene

The Cole Family: Grandpa Cole, Peg and John, Grandmary Cole, Joan, Mary (Shaw's sister), Shaw

Gram + Gramp on the beach with the children

Grandmary Cole surrounded by her grandchildren and their cousins and friends

Pixie and Heather

Pixie, Heather, and Lee

Bruce, Pixie, and Heather, 1945

Letter to Mart while waiting for Mart to give birth

December 1936 - Thursday

Dearest Mart -

Really I am getting sorrier for you by the minute. I can well appreciate the suspense you all went through while waiting for me to hatch. I hope you aren't too uncomfortable, and if it has arrived by now, I hope it's a girl.

I asked the Coles to forward my letter describing our Dayton weekend to you. It was what you might call fancy. Traveling with the Pixie is all very fine but oh - what a washing I have to wade through when I get back. And there is absolutely no place to hang things to dry. I refuse to break down and use the diddy service for with maid service supplied I feel I ought to be able to do the rest - and when I say maid service, it means a good deal. Two gals come in and vacuum, dust, empty garbage, wash "kitchen" + bathroom floors, supply soap, fresh table linen, kitchen linen, 4 hand + bath towels + bed linen everyday. But our two room apartment costs $86.00 per month + 10 cents for each phone call and $10.00 for garage. We took it because there was no lease + won't get stuck for a cent extra as we would elsewhere.

The first week I was absolutely beside myself trying to get everything done right. Unpacking was a terrible problem for there was nowhere to put a thing. There I was also faced with an electric stove with a book of directions the size of Webster's Dictionary - Shaw ate Carbon + Charcoal for a solid week. I had never taken care of the baby for a full day before, making the formula took twice the time it takes to make a good old fashioned fruit cake. How I envied Hanley's their beer and bottle machines.

But now that Shaw is on night work I seem to have developed a system - and what a crazy routine. It goes like this:

6:00 AM. Bottle. (The Pixie is now in the living room.) Back to

MOTHERHOOD

bed to greet Shaw at 6:30 when he comes home.

9:00 AM. I arise, eat breakfast, sterilize the bottles and feed Pixie. Then into the bedroom with Shaw so I can heat the living room.

Next comes the formula + ordering + then 1 P.M. Shaw arises and has his breakfast. As soon as he's off the bed, the Pixie gets on it to prepare for her bath which she takes in the tub after Shaw gets out of the shower.

Shaw stays home while I go to market + do some Christmas shopping, during which time the maids clean, the Pixie being shifted into the living room while they are doing the bedroom.

Dinner is usually at 8 P.M. after which I do the dishes + prepare Shaw's dinner pail. At 9:30 I get Pix ready for bed, feed her, and move her into the living room. Shaw departs + I face the days washing at this crazy hour so it can dry in my room during the night. Then I move a clean set of clothes, oil, cotton etc. into the living room to use when I change her at 6 A.M. then <u>flop</u> into bed about 1 A.M.

My Book of Happy Memories

Letter from Joan about her mothering routine

Wednesday
Toledo, Ohio

Dears -

Victory! My 36 diapers are hanging on the line. I mean on the chandeliers, lamps, radiators etc. One batch is strung out on the rack I brought from your house and I've managed to get it out of the window and onto a cement court, which is one of the big reasons for taking this particular apartment. When that batch is sufficiently frozen it will be replaced by another - and so on, far into the night. I am planning to develop a system whereby I can expose them to the sun for a while at least, for the morning sun streams into our two exposures.

Well, I apologize for dwelling on such a homely subject for my opening paragraph but for the past few days they seem to have been the sole object of my thoughts. The disposable diddies proved somewhat of a failure en route, consequently my supply quickly dwindled. When we settled here I tossed the whole accumulation in the bathtub, hoping to find them all nicely folded by Orley in the morning, but alas - they had multiplied in numbers by morn so I got to work, but suddenly found myself out of soap. Since then I have been constantly thwarted in all attempts to lay my hands on a cake of Ivory. The drugstore downstairs didn't have any, Shaw couldn't get me on the phone to ask for the shopping list, one delivery never arrived and so on. Meantime the tub got fuller + fuller and we shouldn't take a bath for there simply wasn't another piece of space to put them in. So today I started in + have been gaining on them and right now that is until I pick up the Pixie again, the bathtub is unshrouded. Meantime a pail has been delivered (a dollar off floor sample!) and will soon begin its active life.

Oh dear, I wish I had time to tell you of our trip. It was <u>such</u> fun and everything went smoothly. Joy has been an angel + has cried so little that I'd begun to think she was going into a decline until I found a reason for the silence. She's learned to suck her thumb, and finds it so entrancing that rather than open her jaws to cry she'd rather curl her little lips around her right thumb, her fingers sticking out straight and stiff.

Our first night with her in Harrisburg strikes me so funny that I am planning to write down Shaw's and my 4 A.M. dialogue to send on. And also the description of the making of her formula in Ebensburg, PA. The inn we stopped at looked so nice that I thought I'd better grab the chance and make it there rather than wait until reaching Akron. It's lucky I did for the phone operator wouldn't give us Len Firestone's number (at his request) so I telegraphed Polly to say it was okay. In it I said "have made baby's formula", and next morning a maid of the Firestones phoned me to say she was terribly worried about me and that the Firestones were away for a week. I think she thought my wire meant "have babies formula made"!

So <u>many</u> funny things happened but I shall have to wait until we meet again, for I find that all the spare time I used to have is very definitely a thing of the past!

We decided to stay on here, for we would have to wait a few days before moving into the other + in the meantime would've spent the difference in rent. It's a splendid place and our apartment is fine. It's average sized but seems <u>tiny</u> when I think of the trunks we haven't even unpacked yet. I ordered a bathinette which just arrived, but which will go right back for there is hardly room enough for it folded, let alone spread out + ready for action. So the Pixie should have a real swim tomorrow in the tub.

I will match the following with anyone who thinks he's experienced "life's most hectic moment." Two o'clock came, yesterday, and that means only one thing in my life now - the Pixie's bottle, so I put it on to heat. Just as I was about to put it in her mouth, four men arrived to take away the in-a-door bed. Upon their heels a housekeeper arrived to greet me, bringing the maid who wanted to have instructions about cleaning the apartment, and to cap the climax my two Toledo acquaintances dropped in to pay a call. So that made ten of us in a two room apartment. The Pixie, in the meantime, was kicking on the bed and I tell you she is well named for when I left them all bumping into each other in the living room she just looked up to me + grinned a wicked grin as if to say, "Ha, ha, you've got to tend to me no matter what happens."

Time marches on, or rather races on, so this must end. Though everything is very hectic I'm just loving every minute of it. It seems wonderful to be in the swim again. Last night when I jumped into bed I said to Shaw "It seems good to be tired enough to really want to go to bed." He said "Ya - did you set your alarm for six A.M.?" I could have creamed him!

Love,
Joan

Letter when Pixie is 2 months old

December, 1936 - Friday Eve

Dears -

Pixie is two months old today and I'm afraid it hasn't been a very happy birthday for her because her mother has been very cruel to her. For Pixie has learned to suck her thumb, and since my book says no, I am trying to break her of the habit, though it makes me twice as unhappy as it does her! She's had her mittens on ever since I decided this little matter must be attended to before it goes too far. Today the mittens needed washing so she now looks too funny with your little stockings on each arm. How she has screamed her resentment. She yelled so lustily that her daily gain was converted into energy. When she isn't yelling she looks at me so wistfully that it rings my heart. I shudder to think of the thousand and one other things I will have to deny her in the course of her youth!

But in payment for enduring her cross I am going to take her to a dinner dance tomorrow night. Can't you see it in the scrapbook? "Pixie's first party. Aged 2 months and one day. Hotel Biltmore, Dayton, Ohio." Is Orley fainting? Shaw and I decided that Fuigi's party sounded too good to miss so I tried to get a nurse who my friends suggested. Unfortunately, she was on a case so, since the Pixie travels so well, we're going just the same. The dinner is in the hotel where we'll be staying so we're planning to get one of the hotel maids to sit in the room. I plan to go up from time to time to check up but I feel sure she'll be alright, for I've never found anything amiss in all the times I've looked at her in her crib.

A letter from Polly from Miami (!) says she hoped I got her wire saying I was welcome to the house. I'm so glad I took the opportunity to make the formula when it presented itself.

We're fairly well settled now, but I haven't yet organized my time to advantage. The apartment is fine and the maid service wonderful. If it wasn't for her we should be wading in dust by now. My chief problem seems to be <u>where</u> to dry things. My "book" says not to hang them in the room with the baby and that leaves only the living room, for the kitchen is full when I'm in it as is the bathroom. I've hung them on the rack in the courtyard out my window but today I looked out to find the whole business blown out of sight. I squirmed through the window and I must've looked funny harvesting diapers, bibs, shirts. Etc! At night when we move the baby into the living room we move the clothes into the bedroom. In fact most everything we have serves a double purpose - the end table which holds the radio, for instance, is in reality, my tan suitcase, which is not only a table but the baby's closet! The space marked B.C. in the diagram has been converted into a catch all, for we've moved one bureau in there + have squeezed the wardrobe trunk in also. The scales go on top of the bureau so Pixie and I have a tight squeeze when we go in to get weighed. Do you wonder why I've sent the Bathinette back!

We've gotten most of the letters and one package from the Clarendon - also a few irate letters from the management!

Well, because tomorrow will be even a bigger day than the last six have been, I think we'll flop into bed a bit early. My intellectual life seems to be suffering, my chief concern these days being to boil the bugs out of the formulae and ring the soap out of diapers. By the way, I've never heard anyone mention it, but do all young mothers develop diaper muscles such as I'm sure I must be in my shoulders and wrists? Scarlett may have developed callouses from hoeing cotton but she has nothing on me. My harvest is incredibly wonderful though - that's the difference between Pixie and cotton.

Give my love to Celie. I hope to write her next. I do wish Mart would produce.

Loads of love to you all I wish I could write you more in detail for you are always <u>so</u> interested in us.

Joan

MOTHERHOOD

Letter from Joan about their Dayton Dinner party

December 7, 1936 - Monday Eve
The Hillcrest - TOLEDO'S FINEST APARTMENT HOTEL
Toledo, Ohio

Dears -

Well, the Pixie gives great promise of being a golf devotee in the future, for Sunday afternoon she slept in a locker room + seemed thoroughly absorbed by the row of lockers. It was oh, such a fancy locker room, though, more beautiful then she will ever see again so I do hope she took a good look.

But I must commence at the beginning of our gay weekend. We took off in a cloud of diapers and iced formula about one o'clock Saturday aft + arrived in Dayton in time for her dinner. Fuigi had already engaged a room for us. The desk clerk told Shaw that Fuigi had arrived from Florida only that noon, very much the worse for wear due to an auto accident which he had en route.

While I put the Pixie to bed Shaw called on him in his room and returned with the news that Fuigi was decorated with two black eyes + a sad looking nose but was in fine fetter. His Lasalle, which he was planning to take back as a gift to his mother, was in utter ruin and, as he said, it was so worthless that he sold it for junk.

We arranged to have a floor maid go in + look at Pixie every 15 minutes + write me a note each time. The only possible harm which could come to her was a possible fire, as far as we could see, so having the maid take a look every so often relieved our minds.

We went downstairs about 7:30 + met Shaw's freshman roommate and wife in the elevator. They had come 200 miles from the east, another couple whom Shaw knew 200 miles from the west, and we from the north, so you see it was a great gathering of Fuigi's friends from all parts of the region. We were ushered into a cocktail room where all 54 of his guests were gathered, + I must say it was a weird assortment of guests, a collection of his personal friends and his business connections, including many strange looking officials of the National Cash Register Co. We went into dinner and found little Japanese fans for place cards on two long banquet tables, separated by a dancefloor and orchestra. Two of the twenty dozen pink roses now grace our living room, and I might even win a prize for arrangement, for they are poised in a rare old tin waste basket.

Dinner, suffice to say, was from soup to nuts + all the wines, sparkling Burgundy, champagne, cordials, etc. which went with the various courses. During the champagne course I went up to give Pixie hers, and she seemed to relish diluted milk even more than the guests did their fancy drinks. Dinner ended about 11:30 and we danced until 2:30, when I told Shaw I was positively muscle bound and went to bed, but he stayed till the bitter end.

Next morning Fuigi had breakfast for us all in his suite + then invited the out of town guests for dinner at his Moraine Country Club. Seven of us accepted with the greatest of pleasure, including the Pixie, who was all dressed up in dry diapers + a pink rose.

On the way out, Fuigi told Shaw all about his purchase of a full blooded mare who had been put "in a fix" by Gallant Fox. Since foreign horses cannot race in Japan, he is awfully anxious to get her to Japan, so the foal will qualify. If she's born on the Japanese boat it's O.K. but that wouldn't be too good for the baby, so he's having Lloyd's insure him against this possibility. The purchase price of this little souvenir of America is only eight thousand dollars!

The Moraine C. Club is a perfect little gem of architecture and imperial decoration. Shaw may have told you that there are only 84 members, + I assure you we had just about that many waiters. We had a perfectly delicious dinner served with all of the flourishes, + whenever Fuigi asked for something the head Butler would say "It's a pleasure to serve you, Mr. Fugiyama," and he'd practically scrape his head on the floor. The Pixie was bowed into her sleeping corners with the same deference + I doubt if Bobby at his christening was any more of a big show then was Pixie that day! She had her bottle on a chaise lounge in the locker room + soon after that we departed, Fuigi having taken care of our hotel bill! Thank goodness Shaw brought him a couple of neckties for a going away present. We arrived home in time for me to get quickly down to earth by making her formula + though she didn't even seem sleepy, we could hardly crawl into bed. In fact she gained four ounces in her two days away, so it proves that she thrives on excitement.

Life for her has become one constant round of activity, for she has discovered two new past times, besides sucking her thumb. She now blows beautiful bubbles, + has discovered her left arm. When her arm waves by she watches its progress with her cross eyes + sort of blows bubbles at it, simply squeaking in her excitement. It is too funny to watch + Shaw + I get in perfect gales. We think she has become very pretty now that her face is round and her cheeks pink.

It was such fun to get the pictures today. I think they are splendid, and Shaw says Papa Cole has great merit as a photographer. We'd love the negatives for we'd like to send some prints to various people.

Lack-a-day, I fear my manuscript has commenced a checkered career, for it has already suffered one very polite routine rejection slip.

I plan to augment my collection by sending it to Harpers next.

Shaw is working nights this week + thus a different routine must be worked out. The bed has been most necessary to me in working on the Pixie but it would be a little too humpy with Shaw under the covers, so it looks as if the bathroom floor will have to serve. It is washed every day and I plan to double up one of my woolen blankets + place under her. The only other possible spot is the dinette table + I would be in constant fear of her rolling off. She can hardly roll off the floor, though, so I think that's the best.

Shaw has just gone off to night work + felt a little sheepish about walking through our grand lobby in his long underwear + dinner pail!

I do wish I could get all of the things down on paper that I wish to tell you, but tempus fugits something terrible!

Do let Celie read this + send it on to Mart. I <u>hope</u> she'll be reading it in the hospital!

Loads of love to everybody,
Shaw + Joan + Pixie

(I'm collecting hotel letterheads for P's scrapbook. So far, I have 5!)

MOTHERHOOD

Joan's letter about their Toledo Airplane Ride

Dec 1936, after Christmas in New Jersey
Monday

Dears -

Well, we're back to earth again, and in one sense, being on earth again is a <u>distinct</u> pleasure, for our trip back was what the air minded call "bumpy".

You may have seen us take the two rear seats in the plane. We considered ourselves lucky for the view from that position is less obstructed by the wings. Once again, Pixie and I were the only girls and we looked forward to a nice long sightseeing trip. We jounced around a bit as we left Newark, but we knew that would soon be over with for we did the same thing as we neared the airport Thursday. However, we seemed to be flying very low + the jouncing continued. My "innards" began to rebel faintly but I decided I was just getting my sea legs and continued to enjoy the view with a somewhat grim expression. The hostess went up to the pilots' booth + then returned to me, saying that we would probably be more comfortable in the front seats since the tail swayed more than the rest of the plane. Shaw didn't object to it, but I couldn't get there fast enough. When I got settled again the hostess said that if I felt the least bit ill to tell her + the pilot would go higher but that there was a terrific head wind above + if I wasn't uncomfortable he would prefer to fly low all of the way. I was very impressed to think that the course of the plane was in my hands but told her that I'd rather he fly low whatever the effect might be, for otherwise we'd be delayed at least an hour.

Presently she began checking the tickets + when she was near me again I said, "I've no idea of being sick but it would be reassuring if I could hold one of those lovely containers you provide." So for a little while I was holding everything - my stomach, the container, and the

Pixie. We were bumping frightfully, and I know it's bad training to rock a child, the Pix was getting the rock of her life. Suddenly that awful grey, green feeling came over me and I turned my head sideways with great difficulty + made a face at the hostess. She raced toward me + I flung the Pix at her, grabbed up the carton, and gave up the ghost. That is the last I saw of the Pixie - she flew through the air with the greatest of ease and landed in the arms of the hostess, but for all I knew, after that, she might've been left behind sitting on a cloud blowing bubbles. I spent the rest of the trip trying to avoid all thoughts of the Christmas dinner + thanking the Lord that we'd left before attacking the other turkey. But thoughts of all that helping of second joint would recur, and for once in my life the vision of crispy fat was not enticing. I was astounded to hear the landing wheels being lowered for I hadn't had the courage to look out of the window, and suddenly we were landing. Stability brought my health back rapidly and I enjoyed a reunion with my family. It seems that the hostess had held Pixie most of the way for Shaw had been so tranced with the view from the rear seat that he hadn't noticed the goings on up front.

Tuesday - Two friends of mine dropped in and I didn't get back at my desk so - to continue...

We had a twenty minute wait in Cleveland, + since it was way past the Pixie's feeding hour, we discussed whether to feed her or not. I was all for "not", since I couldn't imagine that anyone would ever want to eat again. Shaw was starved - it had been too rough to serve any dinner - so he thought she better eat. The hostess was against it, but one of the pilots said his little baby was always fed no matter how rough, so why not give her half of the bottle? The Pixie grinned at him very winningly so we decided that suited her, and while Shaw went into the airport midst a blinding rain storm, I looked away and poured half the bottle down the Pixie's throat.

Motherhood

Soon the plane filled up again + we were off for the half hour run to Toledo, Shaw beside me this time holding the baby. I rapidly went into my decline, comforted by the thought that "it wouldn't be long now", though there was a possibility that we might have to go on to Chicago if the wind wasn't right in Toledo. A lady who came on at Cleveland + who was sitting just behind me, had quickly lost her health the same as I, and when we came down in Toledo + prepared to leave the plane she looked at me oh so wistfully. Thanking the hostess profusely we stepped on the *terra firma* again + this time Shaw looked a little green around the gills + said he regretted the glass of milk he drank in the Cleveland airport. So the Pixie held the highest score for she alone smiled, ate, + slept during the journey.

But I'm not daunted. I still would fly given another chance, for everything is made as comfortable + convenient as possible + there is always the comforting feeling that soon we will be landing, and it is so much easier than a train with a baby – especially if the hostess holds her!

This description makes me sound anything but grateful to you, Poppa Cole! But please realize that that episode was but a tiny three hours midst four days of continuous happiness at being with you all again. It was indeed a Merry Christmas, thanks to you + Grand Mary, and though I'm sad to think that little Joy will never know a Christmas in my own home, I am more than happy to know that she will have the same kind of Merry Christmas in Shaw's home.

Loads of love from us all,
Joan

Letter after Providence weekend

Fall of 1937 - Wednesday
Cambridge, MA

Dears -

One weekend is hardly over when the next seems upon us. Our many activities keep us hopping and then time flies by. Last week was devoted to getting over our colds - Shaw having caught mine - but now we're fit again. I marvel that Pixie didn't get it, despite the fact, <u>Gramp,</u> she doesn't wear a thick shirt.

The Providence weekend was a great success. Jenny was there to assist with the babies so it was not as hectic as it might have been. We saw loads of people + was glad to find Mart's family in fine spirits.

This weekend promises to be a gay one also. I hope Mary is coming Friday + Genie also. We've been invited to Mable Jones' for dinner but hope that Genie, Dick, Mary and Bill will make themselves at home here. Saturday is the game with people coming over afterwards from the Harvard Stadium!

I guess Bill told you we had Toby for dinner last week. He is a very fine boy, I'd think his natural poise is most attractive and he's full of good boyish sense.

My maid is thoroughly satisfying for though she is totally inexperienced, she will do what I tell her and is quiet and clean. I have her two half days and one whole day.

This being her "whole day" I'm going gadding this afternoon. Through a friend of ours I have an appointment to go through Irving + Cassons wood cutting plant. They, at one time, owned the finest lot of Mahogany in this country + though they make excellent custom made furniture, their main business is church work, carving, etc. So I expect to learn quite a bit about Veneer cutting etc.

Pixie continues to remain adorable. Each day I'm sure she'll walk, but creeping still appeals to her more. She talks a blue streak but says nothing, though she can scold me something fierce. It's very rude to tell you, but she hates her hat and will not leave it on her head.

Your letter just arrived and I'm returning two dollars of the check you sent. Each additional pose was $4.00. Many thanks.

I'm excited at the thought of all these wedding plans - and the possibility of new curtains. Are you looking for plain or figured ones?

I expect to get all of the latest news of you from Mary. It will be fun to see her and I wish you and Gramp were to be here too.

We are still waiting for some of our furniture! I lack a desk which makes writing on a coffee table very inconvenient.

Much love to you all,
Joan

Letter from Shaw (and then Joan) to his mother Mary

October 11, 1937
41 Hawthorne St, Cambridge, Mass

Mother dear –

Back to the night shift this week has given me the morning off + between Pixie's cries Joan + I have put in a heavy morning of desk work, so that we feel quite saintly – all bills paid, checkbook balanced, letters written etc. A clean slate does wonders for the peace of mind doesn't it?

We continue to love Cambridge and dread the day when we will have to leave. The time goes all too quickly, but we are making good use of it and have seen any number of friends. Toby Cambell even dropped in Saturday night + is coming to dinner Thursday.

Yesterday was quite a day which was spent at Uncle John's. He and I played golf in the morning at Oakley + then we had a delicious dinner with Mrs. Curtis and Mabel Jones supplying the conversation which consisted smoothly of drawing + quartering the president. A couple of Boston Beans they are without a doubt. The day was rainy and cold so we spent a nice evening at home - alone for one of the few times since we've been here.

The drastic situation has become acute or became acute at dinner yesterday + what the outcome will be is doubtful but open warfare exists. Miss B opened her heart in the P.M. while Uncle John was making some calls and has been having a hard time of it with the situation. So unpleasant.

Saturday was a perfect football day. Father is probably very proud over the big red team from Ithaca + will no doubt have a chance to gloat over me as well as John after the season is over.

We are looking forward to the weekend in Providence this Sat. when we go down for the Dartmouth game. Just a college boy again it seems, but with a little more work done during the week.

Wednesday the Hoopers came down from Worcester for dinner + we had a pleasant evening with "shop" not taking up all the time.

Joan has a girl who can come in any time + although she is green she will probably be of some help + allow her a little freedom.

We've been trying to figure some way of getting to Montclair + get a few winter things + return some of our summer clothes, but it seems almost impossible at present + expensive. When you get organized do you suppose you could look up a few things for us? I have no coat or hat or mason-working clothes + while sweaters + the old top coat from Sakonnet will do for awhile I feel a little bare. Joan too needs a coat. Would it be too much trouble to put a few of these things in that old suitcase of Mary's + send it express collect to us? The suitcase now contains my working clothes + winter things. I don't need them all. In fact, just a leather coat + pair of heavy underwear will be enough, for I have everything else that is necessary. My brown top coat should be hanging in one of the bags in the upstairs closet + my brown hat is in a marked hat box there also – the hat could go in the suitcase also for a little crushing won't hurt it much – the only thing Joan wants is the tweed coat you helped select for her. If these things are not hanging in the closet they will be in the top of the trunk. If you could get Father to throw in his hydraulics books I would love food for thought – also if he has "Calculus Made Easy" or something like that it would be helpful. The suitcase is probably in the store room. Enough of this.

Pixie looks very cute + grown up in her nice winter suit which she wore yesterday. You know the pink one you bought her? Your birthday card to her has just come + she had the best time with it fingering the faces of the dolls + kitten at the table. Her birthday wire from grandpa was of course her first telegram + while I wasn't here to witness her joy am sure she was very thrilled.

(Joan's writing now appears in the letter)

I see this letter needs the feminine touch. I've been storing up news for you all week + now I'll have to put off writing all the details for I've acquired a beautiful cold. Now, I know you are saying "she got over-tired" which I freely admit this time, but I'm busily dosing myself with 3x tablets + will be fine tomorrow. The temptation of having all our friends over was too much for me but now we're reaping the rewards for we're being asked out for dinner now that I have someone to "sit on" (as the Radcliffe self-help girls term it) The Pix. She's only 18 and green as grass. I quaked the first time I left her alone with Pix and Pixie scowled at her menacingly!

Her birthday was a colossal success - for her parents - but she had much celebration the Thursday before. Helen Dean Floan's daughter was her only guest but we had a very gay party. Chocolate fudge cake with 2 candles which rather bored them, but not us. The toys were all wrapped up in red paper with Harvard stickers all over them. I've subsequently seen both the wrapping paper + bits of the stickers. We went for a walk + posed for pictures until I realized the camera was devoid of film, so her birthday picture in her birthday coat will be taken this Thursday. It's a perfect fit, + would you believe it? – her head has grown to fit the hat! Mary + Genie's birthday gift deserve a separate letter. With a good stiff brush, Mary, she really can have pigtails now. She has developed a habit (which she thinks is very cute) of squinting + blinking at lights + when I presented her with the brush she had the grace to blink at all the silver. I like to think she said "baby" on her first birthday, but it takes Jenny's imagination to believe it. However, she knows what the word means + goes into perfect ecstasy over herself in the mirror. She sticks out her tongue and then howls with laughter.

I was a bit quaky about taking her to Uncle John's Sunday but she turned out to be a lamb. Mabel Jones was completely won over by her smile which she turns on in a shy abrupt fashion. Mrs. Curtis freely

Motherhood

admitted she didn't like children so I kept Pix out of her way. Why the meal went smoothly I don't know, for I was asked to sit at the head of the table to enable the secret to be kept. Uncle John had the bell, a Radcliffe girl was serving, + Rebecca was mad in the kitchen. Uncle John was so busy carving Roosevelt along with the turkey that if the Radcliffe girl hadn't been good we should have starved. Miss Jones + I are neighbors, so I guess we're in the right section!

This letter is full of Pix, but as Gramp says, the world is full of babies. My world is <u>very</u> full, but it is a nice world – especially in Cambridge.

Thank you all ever so much for making Pix's birthday so exciting.

Much love,
Joan

Letter after Thanksgiving

Thanksgiving 1937

Dear everyone -

My desk arrived Saturday, so now that we are contemplating breaking up housekeeping, the apartment contains all of the furniture we contracted for!

Each day I've put off writing for I thought we would have evolved some plan of campaign to tell you about. Grandpa Cole's letter and Hoop's from Worcester, and the remote possibility of more work here have put a halt to the making of any plans for the present. I do want you and Gramp to know how nice it makes us feel to have you hold the doors of 133 open to us. We'll never feel that we're without a home as long as you make us seem so welcome. As soon as we know anything definite about the future I'll let you know promptly.

Such activity this weekend! Friday night Shaw called Harry Ingersol to come down and spend Saturday night. In the meantime I had asked Bill Stearns (Aunt Birtha's nephew) and Hellen Flemming for dinner. While we were waiting for Harry's call to come through, Doc called and said he and Mart would like to come for the weekend - well! When Doc had planned to visit us, that plan had to go through, for he had never darkened any of our doors, so we said come along. I even painted a great big sign - "Welcome Rolly" - and hung it over the mantle. When Harry called we asked him for dinner, and not for the night. Golf plans were made for Sunday morning with Uncle John, and he asked us all for dinner - thank goodness!

Saturday morning I pulled the studio couch into and made a bedroom out of Pixie's room, made a tremendous batch of waffles and then Pixie and I went down to the stadium to see the Westpointers march in. Pix was distantly bored with all the handsome uniforms but loved the band and the horses. I held her in my arms so she could see

Motherhood

and she spent most of the time grabbing for the fuzzy curls on a little boy in front of her. Mary, here's something for you to do in the far future - try wheeling a baby the wrong way on the Lars Anderson bridge ten minutes before the Army Harvard game. When I think of all the times I've walked with the crowd to those games, thinking I was the stuff + how much more the stuff I felt this one Saturday with my little Pix.

Well, Doc + Mart arrived, Harry + Dick + Shaw arrived and finally Uncle John + Belle arrived. Both of my other guests called to say they couldn't accept so we sat down only seven. I had borrowed an extra waffle iron and we split some of the artichokes in two as well as the meringues I'd made for dessert. I think everyone was satisfied.

Next morning the boys played golf with Uncle John + Dr. Hooker. Mart stayed with Pix and I went over to assist Rebecca. Uncle John had engaged two Radcliffe girls. Rebecca gave me complete charge of setting the table, but I was instructed not to use any of the Rose canton. I thought of Aunt Alice as I hunted around for the things and wondered if I was using many things ordinarily reserved for state occasions. It really was a funny situation, for though Ms. Barnes was there, I was the official hostess. The two Radcliffe girls were so cute with their printed directions on how to serve. They knew much more than I did about it. I went through all of the different courses with them + everything was under control when Uncle John came scurrying in, flourishing two bottles of champagne + with the news that there would be no ice cream for dessert. Shaw came in with some cheese from our house under his arm so that changed the courses somewhat and called for champagne glasses etc. About then the Hookers, Mart + Doc and Pixie arrived and Belle hustled upstairs for more fruit knives which were under lock and key somewhere. Finally, we all settled down to what was a veritable feast. Really a complete Thanksgiving dinner from soup to cigars, deliciously cooked + admirably served. By the end of the meal we were all stuffed to the ears and grateful beyond words to Uncle John. Pixie was an angel, staying in her crib all of the time when I know she yearned to inspect the countless gadgets in the various rooms, but the floors were not exactly in condition for a creeping child.

I can't wait for you to see her, for Mart and I cut bangs yesterday morning and she looks more like you than ever Grand Mary. She tatters around the apartment in a rapid fashion now that she has some new shoes with heavy soles.

We're taking her out to see Aunt Mary this afternoon. I had Grace for tea the other day + also cousin Harriet Ellis, thinking it would be nice for them to know each other, but one had to leave before the other arrived.

Mary, I had another "day" in Boston last week + this time I did "arts and crafts", "Irving and Casson", + Beacon Hill. Oh, what fun!

I've tentatively allied myself with the Christ Church guild and tomorrow I'm serving at the Congregational Church Luncheon. Oh yes, there are lots of things to do in this fair city of Cambridge, and now I wish I had crowded my days even fuller.

This is <u>not</u> getting my Monday cleaning done, though there are many more things to say. We may be seeing you soon, though, who knows?

Loads and loads of love,
Joan

Shaw's sister Mary and Bill Jordan get married in February 1938

Letter to Aunt Marion Gilbert, Sister of Mother Edith Getchell

August 30, 1938 - Monday 6 P.M.
Truesdale Hospital
Fall River, Mass.

Dearest Aunty -

I had a long letter started you to[sic] when I was s6ezzed[sic]. But I noow[sic] have much more important news for you (in case you haven't already heard!) A 6 lb. 9 oz boy with no effort at all!

I felt the pangs while making Doc's bed this morning (the maids would be in town) but everybody was around me so we took off in great style – Shaw Mart & me. I had frequent pains all the way up & Shaw couldn't wait to get me there swathed as I was in bath towels all the way but didn't really need to use them. From my very first pain until the baby arrived it was less than 2 hours. When I got here they gave me some stuff to make me sleepy which didn't at all so they gave me another dose. In the meantime the baby gave three big pushes and was born. I remember every minute of it. Saw them hold up the baby & heard it bawl immediately. They were surprised it bawled so quickly. the minute he arrived I felt too wonderful but I have been desraly ful[sic] under the influence of sodium amitol[sic] all afternoon so that's[sic] it's evening now that I have reached a certain degree of coherency![27] I wrote out a list of things I wanted from home & couldn't read it myself afterwards!

The baby was born a half an hour after I got here & believe me I didn't waste any time en route. We had a cop meet us at Tiverton to lead the way & they say he got here punctually after the baby was born! – trailing us instead of leading us.

Everyone was home when I was seized – except the maids. Gram

---

27 This letter is full of spelling and grammatical errors due to the sodium amytal (a type of sedative) that Joan was on for childbirth. We have left these in throughout the letter.

242

Cole came down to take Pixie so she wasn't neglected!

The letter I wrote you was all about your troubles but I must admit I'm a little fuzzy to get down to anything serious.

(for the Coles)

I think we'll call the baby Getchell Brewster Cole or otherwise G. Brewster Cole but keeps[sic] it until your what (aside from family) cause we aren't sure yet.

Well goodbye by Aunty & all. Y[sic] you can decipher this.

I feel wonderful
Joan

List written at Truesdale Hospital (just after Bruce was born)

August 29th, 1938

From letter "Dear Aunty" (8/30): "I wrote out a list of things I wanted from home & couldn't read it myself afterwards!"

<u>First Try:</u>
Suitces slooink
In my crise colest
Bornns pipis yien mit ma
You have trunk scaesboate my room
Matches
Rest in tbmattantin
In
<u>Grood</u> cough
Matches
Ciegrestes (good
They
ABD Taste wonder
Ad to ?!????
Call nurse – Mart
WWire A. Marion
2 good non tashnravle ashtrays
Ripe olives
Get it?

<u>Second try</u>; scrawled but legible,
Bring A.B.D. tablets &….?
Wire At. Marion
Cock.

Motherhood

Cigarettes
Blanket Alva made for baby crib
Trunk suit case in my small closet
Almahin
Get in touch with practical nurse
Glass beerry dishes for ashtrays 4 of th
Long mirror to my make up box
Ripe olives W.H.P.
Wire alsae
Tell Sg bhilly's
Call A. Lenea
Peg Lanpher
A. Blanche
Rader
Check book
Investment
Inp Blaet Ship
Pads
Enchanted byeke
Scisses
Alberts wife

Part of the list Joan wrote, uncharacteristically messy and full of spelling errors

Shaw and Joan the day Bruce was born

Shaw, Bruce, and Joan

Letter to Aunt Marion after Sakonnet Hurricane

September, 1938 - Wednesday

Dearest Aunty -

I had a day letter composed to send you advising that we were safe & sound but by the time I was able to send it via Western Union word had been sent to you and I hated to clutter the wires with unnecessary messages.

Celie has no doubt forwarded my letters by now so you have the story of our flight from Colecot to the Taylor's house. The damage to our house cannot even be mentioned when we look across to the point & realize how many people are really homeless. It was a wild wild storm alright & left Sakonnet a scene of desolation. We've taken countless pictures & if they are <u>ever</u> developed I'll send them to you eventually!

We were planning to reshingle our houses to the tune of a thousand dollars this fall. Needless to say we will spend the money in rebuilding the porch, front yard & seawall!

Did I write you that my nurse got sick & had to leave when the baby was not quite 3 weeks old! Thank goodness she left before the storm. I got an <u>excellent</u> local girl who was with Mrs. Cole this summer & takes entire charge of Pixie. I took charge of the baby & found that a second child was 3 times as easy as a first for I knew this one wouldn't break. Mrs. Cole went to Montclair Sunday for a week & Jessie was to come & stay with me so I wouldn't be alone nights, but she became sick with a cold so Genie came to the rescue. We're really having a beautiful time for the weather is glorious now. I can't say so much for the view from the Cole's house, for the land from the terrace down is strewn with wreckage & P.E.A. workers. You see <u>all</u> of Sakonnet Point came in to this cove and we can recognize most all of the debris.

<u>How</u> about you? We've scanned the papers for Hanover items but

we have found nothing. Where was Lou (a freshman at Wheaton)? I imagine Hat was O.K. except for trees & wire danger. Am wondering if your garden looks anything like the ones around here.

Genie & I spend most of our time sitting in the car listening to the terrible dispatches from Europe. Of all times not to have electricity! The pump goes by electricity so all the water has to be carried in, though we don't have to do it ourselves. You should see Genie holding the flashlight turned on the baby's bottom while I change his diapers. I might say we've enjoyed several illuminated fountain displays – little boys are different, I find, and this one always aims right straight up in the air.

When I see you again I'll tell you more of our experience. We're staying until Oct. 15th. Genie wants to say a word so bye bye.

Much love,
Joan

Article from the Woonsocket Call

Friday September 23rd, 1938

Sakonnet Point Is Scene Of Devastation In Wake
Thrilling Stories Of Tidal Wave Are Told By Residents Of Little Compton Summer Colony

Sakonnet Point in Little Compton, which included many Woonsocket people in its summer colony, is a scene of devastation and ruin.

Thrilling stories of the washing out to sea by tidal waves of cottages, stores, and other buildings at "The Point" are being told. Four fishermen floating out to sea on the roof of the Frank Grinell garage and fishermen's dormitory, a three story structure, were saved by Ray Briggs, another fisherman, whose boat was one of the two at Sakonnet Point wharf which were not washed out to sea and lost. He maneuvered his craft so that he brought it alongside of the floating structure, held it there, while the sea raged, until the four fishermen who were on the roof, jumped to safety into his boat. Veteran fishermen, trained in the dangers of the sea, said that this rescue was the most thrilling episode in all their recollections. The structure had so sunk beneath the waves, that only its roof with its human cargo was visible, and, at times, the waves washed over and almost tore the desperate fishermen from their precarious perch.

Col. Henry C. Card of Greene street, accompanied by his daughter, Miss Helen L. Card of New York City, who has been here for a few days visiting her parents, motored to Sakonnet last Tuesday, as the former desired to care for some minor repairs at the Buell Cottage on Beach road, one half of which is owned jointly by Mrs. Gertrude (Buell) Card and Mrs. Harriet (Buell) Hudson of this city. They arrived home late yesterday afternoon, filled and thrilled by the experiences which they and their neighbors had undergone since last Wednesday, when between 4:30 and 6:30 o'clock tidal waves covered the Beach road section of Sakonnet Point. The waves ripped away heavy sea walls, tore into the cottages and other structures in this section, and carried many of these dwellings and other buildings out to sea.

Buildings Swept Into Ocean

The Buell cottage, half of which is owned as above, and the other half by Miss Louise Mencke of Providence, is still standing, but its porches were washed away and its roof damaged, and half its sea wall torn away. Adjoining sea walls were also washed away.

Further down on the Beach road, the Frank Grinnell house, Thayer's Spa, owned by George Thayer, a native of Bellingham, and his wife, a group of cottages owned by the Thayers, W.H. McCormic's ("Mack's") combination barber shop and variety store building, Wilbur's Grocery, Michael Rogers' Fo'castle restaurant, bowling alley and dance hall, all on the oceanfront, were torn from their foundations by the tidal waves and washed out to sea. This happened also to the Bluff Head fish market at the Sakonnet Point wharf.

Occupants Fled To Safety

Before these buildings were torn from their foundations and washed into the ocean, the occupants, warned by the fury of the storm, had fled to safety, and there were no casualties in the Sakonnet cottage colony.

An automobile owned by the proprietor of the Bluff Head fish market, was swept with other machines into the harbor, and in the machine was a large purse or bag containing the savings of the proprietor of the fish market.

On the harbor side of Beach road, Wilcox's fish sheds were swept away and so was Grinnell's garage, a three-story structure, with garage on the first floor, cooking and dining quarters on the second floor, and also sleeping quarters and fishermen's dormitories on the third floor. Also the large building housing Michael Rogers' big general store on the harbor side of Beach road was carried away by the tidal waves and so were a number of fishermen's homes, as was also a large restaurant building at the junction of Beach road and West Main road, and a number of other structures. The harbor shores were swept.

The tidal waves also swept ten automobiles and two trucks into the harbor where they were submerged during Wednesday night and until yesterday afternoon, when chains and ropes were attached to them and they were hauled out on dry ground.

Wholesale Looting Of Cottages

Soon after the tidal waves had swept Sakonnet Point, scores of automobiles with Massachusetts registrations, many of them from Fall River, swarmed to the scene, and wholesale looting began.

Sides of cottages which were not swept to sea were torn away, doors and windows blown in, and the section afforded a fruitful harvest for people bent on looting. Household furniture, bedding, clothing, etc. were stolen from houses which had been opened by the storm for such nefarious work, and men came in trucks and were carrying away furniture, clothing etc.

State Troopers stopped one group of men who had loaded their loot of furniture, etc. on to two trucks and were carrying it away. The Troopers, busy with highway and rescue work, did not arrest the perpetrators. After this, State Troopers guarded the scene to prevent further robberies. Soon afterwards the Little Compton town council, in a special session, deputized a number of extra constables, and these men, armed with shotguns, stood guard and prevented further looting.

Col. Card and his daughter, as stated, left Woonsocket Tuesday, spent the night in the Buell cottage, and remained there until the storm and the waves had washed away the sea wall and had started to rip off the plaza roof. This was at about 4:30 o'clock Wednesday afternoon.

At that time the Beach road was flooded nearly knee deep, and they and other cottagers were led to safety by volunteers who, despite the fact that they wore hip boots, were drenched to the skin, and were assisted to higher land. Fully 60 to 70 of them were quartered in the McCauley House on the highest point of land in that section. This property, as well as much more Sakonnet real estate, is owned by Dr. Henry D. Lloyd, State senator from Little Compton.

Wade To Safety

These cottagers and others remained at the McCauley house until low tide at midnight, when they were led through water knee deep, and higher in places, by Chief of Police Pettee of Little Compton and other policemen and volunteers aided by State Troopers, and were quartered around in homes in that section and other portions of Little Compton Commons.

Many of the fishermen at Sakonnet not only lost their homes but they also lost all of their belongings except the clothes which they wore.

During Wednesday night and Thursday morning there were heart rending scenes as husbands and wives searched for one another and for their children.

At Little Compton Commons, just before school let out, the steeple fell from the Congregational Church and smashed a hole in the roof, but no one was hurt.

After the tidal waves had subsided, watchers saw several bodies floating by The Sakonnet Point wharf and out to sea. Information was telephoned around that all the school children were saved, although some of them, because of the tornado, were not sent to their homes but were quartered in families near the school house.

Col. Card and his daughter remained at the Sakonnet scene Thursday, until his automobile had been pulled from the flooded Beach road section and they were able to proceed back to Woonsocket, getting here late in the afternoon. He, Mrs. Card and Helen all went to Sakonnet this morning to salvage additional clothing and bed linen from the Buell cottage.

Many Woonsocket Colonists

Among the colonists from Woonsocket and vicinity in the Sakonnet section is Mrs. Arthur Ingraham, formerly of Oakland, whose cottage is located in Taylor Lane.

Cottages at Sakonnet are owned or rented, by Edwin A. Farnell, the H. Eugene Getchell heirs, Mrs. M. Leslie Hough, Miss Jennie N. Sales, John R. Boyden, Rene J.B. Delys, Ariel B. Edwards, Ervin S. Dunn, all of Woonsocket, and Edward H. Rathbun of Providence, formerly of this city, William B. Dunn of Providence, formerly of this city, and others.

None of these structures was seriously damaged, but shingles or slates on the roofs of most of them were "ruffled" and slightly damaged, and other minor damages reported.

Telephone messages to Woonsocket from the Sakonnet section yesterday afternoon reported that all of the Woonsocket people, some of whom had remained in Sakonnet and some of whom had gone down to pick up their belongings, prior to going home at the end of the season, were safe.

Article from The Woonsocket Call

Friday, September 30, 1938

No Cause For Alarm In Storm Warnings, Boston Bureau Says

Boston, Sept. 30, (AP) - The Boston Weather Bureau reported today that storm warnings posted last night should give New Englanders "no cause for alarm ."

The bureau said that high winds would reach a velocity of probably 40 - miles an hour "out to sea," but added they probably would not be nearly so severe inland.

Former Resident Beats Hurricane

Mrs. E. Shaw Cole, Once Joan Getchell Tells Of Sakonnet Experience

Mrs. E. Shaw Cole of Montclair, N.J. who before her marriage was Miss Joan Getchell of this city, is counted among those who fortunately escaped with her life when the hurricane struck with its force along the Rhode Island beaches last week.

Mrs. Cole, her two year old daughter, Joan Shaw Cole and her infant son, Getchell Brewster Cole, had been enjoying the beautiful September days as a guest of Mr. Cole's mother, Mrs. Edward S. Cole at her summer home in Taylor's Lane at Sakonnet. When the storm broke, Mrs. Cole noticed the water rapidly rising around the cottage and hurrying the junior Mrs. Cole and the two children into their automobile, she drove through the storm to the main road only to find it blocked. Driving through fields, with tremendous difficulty she succeeded in reaching the Taylor home, which was on higher ground and safe from the rising water.

Driving close to the door of the home, the two women and the children had just reached safety inside the house when a huge fieldstone chimney fell on top of the automobile and entirely demolished it. Other than the fireplace and chimney the Taylor home, formerly the Dr. Slicer place, was unharmed, and all its occupants safe.

Joan in Sakonnet before the hurricane

Letter to her sister Ceci after the Hurricane

September, 1938 - Saturday aft.
After Hurricane

Dearest Ceci -

Just had your letter & one from Shaw saying you weren't going to Winchester. We've all wondered how we can get in touch with you to tell you we were safe.

Shaw has probably shown you my letter to him so won't repeat anything. Today the roads are being guarded by men in uniforms which I suppose means martial law, and we have to have passes (issued by Mrs. Almy at the P.O.) to get by. The local police have been <u>wonderful</u> & all the natives have been heroic.

Mart Gene & Doc came down to our house yesterday and Dick and Genie later in order to collect stuff in our house. They may have written you about what they did. The day after the storm Mrs. Taylor, Gram & I went down to view the remains and I was honestly thrilled to see the house still <u>standing</u>. Bob Palmer & Evie were guarding it against looters for the glass porch was gone thus the living room door was open. We got Roy Wilbur and he and Bob boarded the door and the skylight and bathroom window which were broken. Evie had actually thrown out a fish which was on the living room floor! They wouldn't let me walk over the debris to the house so I haven't actually been in it, but Mart & Doc say the living room furniture can be cleaned. The upstairs is perfectly O.K. I had Steve Wilbour go down & inspect the sea wall & figure out about filling in the front land. Also he was to bolster up the roof over where the glass porch <u>used</u> to be & inspect the foundations. Those must be tended to right away and we can decide later about further work. Mart & I both burst out with the idea of making one corner of the new porch into a bedroom - cause Celie - there's no great joy in looking across the harbor at a barren wasteland of a point! Everything below the house Lloyd moved across the road is gone, nothing left around the harbor at all. Every shingle on our house is intact, by the way, all of the houses with those fake shingle roofs lost most of the shingles. Needless to say we can wait to reshingle & use the money to repair the house. The garage & cottage are perfectly O.K. Poor Osbornes! Eleanor was there, tears running down her cheeks, for the front of their house just was gone with the wind. <u>Thank goodness</u> I had Kinnicut paint the Point!! Doc & Mart & Genie & Dick are coming down tomorrow. They've got Lawrence cleaning out the mud a foot deep in the cellar - so glad the boys cleaned it out this summer.

We've just come back from Warrens Point to view what was the beach. The bathhouses are in the lot across the road which is now beach also. The whole contour is changed & your eyes get mixed up looking for old nooks & crannies.

The Coles & Thomas lots now contain Sakonnet Point. Tell Margie that the geese she photographed (Mrs. Gray's) were swept by here via the sea & waddled around among the wreckage till claimed. The Sak. Spa sign, the bowling alleys, the Focastle piano etc. etc. etc. were some of the things found among the countless barrels, spas, nets, furniture, bits of houses & 14 boats on the lawn.

Gram was a heroine, taking charge of all of us. We departed when the waves reached the Cole's terrace but we found they never got any nearer. My only bad moment was when they told us we'd have to walk out - with two babies & a recuperating pelvis and formula and snuggle bunnies etc. As Shaw told you we did drive finally, but I sure felt like Tess of the Storm Country.

We were in roses at the Herbert Taylors. Four maids & finger bowls. I was treated as the interesting invalid so didn't lift a finger.

Pixie & Getchell Brewster had a whirl. I had to change his formula and luckily Dr. Harold Taylor arrived on the scene to advise me! He gained ¼ of a pound so I guess he thrives on hurricanes.

The tragedies that befell so many people make our material losses seem like nothing. 5 or 6 fishermen lost their lives & Mr. & Mrs. Fontaine of Woon. were drowned. Also Mrs. Stone Douglas on Long Island. We can hardly feel badly at having lost a front porch and a little furniture!

Yes <u>do</u> get me some shoes. I sent to Ballous in Prov. for some but they were submerged to their second story so don't expect them. Enclosed is a drawing of Pixie's enormous foot! Please send <u>high</u> white ones. I think air mail is the best bet.

Of course there were all kinds of humorous incidents connected with the past week. I'll tell you everything when I see you on the 16th. Until then bye.

Much love -
Joan

I wish the electricity would come back! We need the pump!

Sakonnet Point painted by Richard Kinnicutt in 1938 just before the Sakonnet Hurricane. The original was donated to the Little Compton Historical Society for its permanent collection. It also graces the cover of this book in magnificent color.

My Book of Happy Memories

Pixie's Baby Book Story of the 1938 Hurricane
By Mom Joan E.G. Cole

On the afternoon of the hurricane you were very excited when Grandma + I returned from Warren's Point where we had driven to see the surf. As I entered the house you ran to me and though you couldn't talk very much you called, "Beach, Mummy, Beach!" I looked out of the dining room windows and saw why you were excited for the beach was getting nearer and nearer Grandpa's house. We stood and watched the waves bounding over the lawn and each one came closer to the house. Grandma's sundial blew away and you thought that was very funny. When the heavy terrace chairs blew over the stone wall you thought that was even funnier, but when, within a few minutes, the waves began to curl around the terrace steps, we decided it wasn't a bit funny and we prepared to leave. The wind was howling so hard that we could barely hear the man who dashed in the house to tell us we'd have to wade to Taylor's Lane for the road was washed out.

"Somebody will have to carry my Pixie," I shouted through the wind and looked around to find you just climbing off the dining room table with your hands and mouth full of grapes. I guess you knew we were all too busy and excited to care. What <u>will</u> my Pixie wear, I wondered suddenly, for you didn't have anything but summer clothes. You didn't even have any shoes for your piggies had gotten so big they wouldn't fit. You didn't even have a coat so I grabbed a big blanket to wrap around you. We piled your snuggle bunny + some other clothes in another blanket + tied it in a knot. A man came to the door and said "Can I carry your little girl for you?" He looked big and strong so I was about to say yes when Roy Wilbur, Grandpa's caretaker rushed in the house and said he would break down a stone wall so we could drive through the fields. I was so relieved to know that now you wouldn't get wet and cold and blown around. We hurriedly piled lots of your things in the car and were ready to go when suddenly I looked up and saw your nurse carrying you out to her car. There was no time to lose so Grandma, Bruce and I drove through the wall in her car and you followed with Georgie and Margie in their car. I kept wishing you were sitting in my lap and looked back often to see if you were following. When we got through the fields to the main road I looked again and couldn't see the car you were in. We waited a few minutes and still you didn't come, so we drove back to where we could see your car in the fields, but it wasn't moving at all. Just then, a man appeared in a truck and Grandma shouted through the wind, "My little granddaughter is down there in that car. Could you go and get her?" He went down and towed you out to the main road with his truck and then carried you to me. Your dress was all swirling in the wind, your hair was almost blowing off, and the rain was dashing in your face, making you squint. You did look a little scared! When he put you in the car I hugged you under my coat, and all of a sudden you thought it was fun again. Margie and Georgie dashed in, and so we drove all higglety-pigglety in the back seat to Aunt Harriet Taylor's, dodging electric wires and fallen trees in the road.

We hurried into her warm and cozy house and changed your clothes before a crackling fire. Suddenly, we heard an extra loud crackle and then a big bang. The chimney had crashed down on Grandma's auto. You jumped at the noise and then ran to the window to look – Grandma's car looked so funny – all torn and full of bricks – that you giggled and giggled.

We stayed there three nights. You had a bed right side of Grandma + you used to wake her up very early and make her talk to you. Most of your time was spent in the kitchen with Georgie + Margie and Mrs. Taylor's maids for Mrs. Taylor's living rooms were full of important looking things and you might have wanted to play with them. You seemed very glad to get back home where you could run around + not have to sit on a high stool in the kitchen.

<u>Still</u> you didn't have any shoes, and it was getting so cold that your

piggies were pink most of the time, so one day we went up to Wilbur's grocery store, and sure enough, they sold shoes. So we bought you a huge pair of brown and black boy's sneakers and you stumbled around in them till we came to Montclair. I think I will save them so that when you grow up and tell people what I've told you here, you can show them your "hurricane shoes."

MOTHERHOOD

Bruce's Baby Book Story of the '38 Hurricane
By Mom Joan E.G. Cole

You were sleeping peacefully that afternoon of September 21st. You were only 22 days old so you didn't care if the wind did howl louder and louder. You didn't even notice the waves that broke on Grandpa's lawn and that each one was surging nearer and nearer the house.

But Grandma and I noticed it! We couldn't help it, for soon the ocean was swirling around the terrace and dashing up the steps and we decided we'd better dash too! I was packing your things to put in the automobile when some men hurried into the house and said that the road was washed out so we would have to wade to Taylor's Lane. I had to think quite quickly what to do about you. I put you on the dining room table + wrapped you up in dozens of diapers. Then I folded lots of blankets around you + rolled you up in a steamer rug. The rain was coming down so hard that I tied a big rubber pad around you. Nobody could have guessed that there was a little baby boy inside that bundle. I put one of your bottles in my pocket and was just taking you in my arms when Roy Wilbur, your Grandfather's caretaker, blew into the house announcing that he would break down a stone wall so we could drive through the fields in the car. I was <u>so</u> glad, for I was afraid that I might drop you while we were wading, or that you might blow out of my arms. We jumped into the car very quickly and piled your bassinette, pads, sterilizer, bottles, suitcases, <u>everything</u> in on top of ourselves, and Grandma took us on a very bumpy ride through the fields to the main road. The wind was blowing so hard that Grandma had a hard time keeping the car on the road as we drove under broken electric wires and around fallen trees to Aunt Harriet Taylor's.

Her house looked so nice and safe and felt so warm. You and I went into a cozy room on the ground floor where a fire was crackling. I unrolled + unrolled + unrolled my bundle until finally I found your pink little toes and saw your bright sparkling eyes. It was a little past your feeding time so I gave you your supper in front of the fire. Just as I was putting your bottle in your mouth we heard a rumble overhead, and crash bang came Mrs. Taylor's chimney down into our automobile! Weren't we lucky to have gotten out of it in time?

We spent the next three nights at Mrs. Taylor's and when the road was fixed we went back to Grandpa's house which was unharmed. There wasn't any electricity – so I fed you by candle light. You didn't have any idea how exciting it was – you didn't even know it had happened. I'm pretty certain that you were the youngest person who witnessed the hurricane at Sakonnet, so someday you may be the oldest living survivor. Then you can tell your grandchildren all about what I've told you here. But you better not tell anyone you remember it for you were only 22 days old and you were sound asleep the whole time!

Faits Accompli.

1938

(Pencil rough draft notes)[28]

The Little Compton Summer Association decided to examine its past. Had it lived a good and useful life or had it led an aimless existence. A board member was asked to thumb through the records & tell all. The more she thumbed the more impressed she became with its well-rounded existence. Such versatility!

We have aided & abetted many a cause & we have accomplished some things all on our own. Remember the Sak. Hotel – that obsolete objet d'art? The S. Ass. aided in its obliteration. They dreamed up some sort of a solution to the garbage disposal problem at one time. The early records show that we were instrumental in providing suitable milk for children. Time was when there were no telephones in the Round Pond area but we saw to the extension of phones via the pond. In 1925 we anted up part of the cost of Town oiling, sanding & scraping the Warrens Point road & for scraping the now deceased road from Pruis Ledge to the bathhouses. Finally we refused to allow Long Pond to drain through Warren's Point beach any longer & thus diverted it – to where, the records didn't say.

There was a period during which the S. Ass. organized beach sports for children & arranged for an annual fireworks display at the Golf Club, had spells of violent participation in seaweed removal at the beach. Winter police protection of property was arranged for many a speed caution sign was asked for and obtained from the State Police.

The beach committee advised we purchase life belts for the Life Guards, 4 torpedo floats, an inhalator, & lifeguard chairs & we sponsored a life saving course.

---

28   These are pencil notes for a report Joan was writing for the Little Compton Summer Association.

The yacht club was conceived by the summer ass. & interest in sailing was stimulated.

Come the hurricane we gave $500 to the R.C. disaster relief & $50 toward the restoration of the Cong. Church spire & gave financial ass. toward the reconstruction of the bathhouses & beach facilities.

When the big guns came to be part of our landscape we kept the membership informed regarding the preparation of our houses for practice shots. We also donated $100 to the Army Recreational Committee.

MOTHERHOOD

Little Stories

September, 1940

BON VOYAGE[29]

"But Mummy, on the train going home, can't we sit out with the other people? That little house we had on the train going up was no fun."

The little house wasn't supposed to be fun for the children; it was supposed to be fun for Daddy and me. By the time the Pullman agent had computed the total of all the various tariffs for getting a three year old, a five year old and us to our destination, my husband said, "Lord, let's take a drawing room - it couldn't cost anymore!" So we did, and it was fun, because the children kept going out to heckle the other passengers, and we sat on the seats where you can't look out into the aisle. Because we never urged the children to come back into their little house, we had a most comfortable trip. When we arrived we were met by loving relatives who took us and our luggage on from there.

Then suddenly came Labor Day, and we heard that school began two days afterwards. So again we made reservations, and since Daddy wasn't with us, I acquiesced and got three seats out in the Pullman proper. This proved to be a smart move, because the Pullman Company had put all of the half fares in one car. It was a travelling kindergarten - lots of rich little children with nurses, whose parents knew enough not to budge from the club car. There was a charming Danish refugee with three small children. She was the chic-est refugee I've ever seen, and her children's accents made mine sound like guttersnipes. It was all very broadening and sophisticated to be traveling by her side, and save for the permanent leg injury inflicted on a tired looking grandmother by my three year old who had insisted on spinning his chair around via

---

29 Reprinted for the Junior League's Latest, a newsletter printed by the Junior League of Montclair-Newark, a volunteer organization of women.

her calf at five minute intervals, we had a gala crossing.

Having sent most of the luggage on ahead, I had only to collect one large suitcase when we got to Grand Central. We went to the luggage collection window and waited for it to come up from the train. It didn't come and it didn't come, so finally the luggage master said, "You sure this was a suitcase?" Yes, it was a suitcase, in fact it was a big suitcase. He advised me to try the trunk collection window. The children by now were no longer impressed with the grandeur of the station but they were entranced with the possibilities of the nice slippery floor. I got a porter who got my stub. He came back sweating. "Lady that IS a trunk. You'd know if you had to carry it!" I was in no mood to argue the point as to when a suitcase becomes a trunk, and handed him an enormous tip for putting it on the taxi.

Shortly we arrived at the bus terminal which on that day resembled the General Motors exhibit, but miraculously there was a Montclair bus just pulling in. I threw the children on. They made themselves completely at home, spreading out their dolls, flashlights and sweaters over several desirable seats, while I stood outside waiting to get the bag put on. After another enormous tip the bag landed against the bus driver's shins. "No you don't, Lady, that trunk don't go in here." "Where does it go?" "Nowhere, this isn't that kind of bus." Just then the dispatcher came by. He was kind but firm, "Not a chance, madam, you see we're all jammed up with people coming home from their vacations." I felt like showing him my bathing suit mark.

"All right, children, get off while I check this thing in the bus station overnight. We'll take the next one." "Big stinky-pig bus," they kept saying sotto voce. The porter lugged what was technically now called a trunk to the checking compartments, and it wouldn't fit. I sent him next door to a hotel to see if they would store it. They wouldn't. I paid the porter another week's rent, bought the children a candybar of their own choice, and there we stood, a pretty tableau entitled "Frustration and Her Two Children and a Trunk." First I thought of auctioning the bag off, but I knew nobody would listen. Then I thought of Hoboken. Next I went to the information window. What was the easiest way to get to New Jersey? By bus, madam. No, I mean the second easiest way. Well, you take the Sixth Avenue trolley down to… I simply walked away. I went back and started all over, "I am a problem, not just an ordinary traveler. In fact, I've turned out to be a convoy. Look us over and tell us how to get to Montclair." That was different, so he explained the Hudson Tubes and Hoboken to me. The same porter was lurking around. He knew if I stayed much longer he could afford to retire. He got us in a cab, and I handed him enough to buy the chicken farm free and clear. To the driver I said, "New Jersey, please," and then realized I was getting giddy. I corrected myself in time to stop him at the 34th St. tube entrance. My son tinkered with the meter while the driver went in search of a porter. I hoped he'd break it. A ninety-seven-year old man finally appeared and dragged the trunk down to the subway and heaved it through the open door, for which service he was handsomely rewarded. It was rush hour. Roughly five hundred people lurched over it on their way in and the same number on their way out. The one man in the car who looked at me twice helped me drag it out at Hoboken and swore he'd send a porter down. We all sat on the trunk and waited. "Are we moving and what on?" asked my three year old. "No, we're quiet and still way underneath the ground," I said. (Wouldn't I love to be!) The porter came, and I gave myself up now. At least we were in New Jersey. We got on a nice crowded commuting train full of nobody I knew and fell into a taxi in Montclair.

When we arrived at our doorstep there was a florist box waiting. I opened it and saw it was from my far away husband. "Who sent you those, Mummy?" I thought back to the day when we left for the summer with Daddy in charge of us and the luggage that had been such a lovely, carefree trip. With a tender note in my voice I answered her, "Raymond Whitcomb[30], dear."

---

30   Raymond & Whitcomb Company was an international travel agency based in Boston, MA.

Article from the Elmira Star-Gazette about Shaw

Nov 27, 1941

E. SHAW COLE, engineer in charge of a wastewater survey being made for the Elmira Water Board, is pictured with some of his apparatus. The rod, which he is holding in picture at left is inserted into the water main to measure velocity of the flow. One of the rod openings faces downstream, the other upstream. The openings are connected to a glass device which records changes. Mr. Cole is shown at the right with a listening device used to find the exact location of water leaks after the general location has been determined. Inset photo shows a split main on Morningside Dr. just south of Church St. which discharged 25,000 gallons of water a day before it was discovered.

Youth Today[31]

November, 1941

My just barely four year old son has gone all out for the military. He lugs around all sorts of junky toy rifles, pistols, sabers, and hangman ropes, leaving them conveniently on stairs and across thresholds so that wherever he might happen to be, he can quickly grab a weapon and guard himself against any number of different enemies. I'm supposed to be scared to death of him from breakfast to supper time, and I have to "stick 'em up" under the most impossible circumstances.

Of all his military equipment the pointed weapons stir his imagination the most. A nice clean bullet wound is not to his taste. His mythical hand to hand conflicts have to involve gore, and plenty of it. "Jabbing the enemy" is his most successful technique and he's not above doing it from the rear, as I well know.

In an attempt to supply my children with something besides food, baths, and cross words, each evening after their supper I take off my apron and compose myself on the couch with them. Unconsciously, I suppose it's a desire on my part to have them go to bed thinking that I am the most-fun-mother-in-the-world. Mostly always we read, but on this particular night we had gone in for high art. "Mornings with Masters of Art," was the book and it was full of all the familiar famous paintings; the kind of thing everyone's grandmother used to buy, and I suppose they even used to read it mornings.

The children were starry-eyed at the beautiful costumes on the ladies and the suits of armor on the men. Every spear and sword was scrutinized by my son and their jabbing qualities discussed. But when we came to Titian's reproductions I could see that they were all too tame for his macabre taste when suddenly I turned the page to "Sacred and Profane Love." As you know, in that painting, Profane is totally

---

[31] By Joan Getchell Cole. Reprinted from the League's Latest.

dishabille whereas "Sacred" is all wrapped up. I was fumbling around in my mind for a plausible but expurgated explanation of the allegory when I saw that the significance bothered my son not at all. His eyes were glued on swathed "Sacred." Finally he looked up and whistled with admiration, "Boy, Mummy, she couldn't get jabbed, could she!"

The Leisured Class[32]

February, 1942

Tapering, jungle red fingernails; shiny page boy bob; lips beautifully carved out of what must be red lead; mauve stockinged legs built for trucking - and she trucked right out of my house.

I refer to my last maid servant. Believe me, they are the leisured class. She only had to work here. I have not only to work here, but I have to play here. I have to be awfully glad to see people here. I have to love to read stories out loud here. I even have to look beguiling here.

"It takes a heap o' living to make a house a home". I see what he means now. I have to live through a gulping breakfast, a grubby dinner, a frustrated lunch and a candle-lit failure at night; and the heap he spoke of was the heap o' dishes. Why, if I laid all the dishes I use in a day end to end, I'd still have to do them the next day.

However, it's my home and I'm stuck with it. There are a good many compensations I'm told, but so far, I'm not in a position to quote. Maybe they will manifest themselves when I acquire a certain degree of skill. I may even feel like those lyrical housewives who write articles about "the crispy beauty of carrots"- coming too late for the children's lunch, or the "satisfaction a woman feels as she bends over her cozy stove" watching the cream sauce lump. As I say, though, skill may bring release of nobler thoughts, but in the meantime my musings could hardly be called lofty. As I bump the carpet sweeper into all the ogee feet, I think thoughts like these:

Which shall I do - dust mop, or give the children a bath? If I clean the house the children will get it dirty, and if I clean the children the house will get them dirty. Oh, you know you can't win - you've got to do both.

I see now why soap operas talk about soap on Mondays; it's because

---

[32] Reprinted from The League's Latest.

you do the wash on Monday. I wish I could understand the book of directions about the washing machine. The maid didn't have to wear rubbers when she did the wash.

How does anyone with an allergy dare to shake a dust mop - and how can you possibly get to leeward with the storm windows on?

When I finally get the right nozzle on the right end of the vacuum cleaner I look as if I were playing living statues - you guessed it - the Laocoön.

What were all those stupid reasons I gave for buying an ice box instead of a mechanical refrigerator? Probably some artistic idiosyncrasy about liking nice, big angular chunks instead of all those cloudy little squares. Then there was something about all those moving parts. Since the big freeze came last week, there certainly ARE no moving parts, the water won't even move through the outside drain, and three times a day I have to go out with a kettle of boiling water and thaw it out by hand. It's a funny world when you have to melt the ice so your ice-box will work.

Maybe all those dreamy lotions you hear about on the morning programs do keep hands soft like velvet, but I'm way beyond those. What I need is saddle soap!

And so my thoughts run on - gay and merry and carefree. Just a LITTLE WOMAN IN THE HOME doing her little bit to make her nest a happy one for her little family. It's such a little thing to do, but it's too big for me!

Fireside Chat[33]

September, 1942

Suddenly this issue has to go to press tomorrow morning, days earlier than planned. Your president and I conferred over the phone. Each of us promised to type until our index finger gave out tonight, then call each other tomorrow morning. So I arrange myself as comfortably as possible around the typewriter - shirtsleeves rolled up, green eyeshadow shield and long cigar. I title myself "Genius at Work," and commence. Oh, O, I think, genius is going to become a mother any minute for a gorgeous thunderstorm is brewing, and I have a daughter who prefers to be difficult about them. Space indicates period of time while Genius took off the green eye-shield and soothed the aforementioned with all of the old saws about how harmless thunderstorms are. She's gleeful now at the prospect of wearing her new raincoat to school - a raincoat without a molecule of rubber in it. "It must be magic that keeps you dry," she said. For $6.95 it better be magic.

So, back to the copy room I come. For lack of time and because of a spectacular absence of coordination during thunderstorms this issue will consist of a series of running comments, unedited and unrehearsed. We promise that the next issue will have more dignity and strength.

---

33 Reprinted from The League's Latest.

MOTHERHOOD

Denouement[34]

February, 1943

The other morning I woke up with a scratchy throat. It was a Monday morning - the Monday morning I was going to do the last week's wash too, on account of the holidays. It was the Monday when Christmas was definitely over. I dragged myself out of bed, washed down a handful of aspirin, and came down to get breakfast. The ground floor looked like a victorious scrap drive. The Christmas tree resembled a jaded woman and the crèche looked like any old barnyard. As I walked through the pantry I noted that last week's party hadn't been put back on the top shelves. After gathering breakfast together I glanced at the coffee supply and decided to "splice the main brace", which I think means to the English Navy an extra ration of rum.

When my little family were gathered around me at the table, things began to look up. It wasn't because of the little family, though; it was the coffee dripping down onto the aspirin. As soon as everyone cleared out I went into production. The Christmas tree was hurled out of the front door, the party platters were shoved back into their felts, and the wash went sailing through the ringer spraying buttons in all directions. Meanwhile I had continued to eat aspirin like popcorn, so that when my husband phoned I was a little giddy. "You sound funny," he said. "Oh, I'm alright." I said "I had a sore throat this morning, but it's gone now." "Now, take care of yourself, dear. I don't want you to be sick," he urged. Say, this is good, I thought, and my voice took on a frail note, "I really thought I was coming down with something," "Gee, dear," his voice sounded scared, "I'll be home early."

After lunch I gave myself up to it, as they say, and I stretched out on the bed. When the children saw me their eyes popped out of their heads. Mummy, horizontal, was news. "Are you going to die,

---

[34] The League's Latest - Mrs. E. Shaw Cole, Editor

oh don't!" wailed my six year old daughter. She immediately began to take care of me by pulling my Christmas negligee out of the closet and handing me my lipstick. Apparently I was to die like Camille. My four year old son, very protective and masculine, kept saying get Dr. Mathews. They hovered over me all afternoon and if I had been getting something I would have seemed delirious by the time Daddy came home. "Mummy might die and we're taking care of her!" the children shrieked down the stairs. He lept upstairs and found me looking frail and lovely but definitely of this world. "You stay there," he said. "I'll take over." I couldn't resist it so I said would he mind? I lay there and listened while everybody took everybody over. The conversation was low and soft and all about me. I was beautiful, I was fun and wasn't I the prettiest wife he'd ever have? Oh, yes, and they must always try to be exactly like Mummy. When they came in and said their muted goodnights I was aglow; I was sitting on a cloud in heaven. And then I heard my son jump into bed and say, "Daddy, if Mummy died, who'd cook?"

The Bergere[35]

April, 1943
Montclaire, NJ

We were two brides and two grooms living temporarily under the same roof. I can't seem to remember how we all happened to be there at the same time. The grooms were brothers and their family was abroad. I guess they offered us shelter because we didn't have any homes of our own. I do remember that we didn't have any furniture.

But we were going to. Having been given the cautious go-ahead by our husbands we girls spent the first few days in thoughtful discussions of possible decors. Dream houses were out - that we had on authority - but since our courtships had given us no delusions of grandeur that was no blow. Anyway, it wasn't grandeur we were after, it was atmosphere, and our particular brand of atmosphere, we decided, involved deep rich patinas, mellow fabrics and here and there a unique objet d'art for accent, say an old Roman lamp or something.

When at last our tasks were completely defined we decided we might as well start buying. An auction house seemed to be the most probable hunting ground and when the Park-Bernet Galleries advertised "French and English Furniture - Objects of Art - China and Silverware," we decided we'd better go that day. So, touching ourselves up like connoisseurs, we went.

When we arrived at the Galleries the auction was in full swing. Items of a rare and interesting quality were being whisked on and off the stage. We talked in hushed voices, mightily impressed. It was like being in a museum except you didn't have to walk. Number after number was knocked down before our covetous eyes until finally we realized it was high time we did some bidding ourselves. At this psychological

---
[35] The League's Latest - Mrs. E. Shaw Cole, Editor. This piece was written about a period in February 1935 when Joan and Shaw were living temporarily with Shaw's brother John and his wife Peg at Grandpa and Grandmary Cole's house at 133 Bellevue Ave, Montclair, New Jersey.

moment there appeared a chair. Now this was no ordinary chair. In fact it was a Louis 16th bergere chair. It had a molded cartouche shaped back and gently volute cabriole legs. The frame was carved with acanthus and imbricated ornaments and it was covered with rouge royale brocatelle. For atmosphere it was a natural, so I decided to bid. The bidding was brisk though not for big money but when it began to lag I got scared and stopped. My sister in law nudged me so I bid again. Someone spoiled the deal so I nudged her and she bid. Then somebody else bid so we nudged each other and we both bid. It was ours!

Exactly, it wasn't hers and it wasn't mine. It was ours. I don't remember who paid for it but I do remember struggling down 57th St. on one end of it. She'd driven the car to the nearest parking space and the porter and I wedged most of it into the rumble seat. All the way out I kept staring out the back window at the gently volute cabriole legs, gently voluting in the breeze. She wondered how the rouge royale brocatelle was doing. We still didn't know whose it was.

By the time we got home we had agreed to let the boys decide. It was to go to the husband who looked the best in it, the one who wanted it the most. En route the chair had sort of burrowed down into the rumble seat and it was no small feat to extricate it. Eventually we plumped it into the living room and then hurriedly took off our things. When we came back into the room it gave us quite a start. "Mercy, it looks big! Let's sink it into the room a little deeper," I said, so we stuck it over in a corner. "That looks as if we were ashamed of it," said my sister-in-law, so we decided on another location. We settled some end tables around it and loaded them with ashtrays and magazines. Just then we heard the boys coming up the walk and hastily agreed that if they both wanted it we'd draw lots for it.

We threw them a casual hello from the living room. They took off their things and started in to greet us, but they stopped in the doorway. They just stood there staring. For quite a while they stared. Finally one gasped, "What the H—— is that?" Gladly we told him, "It's a bergere."

The other one looked incredulous. "What's that?" he asked. "It's an armchair - the kind Louis 16th used to sit in," we explained. My husband looked perplexed. "But it's all faded," said he. "Of course it's faded," said I scornfully. "If it was the original rough royale, you'd hate it. It's mellow now." They continued to stare. "You've got the darn thing half buried," one said as he pushed aside the end tables, exposing the imbricated ornaments nicely. They stood off a bit and then they looked at each other a long time. "All right," they dared us, "Whose is it his or mine?" "But you haven't even sat in it yet - go ahead," we urged. The tall one lowered himself into it. He looked like an upset grasshopper, for though the chair was very wide and very big it was very shallow, designed to accommodate hoop skirts. "Now I understand the French Revolution," was all he said. He crawled off and bowed low to my husband who is very thick set and has a broken nose. "Your turn, sire," he said. Sire sat down and the very tall one guffawed. "Charmant," he said tenderly.

Naturally the dinner conversation centered around the bergere. The husbands kept wondering which was stuck with it and because we didn't know, we wouldn't tell them. The very tall one said he didn't know how a chair that was so big could be so uncomfortable. The thick set husband said all right, if he was stuck with it he'd throw good money after bad and insist on a slip cover, rouge royale or no rouge royale. At dessert one of them left the table and came back with Cassel's French-English dictionary. How do you spell bergere anyway? Finally we found it. He read, "'Bergere - a shepherdess, a nymph, or an armchair'." "Now listen," he said, "I'm no shepherdess, he's no nymph, and that's no armchair." That was that.

All the next morning we tried to sell it. We phoned all our friends with interesting houses, then we phoned all our friends with small husbands. Next we called the antique shops but there was no call for bergeres. Finally we called the Park-Bernet Galleries. Yes, they'd resell it that day, inasmuch as they were on the same catalogue, but we'd have to take any loss and we'd have to pay them a commission. That was easy for if the bidding ceased before it came up to the original cost we'd bid on it ourselves. It couldn't cost anything because it was ours to begin with. We had to hurry, though, so we heaved the chair into the rumble seat. It was snowing so we pinned several sheets over the brocatelle and dashed into town. I forgot to say that the roadster was bright red, sort of rough royale before it faded. As we drove up Fifth Ave, I saw our reflection in Arnold Constables, McCutcheons and Saks. The sheets had become unpinned and were fluttering out beyond the exhaust. Connoisseurs, Hah!

We couldn't park very near so we had quite a long carry. We pushed it along 57th St. to the receiving room, then went upstairs to the auction and sat down and waited. I wanted to talk very loudly about a handsome chair that was coming up for resale but my sister-in-law said no, it would look fishy. Finally it appeared and it looked small again on that enormous stage. The bidding began and it kept on without any urging from us. It was brisk. Say, maybe we'll make something on it, I thought. That would be something for the boys. But we didn't. The hammer fell on the exact same figure we'd bought it for. We departed light headed, and empty-handed for a change.

Since then a lot of furniture has come over our threshold. Some of it has come from the Park-Bernet Galleries and some of it has "atmosphere" but one chair is neither Louis nor rough royale. It's legs don't even volute. It's pure club and it came out of a Macy truck.

MOTHERHOOD

Swan Song[36]

April, 1943
Montclaire, NJ

When this last issue is proofread and the printer's ink is dry,
When the copy is thrown in the basket and editor no longer am I;
I shall wait; I can't say I'll be patient, but I'll hold my pen until
The future head of the "Latest" has empty spaces to fill.

Then I who was "We" shall be happy as I sit in a comfortable chair.
I will sharpen my index finger, and then I shall take down my hair.
The typewriter keys will shudder and regardless of where they fall
I'll send my stuff to the "Latest" and I won't correct it at all.

Yet, though the public might praise me - also the public can blame -
For I won't be the news-gathering organ so I'll have to sign my name!
"Editorial we" is a custom to which I was forced to submit,
But many a time as I read what I wrote, I was awfully glad of it.

---

36 The League's Latest. This was one of her last issues as Editor.

A Letter from Joan to Shaw's Parents after Heather was born

November 27, 1943
7:30 AM

The morning after the night before!

Dear Grandparents -

You can now draw a deep breath - & so can I! I feel perfectly splendid. Wasn't it nice that everything went according to Hoyle? I had my turkey & now my baby. I'm sure her skin will be crispy fat!

I have a nice single room with no possibility of having to share it.

Everything is heavenly –

(*Later*)

I've had a good look at Heidi (or is it Heidy?). She's my first round pink baby – but then, she had plenty of time in which to mature! She has Gram's mouth, Pixie's brow, and Abraham's nose!

My torso is in splendid condition (no rip, run or ravel!) & no muscular discomfort except afterbirth pains which are a mere nothing compared to one or two I had last night.

I can't wait to see the night nurse & Shaw to find out what happened. I had the usual hallucinations due to the dope & thought Shaw & Dr. Jones were both drunk (guess who was the drunk one!) I was incensed but thought Shaw was awfully nice to keep plunking the gas bag over my face!

I warned the nurse ahead of time that I'd try & get out of bed & apparently I did! Don't feel you must come down all the time. I'd always love to see you but remember the gas shortage.

Motherhood

Dearest love from a happy Joan

My coffee tasted splendid this morning!

Forgot to say that the modern theory is to be allowed to sit up right away & the more moving around the better. That suits me!

Letters to Mart after the birth of Heather

Dec 1, 1943
4th Day

Dear Multipera para 3 grava 3[37] -

We're twin statistics now – even to the sex. As Bruce said, when he called Gram about the baby, "I have a new sister - <u>another</u> one!"

Well, it was all very routine and unspectacular this time. Shaw got kind of tired, but I came through with no ill-effects. Twelve-fifteen, that first feeling - Shaw leapt into his pants & had me into this room before he'd had time to button his fly I'm sure. Baby came at 3 something while he sat here in an armchair watching the figures in the back delivery room through the window. I remember coming back & quietly throwing up in his face & he said I smelled so of ether he didn't dare open his mouth else he would have too. That would have been a sentimental scene.

At 7:30 next morning I was writing my usual postcards. I'm quite sure they were coherent this time. As usual, I had no muscular soreness - no rip, run, ravel or bust – in fact it says on my bedpan equipment – "Mrs. Cole – Intact."

But yes – after birth pains – one does have them, doesn't one! No matter how bad they are, there is a definite satisfaction in knowing they are <u>after</u> and not anticipatory. I keep hoping that at least they are contracting my stomach – it is <u>so</u> enormous still. A student nurse came in the night after the baby was born & said – "Oh, you still have your baby with you, haven't you!"

I find it a little hard to be whimsical over your third. After I've cooed at her for a while & they take her back to the nursery I get out the hand mirror & find myself brushing grey hairs back into place - I

---

[37] She is addressing her sister Martha, calling them twins in their successful "three for three" pregnancies. Martha was also a mother of 3 children - 2 girls and 1 boy.

Motherhood

feel definitely out of place.

Life in a maternity wing is sure different during war-time, isn't it. Gone are all of the little attentions that used to make the days glamorous. In fact, around here you get the feeling that you ought to be glad there isn't somebody in labor at the foot of your bed. My buzzer is merely obsolete electrical equipment & I pity the gal in the last room on the aisle – she probably won't see a human form till her bill is due. We bathe ourselves on the 4th day, unless a nurse's aid forgets & does it, & we give the baby the formula ourselves. We have our faces washed at five in the A.M. & there is a bedpan <u>schedule</u>. If you want it at all you take it on the appointed hour – particularly if you want it warm. I've written a little essay entitled "Wartime bedpan technique" which I'll copy for your intimate perusal. It will <u>not</u> come out in "The Latest."

I had such a pleasant surprise the other day. Quite a few of our friends are nurses aides here & some of their husbands are the equivalent - assistant orderlies - I think they are called. One of them (Patty Dennison's father) dropped in on me the other evening & I asked him what his duties were. One of them, it seemed, had been to clean up the delivery room after me. Said I had a very good-looking placenta! Can you imagine his ever wanting to speak to me again. (Wouldn't Grandma <u>expire</u> if she thought this had come to pass.) – Such is war.

Well, the home front seems to be doing alright without me, but I can picture the confusion when I got home – everybody talking at once & the nurse leaving in despair. She's wonderful so far but I know she'll give out - it's not possible that my convalescence will be a charming restful one. Remember that first baby & how <u>exhausting</u> it was!

Thanks but I don't need any blankets. You'll get a package soon which should have said "Do not open until Xmas." It's your Xmas gift plus Shaw's "Thank you for taking care of me" this summer. Polly's gift will arrive from a store unchristmas wrapped. It's my baby present to her - finally! Lee's & Gene's are on order & I hope they come before the armistice is signed.

Read any of this to Mackey[38] will you.

Give her my love & same to you –
Joan

---

[38] Mackey Ingram, we called her Aunt Mackey, and her husband Uncle Junie, were lifelong friends of my parents, and lived on Sakonnet Point a few houses away. They had three children, Chris, Jane, and Arthur. Chris married a woman named Lydia, and named his Boston Whaler after her, which later became our family boat.

MOTHERHOOD

Dec. 3, 1943
Wednesday

Dear Mart -

This is too good – I've got to tell you (incidentally I'm on the bed pan & have <u>no</u> hope of being detected till nightfall). A nurse was just telling me that she was sent in to the sun porch early this A.M. to tell a Mr. Dugan that he had a son. She went in & said "Mr. Dugan – you have a son," & two haggard men said in unison, "Good how's my wife?" She said the double talk was sort of startling & asked which was Mr. Dugan. They said "We both are – which of us had the baby?"

This place is wilder than Yale-Harvard weekend. Nine patients came in last night & are in various stages of production – 5 are in the labor room & there aren't 5 beds. I guess they must strap them to the walls. One more just came in & the nurse said they kept her hanging around the hall hoping she'd give up & take a semi private on the floor below. She wouldn't – so they finally had to admit her. Isn't that <u>awful</u>. I hope it's not her first baby.

I can't wait to get home & get some rest. Honestly, you have to have a baby hanging between your legs to get any attention around here. I've been trying to get some hemorrhoid ointment since yesterday afternoon. It seems like such a little thing to ask – but I suppose my burning tail isn't as important as shaving other tails. I ran this hospital personally, from my bed, for the first couple of days (you know how you do) but I've given up even looking into the corridor now. They wheel them down so fast it's not worth looking up.

Heather continues to be my best effort. Shaw hasn't seen her except just after she was born. She didn't look so fancy this morning though! – a little like W.C. Fields.

> You might send my other letter to Aunt M.
> Send any clippings about Harriet Randall, won't you?

Goodbye –
Wanie

P.S. I'm <u>still</u> on the bedpan.

MOTHERHOOD

War Time Bedpan Technique

November, 1943

I am a maternity patient. I came in very maternity, and I'm learning to be very patient.

Time was - in fact two times was (for I'm a multipara three para three) - when all I had to do was snap the buzzer on the end of the black chord and in would bounce a nurse with a bedpan all covered over like a basket of hot rolls. She would hover over me, I would hover over it and then she would depart, complete with equipment. But those were the days when pax was vobiscum, and this is war.

Bedpans, like everything else have been put on a wartime schedule, but I can't seem to convert, I still operate on a peace time basis and it doesn't make for inner harmony. The daily wartime schedule goes something like this (but I don't); the first presentation is at five A.M.

It's the last thing you're dreaming of at that eerie hour but if you're wise you'll hop aboard because your next chance comes long – too long after your morning coffee. The third opportunity does not coincide with the effects of your luncheon tea but it does coincide with your callers. You by-pass that one cause you know they're going to slip one in on you around supper time. There is a certain amount of logic to that, but the really well timed one is in the evening when your husband has just arrived. You've spent the last hour primping before the hand mirror dangling from the bridge lamp. You've put a flower in your hair and you've tucked your breast binder way down. The effect is just registering when in shoots the shroud. Your husband makes a bee-line for the solarium and of course – THAT'S the time you hit the jackpot.

So, as you can see, it's something to establish contact at the proper moment but, it's something else again to call the whole thing off. When you once get on location you're stuck with it, so you might as well lay your plans. It's well to get your props arranged before the nurse darts out, cause from then (and on) you're on your own.

Get your cigarettes and matches handy and be sure you're not down to your last three. If you forget your ashtray all is not lost, but it's awkward. Then your book. (Never the daily paper. The want ads get boring) I am deep in Eve Curie, Time, and the autobiography of William Lyon Phelps and somehow, of the three, Will Phelps is the most satisfactory bedpan companion. Maybe it's because he's nine hundred and eighty pages long. I wish he were still alive. I'd write and tell him that I'd read him from end to end – on my end. It's well to have a little snack handy, too - some salted peanuts, or a box of Nabs. And it's not too dumb to have your cologne within reach.

And there you are. If you've laid your plans well there isn't one thing you have to worry about until your feet fall asleep. When that occurs, don't struggle for it doesn't pay. Relax and try to be philosophical about the whole affair – for after all – hasn't Buddha been sitting that way for thousands and thousands of years?

Joan E.G. Cole

MOTHERHOOD

Letter to Aunt Marion before she was released from Hospital

December 8, 1943
Tuesday

Dearest Aunty –

Thanks for your nice long letter. I'm so glad they like "Heather" - lots of people of course, I for one, backed up by you, shall call her Heather - but I'm afraid it will stick in Shaw's craw. He had named a boy & I a girl, & I won. The Dunclee is on Grandmother Getchell's side.

I go home in a couple of hours & I can't hardly <u>wait</u> to see my "other" children. Of course they are dying to see the baby. It will be a big moment & I shall cry with joy I'm sure. Why is it that I always seem to have such happiness when other people suffer so many bad breaks!

Even to the nurse I'm lucky. She does <u>everything</u>, & I've hired her until Jan. 7th. Had her for ten days before I came & I can tell you I welcomed her with open arms cause Pix had tonsillitis, Bruce a croupy cough & I had hemorrhoids from taking care of them. Can you imagine that it was the first time Pixie had to take a <u>pill</u>! She certainly enjoyed ill health after the worst was over – lying in bed like a queen, finger nail polish, make-up & my best bed jacket. Bruce remained frail as long as possible, enjoying life tremendously, illness being a novelty in our house.

Harriet has certainly had a terrible siege. It was a shame you had to trek across the country & leave your delicious vegetables but on the other hand it was nice that you could see her for a good long time. That must be the first time your house was completely empty since it was built. I'm so glad Lou likes her teaching & that she is near enough so you can get together once in a while. When do you suppose I'll ever meet Beebe?

Isn't it grand about Genie? I confess I was somewhat startled by its suddenness but Jonathan is such a nice guy that she can't be making a mistake. However, I'm glad they aren't getting married till this summer for they should know each other better. Apparently, his mother, though a widow, will pose no problem for she's clever & most independent – like you!

It seems incredible that Hat can't have a child. They certainly are a dime a dozen in this maternity floor. I'll bet she'll get pregnant one of these days & surprise us all. Hope I don't for a while anyway.

It is also <u>too</u> bad that we can't see you more. I don't blame you for not wanting to leave Hanover again, but if you feel the urge do let me know. I'd like to give you the carfare as a present to myself.

Grandmary Cole is as <u>wonderful</u> as ever. I can't believe she is seventy years old, she is so full of life & vigor. Gramp hasn't had a transfusion in a couple of years now, but at the moment he is undergoing a series of tests because several times he has fainted for no good reason. Don't make any references to it for I don't think he wants it known. I'm not too concerned because I imagine it's nerves – he always seems to snap out of his odd sicknesses sooner or later.

Genie & Celie are getting along splendidly together. It is a splendid solution for this year & even better now that Genie has her own home to look forward to. As for Mart, I wish she could find a maid. I still say a great deal of her nervous fatigue is a reaction to Doc's long sickness. I guess he's doing everything he can for her now.

Well, I guess we've covered most everything. Think of me going home to a nice house, to two adorable children, carrying a third & being escorted by a splendid husband. Does he look good to me! Who knows when I'll write again.

Much love –
Joan

MOTHERHOOD

Letter from Joan to her friend Vivian Craig

Postmarked Dec 7, 1943
Monday –

Vee dearest –

I got a message this A.M. that you phoned last evening. Alas, phones in rooms are out for the duration, so we couldn't make contact. Thanks for trying, anyway.

You can well imagine how often you've been on my mind these past days. The morning after you + I talked on the phone I felt a particular wave of gratefulness when we all had our usual morning snuggle – Shaw kissing one cheek + the kids the other, + still another kicking in my tummy.

Dick Hart is finally opening tomorrow night in Brock Pemberton's "Pillar to Post." He has a small part, but if I were fit, I'd certainly go in + see it. Maybe it will have folded before I get around again.

As for me – as usual, things went splendidly. I've forgotten what I wrote you – hope I'm not repeating myself. Oh so slight pains at 12:15 at night. Shaw shot me down here without buttoning his fly, I'm sure, + the baby – Heather Dunclee – came at 3:30. Thousands of pills, hypos + Ether (rectal) prevented undue pains + from this moment on I've been a well woman. No stitches or muscular soreness of any kind save after birth pains. They are <u>something</u> after your third, aren't they! I even got pills for those so I asked for them at every opportunity.

The hospital is so understaffed + so overcrowded that the service is <u>terrible</u>. Everyone has always raved about the joy it is to recuperate here but they had peacetime babies - this is war. I've written a treatise called "Wartime Bedpan Technique" + if I ever get a copy made I'll send one on.

I have a marvelous nurse who does everything. God knows I hope she lasts because I've just got her through Jan 7th + want to go in town a couple of times before I go into domestic seclusion. Surely you'll be in Woon. by then but I'll call you anyway, on the chance that we may meet + talk it over. Incidentally, you <u>never</u> looked as attractive as you did the day you came over (Oh for some French in me!). I'll bet you were beautiful the night Craig left, though!

Please be a pal + keep me posted. I love you sincerely + dearly, Vee, + am vitally interested in you. Darned if I know how, but I can't believe that happiness won't emerge eventually.

Loads of love to you + the children –
Joanie

Poor Butterfly[39]

Joan Getchell Cole

I have just emerged from 10 days of enforced rest in a maternity hospital and I can't help thinking what a "success fou" I would be right now in any intellectual gathering, for after 10 days of uninterrupted reading my mind is in perfectly gorgeous shape.

It seems to me I know practically everything. For the first time I really know where Rabaul is. I know that owner Cox has been kicked out of professional baseball and I know what he used to own. I know what Nimitz is in charge of and I know how far he is from Japan. I know that "Carmen Rose" is a smash hit and I know that Bizet wrote it. I even understand inflation. I know that Dartmouth beat Princeton at basketball and I didn't get that from my husband. I know that British and American press relations are strained like puree over the Cairo conference and I know that Mrs. Henry L. Doherty thumbed her nose at the opening night of the opera. I know that the Gripsholm landed and I know that the press didn't get much out of it. Since the girl who gave birth to the baby on the Japanese ship is a good friend of mine I know even more than the press does about her.

Thanks to Wm. Lyon Phelps Autobiography I could give you an inventory of every man of letters since Aeschylus and I know now that he lived in the 5th century before Christ. I could tell innumerable anecdotes (via Phelps) about every savant you've ever heard of and about many I've never heard of.

Due to my recent environment I could preside over the New Jersey State Medical Conference with the greatest of ease and I could publish a handy guide of obstetrical and pediatrical terms for incoming patients. I can identify the uniforms of each branch of hospital volunteers and I know from the nurses that the hospital couldn't get along

---

39 This piece of writing is undated, but she wrote it after returning home from the birth of Heather.

without them. I know the love life of every nurse for miles around and I have the hot dope on every doctor in town. In short, I'd be a natural as guest artist on "Information Please."

However, that wouldn't be the ideal medium for my capabilities at the moment for I couldn't be seen – and I'm at the peak of physical perfection.

For 10 straight days my face has been creamed and it wears an unweathered aspect. Repeated suffions of bath powder have made me soft as a kitten and I'm perfumed to the hilt. My hands look completely unrelated to potato peelings. My fingers taper off into unbroken fingernails and they are bright red way down to the tips. My feet have taken on the texture of Carrara marble. I'm thinner than I've been for nine months and my face wears that post-natal glow. In fact, mentally, physically and certainly morally I'm a wow.

Yet here I sit – loaded for bear – and I'm confined to the second floor.

Motherhood

On December 19, 1943, at 8:15 A.M. Joan Ellis Getchell Cole died a "sudden death at home", 21 Erwin Park Road, Montclair, N.J.
Age: 35

New Jersey Bureau of Vital Statistics

Joan Ellis Getchell Cole
December 25th, 1907 to December 19th, 1943

MOTHERHOOD

I wrote the following in my book <u>Markings of Mercy</u>. The passage gives a little background, some details, about my mother Joan's death, as seen through my eyes when I was seven years old.

December 19, 1943

It is the week before Christmas, 1943. Holly and new baby bouquets decorate our house in New Jersey. Two weeks ago, Mummy finally brought our new baby sister, Heather, home, our Thanksgiving baby, arriving home just before Christmas.

Mom's been in bed since then with lumbago of the back, whatever that is. Today Mummy, Daddy and I are going to our Congregational Church to hear me sing in the children's choir. Mom and I are getting dressed together in her bedroom.

She is so beautiful. Her tall, soft, warm, cuddly body makes me feel safe as we stand there, the two of us, combing our hair in front of the mirror. She is reaching for her lipstick in a drawer in her huge mahogany bureau, which is covered with all kinds of treasures: a secret penny box, an atomizer, a box of powder, a silver brush and comb, and some jewelry.

Suddenly she sways, grasping for the drawer, and crashes to the floor, yelling out my father's name, "Shaw!"

I dive to the floor where she is lying. My eyes are glued to her face waiting for a sign, waiting for a chance to ask her what is happening. I cannot understand what is going on. Daddy rushes in from the bathroom, his face covered with white foam. Bending down beside her, he calls, "Joan." Again he calls her name but she does not answer him. He reachers in her lipstick drawer for a vial of smelling salts. He snaps it and puts it under her nose. She does not move.

"Stay here," he says to me. "I am going to call the doctor." He runs to the telephone downstairs. I am alone with my mother.

"Wake up Mummy. Wake up," I say. She does not move. I try

again moving closer to her face so she can hear me better. "Wake up Mummy… please… PLEASE. MUMMY. MUMMY. MUMMY-Y-Y." My eyes sting. "Big girl don't cry," I tell myself. Kneeling down, crouched down, I glue my eyes to her eyelids. She will hear me now, I know. "Mummy," I keep calling over and over again.

She did. Suddenly her eyelids flutter and then they open… they are wide-eyed, staring right at me. Quickly, before she goes back to sleep, I ask her, "Mummy, are you going to die?" Now we are talking like we always do, asking questions and getting answers. She answers and says: "No Dear. Of course not, I am not going to die."

Oh no. She went to sleep again. Oh no. Mummy… Mummy.

Daddy and Mrs. Struckman, the baby nurse, come into the room. They hurry over to us. "We are going to put Mummy in her bed now," Daddy says to me. Together they put her there, under the covers.

"I'm here," the doctor announces, as he races up the stairs into the bedroom. Daddy must have left the front door open for him. The doorbell did not ring. He goes to my mother's side and begins to check her out while Daddy says to me, "Pixie, get Bruce and go play downstairs." As I leave the room, he closes the door behind me.

I find my younger brother, Bruce. "Something awful has happened to Mummy," I try to explain. "She fell on the floor and she won't wake up."

We go to Mummy's door and try to listen to what's happening. We hear her snoring… then there are other kinds of sounds, quite loud. It doesn't really sound like Mummy but it is *her* voice. I'm scared. "We'd better go downstairs like Daddy said, "I tell Bruce. I feel bad standing here by the door. I am not supposed to be here. Something awful is happening. I can't stand it.

We scurry down the stairs, head for the kitchen and close the door. It is safe here. We cannot hear those awful sounds any more. We should not have stayed so long. Bruce and I wait for Daddy. Bruce is five and I am seven.

I hear the kitchen door open and Daddy's footsteps slowly come to where we are. He bends down and puts one arm around each of us. He looks at each of us as he says our names. His eyes are sad. He is very serious. "Children, your Mummy has just died. She is gone. She will not come back again."

We huddle on the kitchen floor. I dissolve in tears. My brother stands there wide-eyed, watching.

Bruce and I stay in the kitchen while Daddy does some things. I cannot stop crying. I hurt all over. Daddy comes to us. He tells us, "We are going to Grandmary and Grandpa's house now." They are my Daddy's parents. Mummy's parents died the year before I was born. "Dry your tears and wash your face and hands," he says. I am already dressed in my Sunday clothes.

We leave our house and Mrs. Struckman and the baby. We get in the car and drive to the big brown house on Belleview Avenue, my other home. "Oh good," I think. "Isabelle and Hazel will be there. I can play in the kitchen with them. Maybe Isabelle will have some almond custard in the ice box." Grandpa always tickles me the minute I get inside the door. I giggle so much it's hard to run away but I always do.

I picture Grandmary sitting in her big wing chair in front of the living room window that has curtains you can sort of see through. When Mummy, Bruce and I visit her after school at four o'clock, we have tea. Not us kids, though. We drink grape juice and ginger ale through silver straws. It tastes so good. It gives me something to do while the grownups talk on and on. Grown ups. *Mummy, oh no. She is not here.*

I'm trying to keep myself from making too much noise as I walk up the big front steps. Grandpa doesn't tickle me this time. He hugs me tight. We burst out crying. Then I go to Grandmary whose eyes are red and puffy. "It's all right, dear. I know it hurts. You may cry," she says.

There are other people there. They are all grown-ups. They all talk softly. I go around and hug these big people. My aunts and uncles are there and some white-haired friends of Grandmary's. In the dining room I see Isabelle and Hazel putting food and things on the table. I run to Isabelle for a hug. She doesn't speak. She just hugs, tears rolling down her face. Then pretty Hazel, Isabelle's daughter, holds me tight. "I am sorry that your mother died," she says. "Your Mommy was a special lady and you are too. It won't be the same without her, but you'll be alright, honey, don't you worry. We will be right here. And we will have custard in the icebox whenever you come."

Quick... I need to get away. They make me happy but that hurt is back again. It comes and goes but when it comes I feel all crazy like I don't know what will happen. I find a corner in the front hall just outside the dining room where nobody can see me, or hear the awful sounds I make.

I hear my name. A grown up is talking about me. "Pixie wore her mother out," I hear her say. I try to breathe through all the gunk in my head. Is it my fault all this is happening? If it is, I've never been in this much trouble before.

I think back. *We were getting dressed together. Mummy was going out for the first time. She was going out because of me, to hear me sing in the church children Christmas choir. She didn't have to go. It would have been O.K. Then she fell. I tried to wake her up, but she still died. I was with her. It's all my fault. I wore her out. I made her die.*

I didn't tell anyone this. I leave the corner and walk very slowly toward the dining room table. Carefully I pull out a chair, and slip into the seat. I am hungry. The pancakes taste good, but since I'm soaked in tears and all mixed up, it's hard to swallow. I pick away and watch the grown-ups eat.

MOTHERHOOD

Letter from Shaw to Vivian (Vivi) Craig after Joan's death

January 3, 1944

Vivi dear –

You've been wonderful to us and I can't begin to thank you. Starting with your cheerful phone call that was a great comfort even though I couldn't talk very much, then the <u>beautiful</u> red roses, and then on Christmas the lovely presents for the children, you have practically been here at our side. Honestly, the aeroplane for Bruce + the charm jewelry for Pixie have been just about their favorite presents. I just put Pixie to bed and she was stringing beads (or charms) as usual up till the last minute. I know Joan had things for your girls but they weren't marked and I just couldn't tell what was what. Particularly that week –

You were Joan's oldest friend and you and her other friends are constantly in my mind – for we have all lost so much – at the same time I'm sure she would never forgive us for being sad. My only periods of sadness are purely selfish ones and she didn't have a selfish moment in her life – so when I get feeling sorry for myself I try to remember how she would have done it.

The children are of course a wonderful comfort and the major part of the amazing heritage she has left. When you think what Joan has done in this town alone in only five years in the way of making friends and roots, it is an inspiration and (although I hate the word) a challenge to us all. If only I can bring the children up somewhere near the way she wanted it done + so that they can appreciate and be helped by her example. I will help + make amends for the many things I never did for her. She will always be an inspiration to me – and although it's probably sacrilegious to say so – it almost seems as though she went because her job had been so well done – in order to help some of us to do our jobs better. Wouldn't she laugh at that? – but still I keep thinking of it a good deal –

Vivi, Joan has told me a little of what you've been through and I want you to know how much I admire your courage.

Thanks again for everything + you keep your chin up too –

Love –
Shaw

Two and a half years after Joan's death and the death of Vivi's husband Craig, Shaw and Vivi got married, joining their families into one. My summertime friends became my sisters: Francesca (Cesca), Priscilla (Prissy), and Suzanna (Susu). We were all practically the same age.

The major part of Joan's amazing heritage: Pixie, Bruce, and Heather

In Loving Memory of Joan Cole

February, 1944

Reprinted from *League's Latest*

I like to think that each of us, during our lifetime, weaves a tapestry. Our fears and our courage, our heartaches and our laughter are the threads with which we weave. In some the design is clear, in others the colors clash, while in a few the threads are tangled and broken. Once in a great while someone weaves a tapestry with such loving care that the memory of it is an inspiration that stays with us through the years. Joan's is one of these.

There is strength in each separate strand, an outliving strength that made others strong. And woven all through it are shining threads of humor, graciousness and an intense joy of living. Intelligence is there and tenderness; love and understanding.

So let us get on with our own weaving. It would be her way so let it be ours. No outward show of grief, just remembrance in our hearts, and a deep gladness that we have known her.

Jean M. Strait

A short note regarding the Appendix:

We have added these appendix items to expand on both Shaw and Joan's ancestry and the Pitometer, both of which Joan wrote about extensively throughout her life.

A. John Waldo Ellis is her Grandfather who lived across the street. He was an engineer too!
B. Barbara Gilbert, wife of Joan's first cousin John Gilbert, the son of Aunt Marion Ellis Gilbert, wrote about the Getchell girls in *Birds of a Feather*.
C. Eugenia Rawson, Joan's youngest sister nicknamed Genie, wrote about family origins in *Johnnycakes and Cream*. Another section from *Johnnycakes*, about their family's golf conversations at the dinner table, is in Part I of this book.
D. A genealogy that Joan put together for her Father-in-law for Christmas 1934. #7 features Captain John Cole, our whaling Captain ancestor.
E. Biography of John Adams Cole, Shaw's Grandfather, son of Captain John Cole, from American Society of Civil Engineers.
F. Article about the history of the Pitometer Company on 40th Anniversary of the Pitometer Co. work in the N.Y. Water System. Joan wrote so much about her early married life while Shaw was working for the Pitometer Company.

APPENDIX A

Biography of John Waldo Ellis, Joan's Maternal Grandfather, from the American Society of Civil Engineers[40]

John Waldo Ellis, M. Am. Soc. C. E.
(Member of the American Society of Civil Engineers)
Died October 30th, 1916.

John Waldo Ellis, son of John and Ame Almira Fisher Ellis, was born in Woonsocket, R. I., on September 7th, 1845. He was one of four children, of which three were boys, all noted civil engineers.

Mr. Ellis received his early education at New Hampton Institute, New Hampton, N. H., and at the age of 19 entered the employ of the Boston, Hartford and Erie Railroad, then building from Waterbury, Conn., to Fishkill, N.Y. His advancement was rapid, and he soon became a Division Engineer on the Troy and Greenfield Railroad before the completion of the Hoosac Tunnel. From this road he went to the Norwich and Worcester Railroad then building, and, in 1869, came to Woonsocket, R. I., as Chief Engineer of the Providence and Worcester Railroad, at the same time opening an office for private practice in that place, which he maintained up to within a few years of his death.

Mr. Ellis held the position of Chief Engineer of the Providence and Worcester Railroad, up to the time that road was absorbed by the New York, Providence and Boston Railroad in 1888. Under his direction the road was double-tracked, many branch lines were constructed, the Wilkes-Barre Coal Pier and connection was constructed at Providence, and many bridges, stations, and terminals were rebuilt. During this

---

40   The American Society of Civil Engineers, founded November 5, 1852, is a professional body founded in 1852 to represent members of the civil engineering profession worldwide. Headquartered in Reston, Virginia, it is the oldest national engineering society in the United States.

same period Mr. Ellis' private practice in Woonsocket was at its height, and many prominent engineers of the present day received their first experience in the old Main Street office. The design and direction of the construction of Nourse Mill, of the Social Manufacturing Company, The Alice Mill, of the Woonsocket Rubber Company, and numerous other industrial plants and enlargements in Northern Rhode Island, were a part of the activities of this office.

From 1890 to the time of his death, Mr. Ellis was connected prominently with the various engineering problems of the East. He was Engineer for the Old Colony Railroad Company in the building of the Providence Passenger Terminal, and Engineer Inspector of the Boston and Providence Railroad, from the time of its lease to the Old Colony Railroad, until his death. His connection with various grade crossing matters in Massachusetts and Rhode Island included nearly every important problem that has come up. He was one of the Commissioners for the abolishment of the grade crossings in Lowell, Athol, and Orange, Mass., and was employed as engineering expert by the Cities of Lynn, Worcester, Cambridge, Fall River, Taunton, Haverhill, Readville, and a large number of small towns.

As a Water-Works Expert, Mr. Ellis was among the foremost in New England, serving as one of the Commissioners in the valuation of the Newburyport and Gloucester Water-Works when these were taken over by the City. He was also a member of the Commission in the diversion claims against the City of Pittsfield and the claim of the Nassau Paper Company against the Metropolitan Water Board.

As a Town and City Engineer, Mr. Ellis was very active, and the Blackstone and other rivers in Massachusetts and Rhode Island have many a dam constructed under his direction. The most prominent of these are the Lonsdale, Ashton, and Wilkinsonville Dams on the Blackstone; the Slatersville Reservoir Dam and Middle Dam on the Branch River, and the Georgiaville Dam on the Woonasquatucket, in Rhode Island.

On March 1st, 1901, Mr. Ellis was elected President of the Providence Gas Company[41], and took up the active management of that Corporation, holding the position of President and General Manager to the time of his death. Under his direction, this Company became one of the most efficient of the gas companies operating in the East.

Notwithstanding his many engineering engagements and business connections, Mr. Ellis found time to be a most efficient Director and Manager in other fields. He was a member of the Board of Directors of the Industrial Trust Company of Providence, and Chairman of the Board of the Woonsocket Branch of that Company. He was a Director in the Woonsocket Rubber Company, and many other Corporations. He was also a Trustee of the Woonsocket Institution for Savings, from 1876 to 1908, and a Trustee of the Woonsocket Hospital from its founding, in 1890, to the time of his death. Although a prominent member of many clubs and social organizations, Mr. Ellis had no connection with any fraternal or secret orders. He was a member of the Boston Society of Civil Engineers, serving as President of that Society in 1905. He was also a member of the New England Water Works Association.

His principal diversion in his leisure was that of driving. From the time when he established his home in Woonsocket his stable always contained at least one good blooded trotting horse, and when the roads were good or the sleighing at its best, Mr. Ellis was to be seen among the fastest of those on the speedways. He was a member of the Woonsocket Driving Club, the Roger Williams Driving Club, of Providence, and the Metropolitan Driving Club, of Boston, and it is interesting to note that only three weeks before his death he drove on the track of the latter Club.

Mr. Ellis was a prominent figure in the political field of Woonsocket

---

41   For many years, almost a century later, my husband John J. Pendergast III represented the Providence Gas Company as their labor lawyer from the law firm Hinckley, Allen, and Snyder. Our sons John, Tim, Terry, and Michael had summer jobs as meter readers for the Gas Company in high school.

for many years. He served as Alderman from his Ward from 1895 to 1897 and was President of the Board during the last two years of this service. In 1904, he was elected State Senator from his city and served on many important Committees.

He was a member of the Board of Trustees of the First Universalist Church for many years.

Mrs. Ellis was a man of such marked ability in any of the fields into which he entered that he was recognized as an authority on an unusual range of engineering problems, a public man and a statesman of great ability, and a business man with keen foresight and tremendous energy. The scope of his talents was wide, and indicated a breadth of mentality seldom found in one man.

Mr. Ellis was married on May 23rd, 1870, to Mary F. Howe, who, with one son and two daughters, John, Edith, and Marion, survives him.

He was elected a Member of the American Society of Civil Engineers on July 3rd, 1895, and served as a Director from 1904 to 1906, inclusive.

APPENDIX B

Barbara Brooks Gilbert's husband John Gilbert is the nephew of Grandma Edith Ellis Getchell. He is the son of her sister Marion Gilbert, who lived in Hanover, New Hampshire. This makes John Gilbert Grandma Joan Ellis Getchell Cole's first cousin.

What follows is the introduction and an excerpt from "Birds of a Feather", focusing on the Ellis family.

Birds of a Feather OR It Takes All Kinds
By Barbara Gilbert

We can take pride in the fact that our family tree has, for generations, produced serious, responsible, decent citizens!!...
... Then there's OUR branch!

Introduction

This is a history of a family - our family - which I am writing with love and affection for you, our children and grandchildren and those who will follow. I am writing it because some of you have asked me to write it, but also because I think it is good to know where one has come from in order to better decide where one may be going.

My mother, who was a very wise and modest woman, said to me often, "It is all well and good to be proud of your ancestors, but what is more important, would they be proud of you?" And also, "When you really are somebody, there is no need to advertise."

I have had help from many cousins, both John's and mine, in

compiling this record, and I am deeply grateful to all of you. If there are errors, I take full responsibility. If there is a good deal more in detail about my side of the family than John's, it is not because they were not worthy of a great deal more, but because I never knew any of the older generation, and I have had to rely on others for facts and anecdotes. Also, several people on my side kept very good diaries, which have made good references. When I say, "John remembers," or "John said," this or that, I am of course referring to your dad, John Ellis Gilbert, without whom, this family would never have come into being.

Barbara Brooks Gilbert

Thetford Center, Vermont
Spring, 1983

John remembers as a little boy going across the street to the Ellis compound to watch Nelson, the hired man out at the stables, take care of the horses, harnessing them, grooming them.

He also has wonderful memories of Sunday morning breakfasts at his grandparents' home, with two Swedish maids in attendance. The usual menu was steak, oysters, hot rolls, with all the family gathered around to enjoy!

John Waldo Ellis was a lovely gentle man, beloved by all - Aunt Amy Gilbert told me several times that his grandson, John Gilbert, was more like his Grandfather Ellis than anyone else.

He died on October 30th, 1916, attended by his son-in-law, Oscar Gilbert, M.D., and survived by Molly, his son John, and his two daughters, Edith and Marion, and seven grandchildren.

<u>Mary Francis Howe</u> was born on June 18, 1842 in Hampton, N.H. Her parents were Ebenezer Howe and Hannah Hobbs Sanborn. She went to New Hampton Literary Institute, where she met John Waldo Ellis. They were married on May 23, 1870, and went to live in Woonsocket. She was little, a real fire-ball of energy - "always doing

something"; repose and relaxation were not part of her vocabulary. She loved her garden - especially her roses. John remembers the huge rose arbor, about 40 feet long, with the lawn on one side and the vegetable gardens and stables on the other. There was also a grove of chestnut trees on the property - yielding delicious nuts each fall - the kind that have all but disappeared because of blights.

Marion remembered that Molly used to make her entire family do setting up exercises each morning on the front porch, with Molly calling the signals.

When John was a little boy, both married daughters and their families lived in homes across the street from the Ellis home on Prospect St. After the death of her husband, Grandma Ellis lived two more years under the care of family and servants, increasingly invalid until her death on March 1st, 1918.

There were five children:

1) John Ellis - graduated from M.I.T., and at the time of his parents' deaths, was an engineer on power plant construction and operation in Fall River, Mass. His wife was the former Mary F. Harris. The red and white quilt on our guest room bed was done by her as a story of their courtship. It is a treasure! They had no children.

2) Walter Ellis - also an M.I.T. graduate, he died of typhoid fever at age 26.

3) Harry Ellis - died of diptheria at two years.

4) Edith Almira Ellis was a lovely, serene, scholarly person - with a very infectious giggle when she was amused. John remembers her helping him with his Latin when he was in high school, probably 30 years after she had last studied it. She graduated from Smith College in 1899. Her husband was H. Eugene Getchell, "Uncle Gene". He inherited a very successful business from his father - used to refer to himself as a "tinsmith". They did all kinds of metal works, such as wrought iron. They had a man who ran the household, his name was

"Gerry". John remembers him well, and two maids who held forth at Sakonnet. Uncle Gene was a great bird hunter, down on the marshes along the shore. He would come home from a round of golf about 5 or 5:30, come out to the big open porch, reach over the railing, and remove one of the shingles that enclosed the porch pillars, and reach into his whiskey cache, (this was prohibition, remember), and pull out a bottle of dimple Scotch. At that stage, the association he had with his boot-legger was unknown to John, except that there was much talk among the adult men about the speed of the rum runners off Sakonnet Point. The well-to-do summer population of Rhode Island beach areas were good customers for these specialists.

John remembers the Fourth of July as being a BIG event - fireworks, much excitement, and in midday, shooting clay pigeons. And of course feasts of clam chowder, salmon and peas, fresh from the garden. He also remembers a huge cherry tree in the Getchell garden that produced the most delectable fruit he ever tasted.

Edith and Gene had four daughters:

Martha - a delightful person - quick-witted, clever, generous, and beautiful - a startling honey blond. She was a beautiful diver, would go off the high rocks at Warren's beach - only at high tide, and then having to wait for a big roller to come in - timing her descent just right. She was one of the 20's generation - explosions of energy - dancing the night away. She and "Doc" were very good dancers, John remembers. Doc was W. Roland Harrall, her husband. He wasn't a doctor, he was and still is an invaluable stock broker, having taken care of the whole family's financial interests for many years. Martha was a very good bridge player - and when it was needed - a cool and unflappable, in-control person. She and Doc were always great fun to be with. I well remember my first encounter with the Harrall family. It was the winter of '44. John and I were in Hanover, just finished our internships, John was momentarily expecting his induction into the Army. Martha called her Aunt Marion to say they were all ill, and could she - Marion - come to help. Marion had a very bad cold, but I was fine - and down I went. It was fun - Martha and Polly and Lee all had the mumps, Doc had hepatitis, if I remember rightly, their son Gene was the only one not bedridden - and he showed me how to run the washer, dryer, etc. etc. It was quite an introduction - but I've always felt close to them. Years later when we lived in Easthampton, Lee came to Smith, and we saw a good deal of her and her family during those years.

We last saw all of them when we went to Providence for Martha's funeral service - she had suffered from emphysema for years, and died at Christmas time, 1979 - a great loss!

Joan (pronounced Jo-ann) was always one of John's favorite people. She had boundless energy - thought nothing of two sets of tennis, a round of golf, a swim and then dancing all night. She was very good to the underdogs in life (I think maybe John classed himself as such - he was the only boy of seven first cousins). Anyway, he loved her, she was always good company, full of fun. She married E. Shaw Cole, a 1930 Dartmouth grad., an engineer. His father had been an inventor, invented among other things a device used to measure the flow of water velocity. Shaw worked with him and later ran the company. (Son Brewster now runs the company). Joan went to Smith, but did not finish, she left to take care of her mother who was ill with tuberculosis. She and Shaw had three children, Pixie (who sent me an Ellis-Getchell genealogy which helped me greatly when I was putting this together), Brewster, and Heather. Joan died of a pulmonary embolism when Heather was only a few days old. What a tragedy!

Several years later Shaw married one of Joan's good friends - Vivian, a widow with 3 children. They and their children - 6 of them - were a happy family until Shaw's death 2 years ago from cancer.

Mary Lucille - "Celie" was Gillie's contemporary - always her very good friend. Celie graduated from Smith, majoring in French. She spent her junior year in France, and she married G. Warren "Bud" French, a classmate and fraternity brother of Shaw Cole's at Dartmouth. Bud worked with his father in the family's fruit business - fruit from the Pacific northwest, mostly apples. Their home reflects that interest in apples, the decor is repeated throughout. Celie has made a quilt that outlines Bud's life interests, and it is decorated with apples - it is a beautiful quilt! Celie lives still in Upper Montclair, N.J., Bud died several years ago of aortic aneurysm complications. They have two sons, Wayne and David. Celie and Vivian Cole came to visit us here last fall while up for a mini-reunion at Dartmouth - It was lovely to see them both. We visited her on our way to Annapolis this winter, a lovely, gracious lady.

Edith Eugenia - "Genie" - although younger than John, she and John ran with the same crowd at Sakonnet - they had marvelous times - swimming, sailing, dancing, tearing up the roads (gas was 13 cents a gallon, cigarettes two packs for 25 cents). Many a beach party - clambake - there was a gang of about 10 young people who had a great time together. Richie Hart was one of that gang, and Genie married him. His major was literature and drama, and he went on to Hollywood and Broadway. He died of a heart attack in his dressing room at 35 years! They had one son, Chris. Genie's second husband is Jonathan Rawson. For many years they ran The Stone House at Sakonnet - a gracious mansion which they ran as a boarding house. It made a lovely setting for their daughter Joanne's wedding. Genie and Jon are now retired, still live in Little Compton, R.I. We don't see them as often as we would like to see them.

5) Marion Ellis - John's mother - more about her later.

APPENDIX C

Johnnycakes and Cream
Oral Histories of Little Compton, R.I.

Compiled and Edited by
Lucy A. O'Connor
Printed by America House Design & Communications, Newport, R.I.
(99) *Used with permission*

Eugenie Rawson
Born 1915

Well, my grandfather (Seth Sherman Getchell) used to go fishing over at Westport and he was fishing there one day and got so interested in fishing that he missed the stage home... and he didn't know how he was going to get home and somebody said they would drive him over to Sakonnet Point and he could take the boat home. (Woonsocket, R.I.) So they brought him over and he decided he liked Sakonnet better than Westport so he transferred his allegiance here. I don't know when that was but he stayed at the Lyman House and then, on April 4, 1913, my Aunt Blanche Getchell Robinson (according to town records) bought the Davis boarding house down at the Point. I think probably my grandfather bought it in her name and we always understood that, but the title was in her name, Blanche G. Robinson.

The story is that I was born in September of 1915, and the next summer (I was kind of a sickly child) my mother took me down to visit my Aunie Blanche in the Davis house and I apparently squalled all the time and my cousin got a little annoyed and said, "What did she come down here for?" And my aunt said, "Well it's saving her life getting her out of the hot city." He said, "I don't think she's worth saving!" (Chuckle) That was a great family joke for some time.

APPENDIX D

A Genealogy that Joan put together for her Father-in-law for Christmas in 1934

1934

For Father Cole
A few roots of the family tree.
May you make them sprout!
With love and Merry Christmas,
From Shaw & Joan

Addenda

(The numbers correspond with the generation number beside each bracket. Disregard the printed number.)

1. Thomas Cole. Recorded as a husbandman in Salem, 1649-1650. There was a Thomas Cole who came on the Mary and John, March 24, 1683, and was an original proprietor of Hampton, and is mentioned as there in 1632. Whether he is this Thomas Cole is unknown to this writer.
2. John Cole. One of the inhabitants of Salem who protested against imposts in 1668. He was a cooper by trade and left Salem about 1675 for Malden, from which he departed to about 1684 for Lynn where he died. Sarah, his wife, was tried for witchcraft at Charlestown and acquitted Feb 1, 1693.
3. John Cole. Chosen surveyor of highways in Boxford in 1726 while residing there.
4. Jonathan Cole. He and his wife were dismissed from the First

Church in Boxford to help form the Second Church in 1736-1737. He was chosen tithingman 1742, and was taxed from 1721-1744. On going to Harvard he bought a farm of 65 acres on the north side of "Pine Hill Brook," from Joseph Darby, paying therefore 410 pounds.

5. Abijah Cole. Very little is known of his brief life. He probably died when less than thirty years of age. It is related that at the time of his death his wife was overwhelmed with her loss and refused to be comforted, but finally, before the funeral, she took her Bible and went out into the orchard alone, and after some time returned calm, resigned, and peaceful. The following, in possession of the Maine branch of the family, is supposed to be a copy of a will: "I, Abijah Cole, having joined a company or regiment for the capture of Quebec, in view of the uncertainty of human life, do give and bequeath to my father, Jonathan Cole, and to my brothers, Jonathan and John Cole, certain lots of land situated in Harvard, and to my friend Sarah Kent, personal property, consisting of a watch and money." - about 1755.

6. Asa Cole. At age 14 he went to live with his step father, Samuel Garfield, in Harvard, Mass., and learned his trade, that of a millwright. Later, they moved to Rindge, New Hampshire and there owned and operated a saw and grist mill for some six or seven years. He then moved to Westmoreland, following his trade as a millwright in that region, working one season on a mill in Coventry, Vermont, and also living some two years in Putney, Vermont. About 1810 he built the Pierce Mills in the south part of Westmoreland, and lived near and managed them for some four years. He sold the mills in 1814. In March, 1815, Ephriam Brown, of Westmoreland, who had purchased a large tract of land in Ohio, and was about to emigrate thither, applied to him (Asa) to join the party. He accepted the

proposal and made arrangements for his third son to go with him, but just one week before the party started he was taken with bleeding of the lungs, and was compelled to give it up. On his recovery from this illness he determined to go Eastward and went to Gouldsboro, Maine, where his brother had settled, hoping to find some place where he could do business to his advantage, and also hoping that the change of climate would improve his health. But it was all in vain. He took passage for Boston in 1816, arriving home in November, sick, emaciated, and prostrated. Two weeks afterward he died. His wife was a superior woman. Thus left alone with a family of eleven children she managed to keep her family together until they were able to care for themselves or find a good home. In 1838 she married Amory Pollard of Bolton, Mass. and survived him. She was buried in Westmoreland, N.H. on Sept 4, 1852.

7. (Captain) John Cole. After his father's death at the age of eight became a "chore boy" on a neighboring farm in Westmoreland. A few short terms during the winter season was all the schooling he received. As a boy he was noted as a good wrestler and was good company everywhere. When he was 15 years old he left the farm and sailed before the mast on a coasting vessel. Although seasickness, homesickness, and a siege of smallpox befell him, he decided during this voyage to become a sailor and a master of a ship. He studied navigation and was promoted rapidly so that at the age of 27 he was placed in command of a fine New Bedford whale ship, and commenced upon a series of very successful voyages. On March 6, 1838, upon his return from a 3 years voyage as master of the "Hibernia," he married Miss Elizabeth Shaw of his native place. That lady of his choice possessed not only rare physical beauty but also a heroic spirit, this can be seen in the fact that a former proposal of marriage made by him had been rejected solely on the ground that he

was not a Christian. This humbling defeat doubtless had much influence in leading him to a close study of the Bible, with which he became thoroughly conversant. After a few months of wedded life he again sailed another voyage. On the 16 of December 1838 his son was born. After his return from sea, at the most earnest entreaty of his wife and friends, he resolved to give up a sea life and settled first in Hartford, Conn. where his twin daughters were born, and afterwards in Boston. But the difficulty experienced in obtaining congenial business on land, while flattering inducements were ever drawing him back to his accustomed profession, finally resulted in his accepting the command of the ship "Wm. Hamilton," intending that this should be his last voyage. Before leaving, he purchased the Carey Cottage in Medway where he left his family for a 3 year absence. His wife and daughter died of consumption - 1843, but he did not hear it until long afterwards while he was cruising in the North Pacific, when he received a letter from the home pastor. On October 9th, 1845, he married Miss Mary Wells of Westmoreland and soon after settled in Walpole, N.H. He was one of the few "free sailors" of the town and was a member of the convention that nominated their Presidential candidate in 1848. He was an ardent worker for human rights, and many colored fugitives found a helper in him on their way to Canada. At this time he became a member of a Masonic Lodge in Keene. He was also, as a "Son of Temperance," active and successful in efforts to reclaim intemperate men and restrict the liquor traffic in Walpole. Taking his wife with him, he sailed on the ship William Penn, of which he was part owner, from New York to San Francisco. On the return voyage he met the first disaster in his business life in the loss of his ship, which was wrecked off Cape Hatteras Sept 13, 1855. The last to leave the ship, he floated on a spar for 19 hours before being rescued by a passing vessel. His wife was rescued as well by a different vessel. He and his wife were united in New York after many days of suspense. In 1856, after the birth of Arthur Wells in Westmoreland, they once more moved to Medway and remained until 1872. His last years were spent at the Shaw homestead in Westmoreland during which time he earnestly labored to bring about a harmony of feeling among the churches of the town which had been divided by a feud. In this he was successful. On December 29th, 1874 he died very suddenly of apoplexy and was buried in the Westmoreland Cemetery.

APPENDIX E

Biography of John Adams Cole, Shaw's Grandfather, son of Captain John Cole, from the American Society of Civil Engineers

John Adams Cole, M. Am. Soc. C. E.
Died November 16, 1932

John Adams Cole was born in Westmoreland, N.H., on December 16, 1838, the son of a whaling captain John Cole and Elizabeth (Shaw) Cole. He was educated at Kimball Union Academy, at Meriden, N.H., and began his technical career as a student in the office of the late Thomas Doane, M. Am. Soc. C. E., in Boston, Mass.

In 1861 and 1862, Mr. Cole was with the late J. Herbert Shedd, M. Am. Soc. C. E. He was engaged also on the State survey of the Sudbury Meadows (Mystic) Water-Works.

In August, 1862, Mr. Cole volunteered as a Delegate of the United States Christian Commission, a voluntary organization for carrying on religious work among the soldiers and aid to the wounded, during the Civil War. He went to the Army of the Patomac then on the Peninsula. After the Battle of Antietam, he returned to New England and spent three months addressing public meetings in the larger cities, and organizing societies for Commission work. In January, 1863, Mr. Cole was appointed General Field Agent for the Commission for the Union Armies east of the Alleghenies, and was engaged in the field until the end of the war. More than $3,000,000 were donated and expended for supplies for the wounded and for hospital work, and hundreds of clergymen were delegates at the front. The course of his duties took Mr. Cole to the battlefields on Antietam, Gettysburg, The Wilderness, Cold Harbor, and many other historic engagements, and he was present at the surrender of Appomattox. His letters from these historic scenes, carefully preserved by the family, are of thrilling interest.

After the Civil War Mr. Cole opened an engineering office in Washington, D.C. He removed to Chicago, Illinois, in 1872, and established himself in private engineering practice. Among other important works, he designed the original Lake View Pumping Station (later, a part of the Chicago Water-Works) and the Hyde Park Water-Works, including an inlet tunnel a mile out under Lake Michigan.

He also designed much of the sewerage system of the then separate municipalities of Hyde Park and Lake View; also, important Lake shore protection works, as well as other municipal improvements. Later, his practice was extended to many cities in the West and, for years, he was widely known as a Consulting Engineer of prominence. He resided in Ravenswood, Illinois, for some years, but later removed to Hyde Park, a suburb of Chicago.

For many years Mr. Cole was engaged as a Consulting Engineer in making expert reports for bankers on public utilities throughout the Middle West and the Far West. In 1896, he became associated with his son, Edward S. Cole, M. Am. Soc. C. E., in the development of the pitometer.

Mr. Cole was always a devoted church worker. He served as Elder in the Hyde Park Presbyterian Church for more than forty years, and as an Honorary Trustee of Howard University, from which he received the Honorary degree of Doctor of Laws. He was also President of the Chicago Tract Society from 1911 to 1913; and of the Training School, in 1912 and 1913. He was a member of the Western Society of Engineers, and of the Chicago Literary Club. He was survived by his widow, Mrs. Julia (Alvord) Cole, to whom he was married on December 15, 1870. Mrs. Cole died late in 1932. His immediate survivors are a son, Edward, and a daughter, Elizabeth (Mrs. D. J. Fleming).

Mr. Cole was elected a Member of the American Society of Civil Engineers on March 7, 1894.

APPENDIX F

Article from Water Works Engineering on the 40th Anniversary of the Pitometer in the NY Water System

December 16, 1942

START OF PITOMETER WORK IN NEW YORK CITY IS MARKED
Measurement of Flows in Mains Was Commenced Forty Years Ago Using a Then Novel Instrument

Forty years ago, Edward S. Cole started to measure the flow in the New York City distribution trunk mains, by using what was then a new instrument in the water works field called the "pitometer".

At that time, the late Nicholas S. Hill, Jr., was Chief Engineer of the New York City Department of Water Supply and employed Mr. Cole on his staff, to make a pitometer water works survey. Such surveys since that date have formed a part of the New York water supply practice.

This fortieth anniversary of the use of the pitometer on the New York Water System was marked by a surprise luncheon for Mr. Cole. The party was arranged by some of his business associates, and held at the Machinery Club in New York on December 4th.

Cole Presented with Gifts

As mementos of the occasion, Mr. Cole, now President of the Pitometer Company, was presented with two bound volumes containing technical papers and other documents relating to his pitot tube inventions. He also received a pen and pencil set, the toastmaster being Egbert D. Case, Vice President of The Pitometer Company.

The pitot tube for measuring the flow of water derives its name from the French hydraulic engineer, Henri Pitot, who in 1730, experimented with a glass tube, bent at right angles near one end, which, when inserted into the River Seine, showed that the velocity of the stream flow raised the water in the glass tube above the level of the stream.

In 1896, this principle was successfully applied by Edward S. Cole, at Terre Haute, Ind., for measuring the flow of water in closed pipe, the instrument in this form being called the pitometer.

Mr. Cole graduated in 1894 from Cornell University with a degree of M.E., and was associated with his father, the late John A. Cole, Consulting Engineer, Chicago, on the appraisal, design, construction and management of municipal water works plants in the Middle West.

Company Formed in 1904

In 1904, this partnership was incorporated as The Pitometer Company, the specialty work of the company being surveys to locate underground leaks in water works systems.

Since that time, approximately 850 such surveys have been made in the United States and Canada, including practically every major city east of the Rocky Mountains.

While the pitometer as originally designed has not been essentially changed, since the early days of its development, much experimental work has been carried on in relation to perfecting its accuracy. It has been approved by the American Society of Mechanical Engineers as an accurate means of testing hydraulic prime movers.

Work of Company Expanded

In 1925, The Pitometer Company expanded its activities to include engineering studies for the re-design of distribution systems and trunk main surveys for obtaining flow characteristics of main feeders in large cities.

About twenty years ago, Mr. Cole began experiments on developing a device, based upon the pitot tube principle, for measuring the speed and distance traveled by ships. As the results were promising, in 1927, a new company was formed. The Pitometer Log Corporation, Mr. Cole being also President of this company.

The Pitometer Log was first suggested by E.R. Howland, a Pitometer Company Engineer, who collaborated in the development of this instrument. The instrument has been approved by the U.S. Navy and approximately 600 of the logs have been made for all types of naval vessels. The high degree of accuracy secured by this log has proven very valuable both as an aid to navigation and to effective firing of naval guns.

In arranging the surprise party, Mr. Case was aided by Mr. Cole's two sons, E. Shaw Cole, Chief Engineer, The Pitometer Company, and John R. Cole, General Manager of the Pitometer Log Corporation.

CPSIA information can be obtained
at www.ICGtesting.com
Printed in the USA
JSHW020928110623
42912JS00002B/75